W9-AGM-887

The Apes

THE APES

THE GORILLA, CHIMPANZEE, ORANGUTAN,
AND GIBBON—THEIR HISTORY
AND THEIR WORLD

VERNON REYNOLDS

E. P. DUTTON & CO., INC.
NEW YORK   1967

FIRST EDITION

Grateful acknowledgment is made to the following for permission to reprint copyright material:

C. E. and M. L. J. Akeley. From *Lions, Gorillas and Their Neighbours*. London: Stanley, Paul & Co., Ltd., 1933.
B. J. Benchley. From *My Friends the Apes*. Boston: Little, Brown & Co., 1942.
Barbara Harrisson. From *Orang-Utan*. London: William Collins Sons & Co., Ltd., 1962. New York: Doubleday & Co., 1963.
Catherine Hayes. From *The Ape in Our House*. Copyright © 1951 by Catherine Hayes, published by Harper & Row. Reprinted by permission of McIntosh and Otis, Inc.
C. Hose and W. McDougall. *The Pagan Tribes of Borneo*. London: Macmillan & Co., Ltd., 1912.
A. M. Hoyt. From *Toto and I: A Gorilla in the Family*. Philadelphia: J. B. Lippincott Company, 1941.
W. N. Kellogg and L. A. Kellogg. From *The Ape and the Child*. Copyright 1933 by McGraw-Hill Book Company. Used by permission.
Wolfgang Köhler. From *The Mentality of Apes*. New York: Humanities Press Inc., and London: Routledge & Kegan Paul Ltd., 1956.
E. M. Lang. From *Goma the Baby Gorilla*. London: Victor Gollancz, Ltd., 1962. New York: Doubleday & Co., 1963. The original German-language edition was published by Albert Müller Verlag, Rüschlikon-Zürich (Switzerland) under the title *Goma, das Gorilla-Baby*.
R. M. and A. W. Yerkes. From *The Great Apes*. New Haven: Yale University Press, 1929.

Sources and Credits for Illustrations

Courtesy J. C. Abreu and Roberta Yerkes—Plate 104. Courtesy Aldine Publishing Company, from original by H. P. Klinger, J. L. Hamerton, D. Mutton, and E. M. Lang

[[5

SOURCES AND CREDITS [[6

—Plate 37. ATV, photo by permission of—Plate 91. J. B. Audebert, *Histoire naturelle des singes et des makis*, 1800—Plates 15, 16. From original by J. Biegert—Plates 32, 33. From A. E. Brehm, *Tierleben*—Plate 60. British Museum—Plate 1. From E. R. Burroughs, *Tarzan, Lord of the Jungle*—Plate 90. C. R. Carpenter, *A Survey of Wild Life Conditions in Atjeh, North Sumatra, with Special Reference to the Orang-Utan*, 1938—Figure 8. R. W. Chaney—Figure 13. Courtesy Conservative Research Department—Plate 92. Ken Coton—Plate 109. R. K. Davenport, Jr.—Plates 70, 71. From P. du Chaillu, *Explorations and Adventures in Equatorial Africa*, 1861—Plates 57, 58, 59. J. Ellefson—Plates 65, 66. From W. Fiedler, *Übersicht über das System der Primates*, 1956—Figures 2, 4, 9. Fox Photos Ltd.—Plate 97. From R. L. Garner, *Gorillas and Chimpanzees*, 1896—Plate 45. E. Geoffroy Saint-Hilaire and F. Cuvier, *Histoire Naturelle des Mammifères*, 1824—Plate 20. From K. Gesner, *Historiae Animalium*, 1551—Plates 8, 9. From original by M. Goodman—Plate 36. Kenneth W. Green—Plates 26, 27, 98, 99, 100. From W. K. Gregory—Plate 41. B. Grzimek—Plate 106. Barbara Harrisson—Plates 72, 73, 74. C. Hayes, *The Ape in Our House*, 1952, Harper & Row—Plate 80. From C. E. Hoppius, *Anthropomorpha*, 1760—Plate 13. W. T. Hornaday, *Two Years in the Jungle*, 1885—Plates 64, 67. A. M. Hoyt, *Toto and I: A Gorilla in the Family*, 1941, J. B. Lippincott Company—Plates 78, 82, 83. *International Zoo* Magazine—Plate 110. Ida Kar—Plate 24. W. N. and L. A. Kellogg, *The Ape and the Child*, 1933, McGraw-Hill Book Company—Plates 75, 79, 81. W. Köhler, *Intelligenzprüfungen an Menschenaffen*, 1921, Springer Verlag, Berlin—Plates 84, 85. A. Kortlandt—Plates 46, 47, 48. From G. L. Leclerc, *Count Buffon, Histoire Naturelle*, 1766—Plate 14. From D. Livingstone, *Last Journals*, 1875—Plate 54. The Metropolitan Museum of Art. The Cesnola Collection; purchased by subscription, 1874–1876—Plate 4. Museo Nazionale di Villa Giulia—Plate 5. National Museum, New Delhi; photo Mansell Collection—Plate 3. The Pierpont Morgan Library—Plate 6. From J. Piveteau—Plate 40. From A. Portmann, *Documenta Geigy*, Bulletin No. 8. 1961—Figure 10. Drawing by Arthur Rackham in Edgar Allan Poe's *Tales of Mystery and Imagination*, 1935, Harrap—Plate 89. *Red Data Book*—Figure 7. *Report of the Maias Protection Commission*, 1960—Figure 6. Sculpture by Hugo Rheinhold—Plate 18. A. H. Riesen and E. F. Kinder, *The Postural Development of Infant Chimpanzees*, 1952, Yale University Press—Figures 11, 12. After J. T. Robinson, in W. E. Le Gros Clark, *History of the Primates*—Plate 42. San Diego Zoo—Plate 23. G. B. Schaller, *The Mountain Gorilla: Ecology and Behavior*, 1963, The University of Chicago Press—Figures 5, 14. G. B. Schaller—Plates 61, 62, 63, 68, 69. From G. von Schubert, *Naturgeschichte des Tierreichs*, 1886—Plate 19. From drawings by A. H. Schultz—Plates 25, 29, 30, 31, 34, 35. Elsbeth Siegrist—Plates 76, 77. Siftung Preussischer Kulturbesitz, Staatliche Museen, Skulpturenabteilung, Berlin—Plate 7. From E. L. Simons—Plates 38, 39, 43, 44. 6571st Aeromedical Research Lab, USAF—Plates 21, 22, 86, 87, 88, 95, 96, 101, 102, 103, 107, 108. From H. M. Stanley, *My Dark Companions and Their Strange Stories*, 1893—Plates 93, 94. Paul Steinemann, Zoological Gardens, Basel—Plate 105. N. Tulpius, *Observationum Medicarum*, 1641—Plate 10. From E. Tyson, *Orang-outang, sive homo sylvestris*, 1699—Plates 11, 12. From G. Vandebroek, *Notes ecologiques sur les anthropoides*, 1958—Figure 3. From A. Vosmaer, *Description de l'espece de singe aussi singulier que tres rare, nomme orang-outang*, 1778—Plate 17. Sir J. Gardner Wilkinson, *The Manners and Customs of the Ancient Egyptians*, Vol. 1, 1878—Plate 2. R. M. Yerkes, *The Mental Life of Monkeys and Apes*, 1916—Figure 15. Yerkes Regional Primate Research Center, Emory University—Plate 28.

Photographic copy work on Plates 8, 9, 11–17, 19, 25, 29–33, 35, 36, 38–45, 57–59, 64, 67, and 92 by Ken Coton

Figures 1–10 rendered by Brian Lee

Plates 49–53, 55, and 56 were taken by the author.

TO E. M. R.

Contents

[[9

CONTENTS [[10

LIST OF ILLUSTRATIONS

[[11

following page 256

List of Illustrations [[15

Acknowledgments

I AM DEEPLY grateful to the following people for help of many kinds: to Dr. John Napier for reading and commenting on the whole manuscript; to Dr. George Schaller, who originally created the opportunity for me to write this book and later read parts of it; to Roberta Yerkes for photographic help; to Dr. Fae Hall, Professor William Montagna, Dr. David Pilbeam, Professor Elwyn Simons and Barbara Harrisson for personal communications and in some cases reading and commenting on parts of the manuscript; to Professor Adolph Schultz, Dr. Peter Ucko and my wife for critical readings of parts of the manuscript; to John Ellefson and Dr. Richard Davenport, Jr., for making available to me reports on their fieldwork and photographs prior to publication; to Dr. Morris Goodman for helpful discussion; to Dr. Clyde Kratochvil for reading part of the manuscript critically and for photographic support; to David Haworth of *The Observer* for constant encouragement; to my mother for her help with picture research; to Ken Coton for photographic help and Brian Lee for drawing the maps. In addition, I am greatly indebted to all those authors, publishers and owners of illustrative material who have allowed me to reproduce their work. Final responsibility for all statements in the book rests, of course, with the author himself.

Introduction

IN THE JUNGLES of Africa and Asia, hidden among cool leaves, live the apes. Hard to find, harder still to observe, they lead their independent, foraging lives. Man's wars do not concern them. Each day gibbons leap among the trees, solitary orangs climb from branch to branch, groups of chimpanzees gather, and gorillas peer over giant lobelias. Theirs is a world of greens and browns, a friendly world where only Cousin Man is to be feared.

For Cousin Man has turned traitor. When the mother ape is shot, the infant will cling to her body, and can then be prized off, and caged. Packed in a cage, one or two out of six will survive to reach a strange new jungle, one inhabited by human beings who will observe, train, and experiment with them. They will lead a new life, with regular mealtimes, friendly keepers, a cagemate—but for most of the apes, a lifetime of frustration and boredom, that gradually becomes less and less tolerable as full size and maturity are reached.

Not everywhere are conditions so bad. In 1966 I visited the Holloman

Air Force Base, New Mexico, where an enlightened team had found a solution to the problem of how to house captive apes. I watched some of the large number of chimpanzees kept there being released into a thirty-acre moated area constructed especially for them. Thirty acres! Big modern zoos are often packed into little more space than this.

Now that Cousin Man has become patron, emphasis is shifting from wasteful slaughter to breeding. Far too many mothers have been shot, apes are harder than ever to get, and more expensive, and the need for them, especially in the medical sphere, is greater than ever before. But man's attitude to the apes is still fundamentally one of exploitation. Perhaps at some time in the far distant future, man will mature sufficiently to realize how primitive this exploitative attitude is; but that day is a long way off, and the apes will probably be extinct before it arrives. I call the attitude "primitive" because it is the same attitude that man has always had toward animals ever since he began to use them for ends other than that of killing them for food. Apes are often treated about the same as farm livestock, and a good deal worse than household pets.

Yet they are almost human beings. Not so long ago, in geological time, there were forms, now extinct, that were the ancestors of both men and apes. Our heritage has left us and the apes with much in common, in our body structure, our behavior, our emotions, and even our intellect. What man has developed, what makes him dominant, are his upright posture, his culture, his tradition, and his extra brainpower, evolved over the last few million years. These are our human specializations, the source of our progress. But beneath the veneer we are still animals, and that is largely why apes fascinate us.

Much research has been done, and much continues to be done, on the intellectual capacities of apes. Chimpanzees have succeeded in "counting" up to eight, that is, in pressing a lever the correct number of times in response to a number flashed on a screen. Having pressed the lever, the ape "applies" for his reward (a food pellet) by pressing on a second lever. Naturally, he gets the reward only if he has pressed the correct number of times. In this way, a performance efficiency of 90 percent has been built up over a number of years. Puzzlingly, however, one ape who mastered this counting technique did not maintain his high standard in later years, as if he had "forgotten."

Far less is known about the emotional makeup of apes. There is no objective technique known to man that is capable of registering the precise emotional state of another creature—whether it be a fellow human being, an ape, or any other animal. We can draw deductions from observation of the animal's behavior—the noises it makes, the expressions on its face, the way it moves its body. But such deductions are likely to be wrong, because they are usually not based on objective measurements of any kind. They may be based on the "anthropomorphic" reasoning that similar expressions in ape and man indicate a similar emotional state. But a screaming chimpanzee may not be in pain, for it is part of their normal life in the wild to scream, when excited, several times a day.

A more accurate way to make deductions about emotions is to associate expressions with certain actions whose meaning is clear. If one ape chases and savagely bites another, we need not hesitate in describing him as "angry." If he flees from a water hose, screaming, and defecating loosely, we can say he is "afraid." But such an understanding remains a crude one. We need more subtle techniques to enable us to determine just how closely the emotional structure of the mind of the ape resembles our own. Only when we can acquire such data will we begin to have scientific grounds for the application of humanitarian methods to the keeping and using of apes, and only then will we be able to understand the true nature of the similarities and differences between ourselves and our closest animal kin.

But this will not be possible if we continue to exploit apes at the rate at which we are presently doing so. The orang is in danger of becoming extinct. We are depleting the African apes wherever license for export allows us to do so. Only the gibbon is really safe at present, and this may not always be so. I have suggested a way of conserving the apes. In a sense, the whole of this book is an argument in favor of their conservation. If it contributes in any way to that end, it will have been amply justified.

The Apes

CHAPTER 1

The "Ape" in Ancient Times

IN THE PRESENT scientific era, most of us are aware that there are dozens of different species of primates, belonging to a series of different zoological groups: there are the lower primates—lemurs, lorises, and tarsiers—and higher primates—monkeys, apes, and man. The true apes—gorilla, chimpanzee, orangutan, and gibbon—are distinguished from the monkeys by their large size, their lack of a tail, their relatively large brains, their ability to swing from their long arms, and a host of other characteristics. The ancient historians knew little or nothing of them. In fact, few of the primate species known today were familiar to the peoples of earlier civilizations. The apes themselves were not generally known until the eighteenth and nineteenth centuries of the Christian Era. Monkeys, however, were widely known from very early times.

The civilizations from which our own is descended were in the ancient Near East and, later, in the lands around the "Mediterranean" —the sea "in the middle of the earth"; beyond lay mysterious land, unexplored and unknown. The only common primate species that inhabited this "world" in ancient times were the Barbary "ape" (a monkey, not an ape at all), living along the north coast of Africa; the hamadryas and the yellow baboon in Egypt and Ethiopia; and a few guenons, the patas and Colobus monkeys in Ethiopia and beyond. None of these was an ape.

Of course, the inhabitants of Ethiopia, equatorial Africa, and peoples in tropical lands elsewhere knew of many more kinds of monkeys, and of the "anthropoid" (manlike) apes as well, but their cultures did not produce written or artistic records for us to study today; whereas the peoples of the ancient civilizations have all, to a greater or lesser extent, left behind them written statements or pictorial representations of the monkeys they knew. Their knowledge came from their own experience of locally living primates, from observation of imported specimens, and from the reports and tales of those few bold travelers who ventured into unknown lands.

Man created his first civilization in the Near East. At sites such as Jericho, near Jerusalem, in present-day Jordan, the birth of this civilization can be seen, from its Stone Age antecedents of 7000 B.C. to the civilization of the early Bronze Age, around 3100 B.C., and on, through biblical times, to the present day. From the lowest levels of such ancient cities nothing but broken pots and tools and walls remain, and we have no way of knowing the extent to which people were engaged in activities such as the keeping of pet monkeys. It is not until the reign of Solomon, King of Israel during the tenth century B.C., that we know of monkeys in western Asia, for according to the Bible it was during his reign that a shipload of wild animals, including monkeys, was brought into his country.

Monkeys were a common form of tribute to kings, doubtless because where they did not occur naturally, they were highly prized. We next know of them in this area from the reign of Shalmaneser II, King of Assyria from 860–825 B.C. This king set up a black limestone obelisk in his capital city, Nimrud (the biblical city Calah), to record his expeditions and conquests. The obelisk was found by the English archaeologist Henry Layard in the last century, and is now in the British Museum (Plate 1). On it can be seen several monkey-like creatures being led on leashes, probably as gifts of tribute to the king. Two, perhaps three, kinds of monkeys are shown, of which one is most probably the hamadryas baboon, for it has a mane.

Although the beginnings of civilization in western Asia antedate those of ancient Egypt and ancient India, both the latter provide evidence of monkeys long before the time of Solomon and Shalmaneser. In Egypt, we have evidence of them in predynastic times, before the Old Kingdom of 3100–2200 B.C.

By Old Kingdom times, Thoth, the Sun God, had as his sacred animal the hamadryas baboon. Egyptian deities (themselves often part animal) were frequently associated with holy animals, and there is no reason to suppose that the hamadryas baboon was chosen because of any human-like attributes. As well as the hamadryas baboon, many of the other species of monkeys of north and northeast Africa are represented on Egyptian paintings and sculptures (see Plate 2). We can tell something about the Egyptian people's attitude toward these monkeys. We know that they were the object of religious devotion. We know, too, that they were kept as pets, and they are often shown seated under the chair of their owner. Besides, they were specially trained to help with such tasks as picking figs. But ancient Egypt produced no zoologist—no one, that is, who sought to classify animals in the way the Greeks subsequently did.

At the same time that the Old Kingdom was flourishing in Egypt, a magnificent civilization was alive in northwest India, in the Indus Valley. And from its principal city, Mohenjo-Daro, we have evidence of monkeys in the form of little clay seals and models like the ones from predynastic Egypt. A good example is the little monkey shown in Plate 3. It is probably a rhesus monkey. It was found at a very low level at Mohenjo-Daro, and is similar to monkey models found in Ancient Egypt.

It is indeed an odd coincidence that such similar models of animals were being made in both India and Egypt at this early time, during the fourth millennium B.C. There is no direct evidence that the civilization of ancient India was known to the ancient Egyptians, although the other peoples of the Near East were trading with both areas and may have acted as intermediaries. Mohenjo-Daro ceased to exist in 1500 B.C., when it was destroyed by peoples invading from the northwest. Neither the ancient Jews nor the ancient Greeks of the first millennium B.C. knew of it, nor, indeed, did anybody in Europe until it was discovered by archaeologists at the beginning of the present century.

It is from the early Jewish writings that we can catch our first glimpse of a new human attitude toward the monkey. An old rabbinical script tells how, when Noah tasted the first wine, the Devil sacrificed a sheep, a lion, a monkey, and a pig, in that order. These symbolized the stages of man in drunkenness—mild, wild, foolish, and finally disgusting. Already at this early date, the monkey symbolized an aspect of the baser side of human nature—an idea that, as we shall see, was to persist throughout the Christian Era.

The ancient Greeks, too, were familiar with monkeys. The early Greek poets of the seventh century B.C., Archilochus and Simonides, refer to them, Archilochus telling a tale of a monkey that is tricked by a fox, Simonides using monkeys as a type of evil in a satire. A seventh-century B.C. kylix with a monkey's face (see Plate 4) has been unearthed in Cyprus. Several of the Aesopic fables, which were being told in Greece in the fifth century B.C., were about monkeys. The story of the "ape" tricked by a fox is repeated; in one tale the monkey asks the fox for his tail, but the fox declines (the monkey here must be a Barbary ape); one story tells how monkeys that have been taught to dance in purple robes forget their tricks when thrown some food by a spectator, whence comes an old English moral:

> "An ape's an ape, a varlet's a varlet,
> Though he be clad in silk and scarlet."

One monkey fails to imitate a fisherman; another is rescued by a dolphin (a story taken up by La Fontaine). But the Aesopic story that was to have the most interesting history is the one about a monkey mother with twins, which, in a later English translation, runs as follows:

An *Ape* brought forth Twins, one of which She was extreamly Fond of, but the other She as little regarded. Being once Surpriz'd, and in imminent Danger, She ran away in great fear, and took up the Beloved Brat in her Arms, and toss'd the other over her Shoulder to ride Pick-a-back. In the Hurry She Stumbled over a great Stone, and knockt the Fondlings Brains out; but the despised Baby at her Back, came off without any damage.

The Christians made much of this tale, as we shall see.

Just what kind of monkeys these were is uncertain. The clue in Aesop indicates that some of them, at any rate, were Barbary apes. These must have been imported from the southwest, for North Africa is the home of this species. They probably came by way of Carthage.

Carthage was founded about 850 B.C. and was already a power at the time of the early Greek writers. Ships crossing the Mediterranean could easily have taken numbers of Barbary apes with them. In the Etruscan art of Italy, pet Barbary apes are common by the fifth century B.C., and this species was probably the one best known to the Italians. But in Greece it is certain that more species were known:

Plato and Aristophanes wrote of the baboon in the fifth century B.C., while in the fourth century B.C. Aristotle was able to divide the known monkeys into three groups:

1. Barbary apes (no tail)
2. Monkeys with tails
3. Dogheaded baboons

In the first century B.C., the tales of Phaedrus, who wrote down in Latin verse the Aesopic fables current in his day, include the story of the monkey that begs a fox for its tail. So it does seem that the monkey in popular story was the Barbary ape rather than either of the other known groups.

Whatever its species, the "classical" monkey had a distinct character—it was clownish, ugly (it lacked buttocks, and large buttocks were a sign of beauty to the Greeks), wily, greedy, vain, and above all imitative.

Greece produced thinkers and poets; Carthage, generals and explorers. So, while leaving fewer records than the Greeks, this seafaring people nevertheless came to know much more about the outside world. Early in the seventh century B.C., a silver bowl was made by a Phoenician craftsman, and this bowl was found by archaeologists in Italy a hundred years ago. Around its sides were depicted a variety of hunting scenes. One scene shows a hunt for the red deer of the Atlas Mountains in Northwest Africa. Another shows a creature (Plate 5) that, it has recently been suggested, is a true ape—perhaps a mountain gorilla. The creature certainly has apelike features; it is hairy and manlike, with an ape-shaped head. It could be a reconstruction by an artist working from a head and a skin brought in by the hunter, together with a description of the beast. The "ape" is shown standing upright, holding a rock in one upraised hand, as if ready to throw it, and a branch in the other hand.

Were there indeed apes in the Atlas Mountains in the seventh century B.C.? We do not know. The picture on the bowl certainly calls for explanation. Perhaps, however, if it really is an ape, we should bear in mind that it may have been imported from farther south, aboard a trading ship. Also, its stone-throwing, stick-carrying propensity tends to identify it as a chimpanzee rather than as a gorilla (see Plates 47, 48). However, the creature on this bowl is certainly the earliest representation known of what *may* be an ape.

Early in the fifth century B.C., Hanno, a Carthaginian navigator, made a voyage along the west coast of Africa for the purpose of exploration and colonization. His Punic log, which survives today in a Greek translation, tells how, at the end of the outward voyage, after passing a high mountain, the voyagers came to a gulf in which there was an island, and in this island was a lake with a second island,

full of savage people, the greater part of whom were women, whose bodies were hairy and whom our interpreters called Gorillas. Though we pursued the men, we could not seize any of them; but all fled from us, escaping over the precipices, and defending themselves with stones. Three women were however taken; but they attacked their conductors with their teeth and hands, and could not be prevailed on to accompany us. Having killed them, we flayed them and brought their skins with us to Carthage. [Translated from the Greek document *Periplus,* by Thomas Falconer, 1797. *Periplus* is believed to be a translation of Hanno's Punic original, which is lost.]

What were the creatures Hanno saw? Can they have been true apes? It is probable that he had reached what is today Sierra Leone. This would bring him within the range of the chimpanzee today, but leave him far short of the gorilla's present-day range. However, we do not know the whereabouts of gorillas or chimpanzees in the fifth century B.C.

It is unlikely that the "gorillas" were pygmies. Pygmies were already known in Egypt, Greece and, probably, North Africa at this time. Also, of course, they are not hairy. It is unlikely that they were monkeys, with which Hanno was already familiar. In any case, names already existed for these, and so there was no need for a new one. Thus it seems likely, from the details and from the behavior described, that Hanno gave us the earliest verbal description of a true ape.

Pomponius Mela, a first-century B.C. Spaniard who wrote a geography of the known world in Latin, *De Situ Orbis,* mentioned Hanno's tale and introduced the Gorgons—monsters of Greek mythology, dwelling in the far west—to explain what Hanno found. While this was just confusing the issue, to Mela it was a sufficient explanation, for to him Gorgons were much more familiar than gorillas or chimpanzees. At any rate, Gorgons they remained as far as the ancients were concerned, for Pliny the Elder (first century of the Christian Era) was content to write that Hanno had collected two skins of Gorgons that could be seen in a temple at Carthage, and Pliny was widely regarded as the wisest man of his age.

In Carthage itself, and in the surrounding cities, the Barbary ape was the monkey or "ape" of Hanno's day, and no one appears to have found the "gorilla" skins worthy of note, so that to the north, a hundred years later, Aristotle knew, or wrote, nothing of them.

In the second century B.C. the Greek historian and geographer Agatharchides wrote a work *On the Red Sea* in which he described Ethiopia and its peoples. This work no longer exists in the original, but two later Greek authors, Photius and Diodorus, both quoted from it, and their quotations survive. One passage that both of them quote concerns two strange "peoples" of Ethiopia, the "wood-eaters" ("Hylophagoi") and the "seed-eaters" ("Spermatophagoi"). Here is what Agatharchides has to say concerning the "wood-eaters" (Photius's version):

The Hylophagoi on the other hand eat the soft parts of the wood of trees. At nights they sleep in places which they choose because they afford a strong protection against the wild beasts of the area. Then as soon as it is light they climb—women and children as well—into the trees, eagerly stretching to reach the highest branches. There they crush the softest bits of wood and then eat them without trouble. Their way of life is quite remarkable—it is incredible to see how they can climb and how their whole limbs, not just their hands, fingers and feet, have been stretched out. They leap easily from one branch to another and snatch the branches from each other even in the most dangerous places. Indeed, such characteristics do they display that everyone who sees them is astonished and hardly dare talk of them to people who have not seen for themselves for fear of being disbelieved. They chew all the juicy branches with their teeth and then can digest them in their bellies without trouble. If they happen to fall from a high branch, they come to no harm because of their great strength. They go about naked and share their wives and children. They make war with each other about their territories and the majority die of hunger at about 50 when cataract spreads over their eyes.

Diodorus adds little to this, except that he specifies that "if they happen to slip with their feet they can catch hold again with their hands." Also, he states that they fight each other "armed with rods, and they tear apart their enemies once captured." He does not mention their sleeping habits, nor does he say that people do not care to talk about the creatures.

It has been suggested that the "Hylophagoi" were chimpanzees. Owing to the similarity between the two quotations, there is no doubt that we have here an accurate rendering of what Agatharchides wrote. Was he a reliable observer? Or was his description based on hearsay? We cannot be sure. He mentions in his account certain habits that indicate chimpanzees rather than monkeys, although, of course, he thought they were a race of people.

Wood eating, for example, occurs in chimpanzees at certain times, when they tear off strips of bark and chew them up. Monkeys do not do this, nor do Ethiopians. The lengthening of limbs and hands, the catching hold of a branch in a falling flight, and the ability to survive a fall fit well with what is known of chimpanzee behavior, as does the mention that these creatures sleep in places that are protected from wild beasts, for in fact chimpanzees make nests in the trees. The idea of rival groups going to war with each other may perhaps refer to the wild hootings and shriekings chimpanzees make. And lastly, the observation that old Hylophagoi succumb to cataract fits with what my wife and I saw in Africa (see page 131).

Today, chimpanzees occur in the southern Sudan, which is just to the west of present-day southern Ethiopia, but a long way from the Red Sea.

On balance, I think we have enough evidence to say that Agatharchides' Hylophagoi probably were chimpanzees. In that case his report ought to be considered as the second account of an ape in the literature of the Western world. That was in the second century B.C. It made no impact on classical thoughts about monkeys, for from the start the species was taken to be a new race of men. Greek legend already had a race of monkeys—the Cercopes—who were originally men but were turned into monkeys by Hercules because of their trickery. So the Hylophagoi fitted more easily into Greek thought as a race of submen than as a new species, as we now see it, of higher primate. The Greeks lacked the conceptual framework for a form of *animal* between monkey and man that was neither one nor the other.

In the first century C.E., as we have noted, Pliny of Rome was the authority on most things, including monkeys, submen, and men. In his *Natural History* we find the following:

Among the Westerne mountains of India the Satyres haunt . . . creatures of all other most swift in footmanship: which one while run with all foures; otherwhiles upon two feet only like men.

He also described another people of India, called the *Choromandae*,

a savage and wild people: distinct voice and speech they have none, but in steed thereof, they keepe an horrible gnashing and hideous noise: rough they are and hairie all over their bodies, eies they have red like the houlets, and toothed they be like dogs.

The "Satyres" or the *Choromandae* may just possibly have been gibbons, but we cannot be sure. Satyrs in Greek legend were creatures of the woods and mountains, half man, half goat, and were derived from Pan, an early Greek nature god; their character was indolent and lascivious. Satyrs were again described by the third-century C.E. author Aelian, who placed them in India. According to Aelian, they lived on leaves and fruits, and when pursued fled to the mountains and rolled down rocks on their pursuers. These strange and ancient references to wild-beast-like races of people, persisting through the centuries, belong to a framework of thought and religion where monsters and weird races of people living in remote corners of the world were accepted by all. But certainly these stories may have been based on *some* facts, and it could well be that our now familiar apes—chimpanzees and gorillas in Africa, gibbons and orangs in Asia—were what gave rise to them. Within the framework of Greek mythology and belief, however, each form came to possess independent and unique existence.

Besides these exotic forms, however, Pliny described what was known of the commoner monkeys in his day:

The different kinds of apes, which approach the nearest to the human figure, are distinguished from each other by the tail. Their shrewdness is quite wonderful. It is said that, imitating the hunters, they will besmear themselves with bird-lime, and put their feet into the shoes, which, as so many snares, have been prepared for them. Mucianus says, that they have even played at chess, having, by practice, learned to distinguish the different pieces, which are made of wax. He says that the species which have tails become quite melancholy when the moon is on the wane, and that they leap for joy at the time of the new moon, and adore it. . . . All the species of apes manifest remarkable affection for their offspring. Females, which have been domesticated, and have had young ones, carry them about and shew them to all comers, shew great delight when they are caressed, and appear to understand the kindness thus shewn them. Hence it is, that they very often stifle their young with their embraces. The dog's headed ape is of a much fiercer nature, as is the case with the satyr.

This wonderful hodgepodge of fact and fable is an agglomeration of all the information Pliny could glean from earlier sources.

Between Pliny and Aelian in time lived Galen, one of the first anatomists, a second-century C.E. Greek physician whose medical writings were outstanding in their time and were standard works of reference until the Renaissance, over a thousand years later. Galen dissected monkeys, preferring to use Barbary apes but also using baboons and other species, and it is possible that he dissected an ape as well. In his own words:

An Ape is the most like a Man of any quadruped: In the Viscera and the Muscles, and in the Arteries, and Veins and Nerves, because 'tis so in the structure of the Bones. For 'tis from their make, that it walks on two Legs, and uses its fore-limbs as Hands. It hath the largest Breast of any Quadruped, and Clavicles or Collar bones like a Man, and a round Face, and a small or short Neck.

As far as knowledge of monkeys and apes is concerned, Galen was the last bright star in the fading heavens of the ancient world. There were no more contributions to primate knowledge for a long time. Monkeys were kept as pets, and used commercially to do tricks—they were taught to dance, play the flute and harp, walk on stilts, drive a chariot, hurl the javelin, and shoot the bow and arrow. Some were dressed. They performed at roadside shows and perhaps in theaters. People found their "aping" of human behavior very funny. Both sympathy for captive animals and disgust at the monkey's natural sexuality came later; these seem to be essentially Christian ideas.

The rise and spread of Christianity in the Near East and southern Europe had a profound effect on the thinking of ordinary men and women. Quite apart from the newly imposed structure of supernatural ideas derived from Jewish thought, it imposed severe restrictions on actual day-to-day behavior. Moderation of all the "appetites" became a commendable virtue; gone was the freedom to enjoy wine, women, and song that the ancients had understood so well. The early Christians, like militant groups the world over, needed all the strength they could get, and derived it from self-denial.

Early Christianity, and St. Paul in particular, taught that sexual behavior, except in the cause of reproduction and within the bounds of marriage, was a sin, and although the idea must have been frustrating to most level-headed pagans of the day, it gained currency with the spread of the new religion and is still widely held in the Christian world today. This frustration found some relief in the aggressiveness of the Christians toward other religious groups, most of which were more tolerant of man's natural desires. And it showed itself in minor ways too, including man's attitude to the monkey. For those characteristics of the monkey that amused the ancients—its imitativeness, greed, and sexuality—failed to amuse the Christians; these qualities now took on sinister proportions as sins, for which the soul of man would be eternally condemned to hellfire. From being an object of fun and games, the monkey became nothing less than a symbol of the Devil himself.

We know this from a few documents that have survived from the early Middle Ages, and from the symbolic role of the ape on the margins of illustrated Bibles and other manuscripts. In all, the ape is associated with pagan ideas deriving from ancient Egypt. Egypt was evil; it was the Old Testament "land of darkness" from which Moses escaped, and it was the land of idolatry. In the *Physiologus,* the first bestiary—a compendium of "Christian zoology" that was written during the early part of the Christian Era—the "ape" and the wild ass are said to represent the Devil because both announce the autumnal equinox—the ass by braying twelve times, the "ape" by urinating seven times. This was a time of special significance to the early Christians, who interpreted it as meaning that the night (that is, the pagans) had become equal to the day (that is, the faithful)—a condition rejoiced in by the Devil.

We have another fine example of the attitude of the early Christians toward the monkey in the action of Theophilus, Christian leader of an antipagan revolt in Alexandria in the year A.D. 391. He destroyed every vestige of idolatry he could find except one monkey statue, which he ordered to be set up as a monument to heathen depravity.

Throughout the first millennium of the Christian Era, a feature of Christian writings was the attempt to find new explanations for man's problems in terms of the framework of biblical thought. While Aristotle had been content to say that monkeys resembled man very closely, and Galen worked out the idea in detail and showed it to be true anatomically, neither of them was preoccupied with the problem of *why* this should be so. But the Christian philosophers always searched for reasons—to them all things could be explained in terms of the Bible. And so, in the *Physiologus,* there is a strange passage stating the connection between the Devil and the monkey. This was based on the monkey's supposed physical resemblance to the Devil. The passage concerned reads as follows:

He [the Devil] had a beginning, but he has no end [that is, no tail]; at the outset he was one of the archangels, but his end is not in view. Now the ape, not having a tail, is without species, and his rear, without a tail, is vile; like the Devil, he does not have a good end.

St. Augustine, the great Christian philosopher of the fourth to the fifth centuries, asked the question: What criteria can be used to distinguish man from the monkeys, the submen of classical writings (which were still believed, on the authority of the ancients, to exist in remote parts of the earth), and the creatures of Greek legend—for example, the satyrs and centaurs? The criteria of man, he answered, were *mortality* and *reason*. Legendary beings lacked the former; monkeys and submen lacked the latter.

At the end of these so-called Dark Ages, in the eleventh and twelfth centuries, international trade was on the increase and cities were developing, attitudes were softening and the Christian world was awakening to a new fullness of life and thought. Pictures of monkeys became more common, even in church on misericords, and monkeys were more frequently mentioned in writings. This was perhaps because more monkeys were coming to Europe as pets and performers. Increasing familiarity seems at this time to have led to a change of attitude toward the monkey: from being a symbol of the Devil himself it became a symbol of the human sinner, the Devil's victim.

Sermons are our chief source of information at this time, and we find that the Aesopic tale of the mother monkey with her two babies (see Plate 6, dated about A.D. 1170) has been adapted into a Christian morality tale. The story was used in two versions:

First version: Here the mother monkey is fleeing from hunters; she is forced to drop her loved youngster, but carries the hated one on her back to safety. This tale was interpreted as follows: The mother monkey is the lustful sinner; the loved young is the sins of the flesh; the hated young represents virtues; the hunters are the devil. Moral: Only by abandoning the pleasures of the flesh can man escape the Devil.

Second version: Here the mother flees Satan, clinging to her sexual pleasures; but the young on her back, which now represents her sins of the flesh, grows and grows until finally it becomes so heavy that she is caught.

Now people could laugh at monkeys; their capacity as mimics was again widely appreciated, and some classical stories on the subject were revived. One such was Pliny's tale that the way to catch a monkey is to lay out birdlime and pretend to rub it into your eyes while a monkey is watching; the monkey will imitate you, and can then be caught. To the Christians it was Satan who laid out the lime as temptation to sinful behavior, and man, the sinner, who rubbed it into his own eyes.

With the development of commerce, Christians had a new kind of greed to preach against—the amassing of material wealth. We now find the tale of the mother monkey in a new guise: now, changing from her role as the lustful sinner, she becomes the rich man; the loved infant to which she clings is wealth, and the infant on her back, the mounting burden of sin. The hunter is death, and the moral, "You can't take it with you."

On this level, the level of pulpit oratory, the monkey's place in the medieval scheme of things was fairly clear-cut. But behind the pulpit the similarity between man and monkey remained a problem for honest Christian thinkers.

Albertus Magnus, the thirteenth-century theologian, took matters a stage further than Augustine had done. Instead of dividing mortal beings into two groups—man, who has reason, and animals, which do not—he distinguished an intermediate category of creatures "similar to man," and in this category he put the pygmies (known since the time of ancient Egypt) and the monkeys. While lacking reason, these creatures were superior to all other animals in having some control over their animal desires, in the form of memory and imitative abilities. Thus Albertus Magnus was the first man in history to suggest that monkeys provide a link between man and the animals. Aristotle had remarked on the similarity between man and monkeys, but had gone no further. Albertus Magnus now saw that monkeys combined some of the qualities of mind and body found in the lower animals with some found in man. But he was nowhere near the modern evolutionary position, lacking the concept that the forms of animals can change over time. His interpretation of the three levels of living things: beasts, monkeys, and man, was essentially Christian, for the stages differed according to the extent to which mind had supremacy over body, an idea based on the concept that God and the angels were totally without animal desires, as indeed was Adam before the Fall.

Close to the core of Christian thinking on the nature of man is the story of the Fall of Adam. Originally pure, he fell in the Garden of Eden by succumbing to the temptation of eating a fruit, a very special forbidden fruit, which grew on the Tree of the Knowledge of Good and Evil. The Devil, in the form of a snake, induced Eve to defy God and eat the fruit. Adam ate too. The first consequence of their eating was that Adam and Eve became aware of, and ashamed of, their nudity. So it would seem that the knowledge acquired by eating the fruit was consciousness of sex. (The acquisition by man of consciousness of sex is also a theme in the original Engidu myth—the ancient Gilgamesh story of western Asia, dating from around 2000 B.C.—from which the myth of the Fall was derived.) The fruit is a direct symbol of sexual knowledge; and the whole story is an attempt to explain where man's animal desires originate from, and why he finds it so difficult to be virtuous.

The reason I have dwelt on this interpretation is that unless it is accepted, the appearance of monkeys in illustrations of Adam, and the special role they play, cannot be fully appreciated. The frontispiece of a medieval English bestiary shows Adam naming the beasts, and in front of him sits a monkey holding an apple. By the early sixteenth century the monkey is often seen in the Garden of Eden with Adam and Eve and the snake, and it is always eating an apple. In Ludwig Krug's woodcut of the Fall (see Plate 7) there is a snake, but the monkey occupies center stage, and the message is clear: as Adam bites the apple, he becomes, like the apple-eating monkey, sexually aware.

Oddly enough, there is no written authority for the occurrence of monkeys in the Garden of Eden. We have seen that, in the sermons of the Middle Ages, monkeys were most often symbols of the lustful sinner. Here, in the sphere of art, the idea is repeated. It was the fact that the ape so splendidly fulfilled the requirements of a symbol of sexual sin that led one artist after another to put the monkey into the Garden. Monkeys love fruit, and they are freely sexual. In eating the apple before Adam's very eyes, the monkeys mock him and tempt him. They are the very instruments of his temptation.

With this flowering of the monkey as the archculprit of all our ills, we reach the late Middle Ages and the end of the monkey as an object of special treatment in religious art and writing. Certainly it continued to be written about and painted. But from the sixteenth century onward there were greater tolerance and amusement at its antics, and a secular attitude much more like that of ancient times prevailed.

The sixteenth century, too, saw the rebirth of zoology in the work of Konrad von Gesner, the German scholar. During the latter half of the century, he compiled the *Historiae Animalium* in which every known fact he could unearth in the libraries of Europe about every known living beast was faithfully recorded. Some of the creatures he described have since passed into the realm of legend; others have not. He distinguished several varieties of "apes":

There are apes in *Troglodytae* which are maned about the neck like lions, as big as great Belweathers. So are some called *Cercopitheci, Munkies,*

Choeropitheci, Hog Apes, Cepi, Callitriches, Marmosits, Cynocephali, of a Dog and an Ape, *Satyres* and *Sphinges,* of which we will speak in order, for they are not all alike, but some resemble men one way, and some another.

All these are described, and most of them are illustrated (see Plates 8 and 9). We can distinguish all the well-known sources of antiquity in their creation—indeed, Gesner often takes pains to say who his sources are. Among the stories he tells is the one of the monkey mother, told in a rather matter-of-fact way, without moralizing:

They bring forth young ones for the most part by twins, whereof they love the one and hate the other; that which they love they bear in their armes, the other hangeth at the dam's back, and for the most part she killeth that which she loveth, by pressing it too hard; afterward she setteth her whole delight upon the other.

This is the last time the tale of the monkey mother, which we have traced all the way from Aesop, achieves prominence. It had a run of no less than twenty centuries. And in all that time, not one author perceived the truth behind the story. This I believe to be as follows: when her infant dies, for whatever reason, the typical female macaque, of which the Barbary ape is one kind, holds on to the body tenaciously and carries it around with her wherever she goes. Surely it was the sight of a mother Barbary ape clutching the corpse of her baby that gave rise to this story. The idea that she herself killed it by too much love, and the idea of the hated twin on her back, belong, on the other hand, to the realm of fancy. True twins are rare, although female monkeys do sometimes carry two infants, one on the belly and one on the back.

Gesner is commonly considered to be the founder of modern zoology. Today we note with wonder the absolute lack of any distinction between fact and fantasy in his descriptions. Commonplace trivialities and the wildest exaggerations were set down side by side. His concern, with an objectivity to be admired, was to collect the known beliefs, tales, facts, fables—any information whatsoever—pertaining to all living beings. This, then, was the total extent of man's zoological knowledge at his time. In the next chapter, we shall see how zoology, and knowledge of the apes, developed on the foundations Gesner laid.

CHAPTER **2**

Finding the True Apes

IN THE SIXTEENTH century, man's visions of the world began expanding, liberating ideas that were to lead to big changes in governments, in religions, and not least in science, including medical and zoological knowledge.

At this time there was a tremendous increase in navigation, with the ocean-going sailing ship coming into its own, and opening up the seas of the world. The great powers in Europe were the seagoing nations, foremost among them Spain and Portugal. Spain discovered the Americas, and the Portuguese pioneered the route to the Indies round the south of the African continent. The Dutch were also a power to be reckoned with, while the English began taking seafaring seriously under Henry VIII, slowly building up supremacy on the seven seas, after crippling the power of her enemy, Spain, at the end of the sixteenth century.

A succession of small trading posts was established along the coasts of West Africa and the Indian Ocean, mainly by the Portuguese, and later by the Dutch and the English. Then, with the invention of the

[[41

printing press, which rapidly brought about the dissemination of information to wide audiences, Europe was the seedbed for a great growth of new ideas. It was now that the true apes were finally distinguished from monkeys on the one hand, and from men, monsters, or mythical beings on the other.

About this time, an Englishman named Andrew Battell, who lived about 1589 to 1614, had gone adventuring to unknown lands, and had been imprisoned by the Portuguese in South America, whence they sent him to one of their settlements at São Paolo de Loanda, in Angola, and along the West African coast. While he was there, he obtained knowledge of, and perhaps also saw for himself, both gorillas and chimpanzees. His report, published in 1625, called them the "Pongo" and the "Engeco," these names being corruptions of African tribal names "Mpongwe" and "Nshiego." He wrote:

The Woods are so covered with Baboones, Monkies, Apes, and Parrots, that it will feare any man to trauaile in them alone. Here are also two kinds of Monsters, which are common in these Woods, and very dangerous.

The greatest of these two Monsters is called, *Pongo*, in their Language: and the lesser is called, *Engeco*. This *Pongo* is in all proportion like a man, but that he is more like a Giant in stature, then a man: for he is very tall, and hath a mans face, hollow eyed, with long haire vpon his browes. His face and eares are without haire, and his hands also. His bodie is full of haire, but not very thicke, and it is of a dunnish colour. He differeth not from a man, but in his legs, for they haue no calfe. Hee goeth alwaies vpon his legs, and carrieth his hands clasped on the nape of his necke, when he goeth vpon the ground. They sleepe in the trees, and build shelters from the raine. They feed vpon Fruit that they find in the Woods, and vpon Nuts, for they eate no kind of flesh. They cannot speake, and have no vnderstanding more than a beast. The People of the Countrie, when they trauaile in the Woods, make fires where they sleepe in the night; and in the morning, when they are gone, the *Pongoes* will come and sit about the fire, till it goeth out: for they have no vnderstanding to lay the wood together. They goe many together, and kill many *Negroes* that trauaile in the Woods. Many times they fall vpon the Elephants, which come to feed where they be, and so beate them with their clubbed fists, and pieces of wood, that they will runne roaring away from them. Those *Pongoes* are neuer taken aliue, because they are so strong, that ten men cannot hold one of them: but yet they take many of their young ones with poisoned Arrowes. The young *Pongo* hangeth on his mothers bellie, with his hands fast clasped about her: so that, when the Countrie people kill any of the femals, they take the young one, which hangeth fast vpon his mother. When they die among themselues, they couer the dead with great heapes of boughs and wood, which is commonly found in the Forrests.

A note by the editor of Battell's book, Purchas, is interesting:

The *Pongo,* or Giant-ape. He told me in conference with him, that one of these *Pongos* took a *Negro* Boy of his, which liued a moneth with them. For they hurt not those which they surprise at vnawares, except they look on them, which hee auoyded. He said, their highth was like a mans, but their bignesse twice as great. I saw the *Negro* Boy. Their strength. What the other Monster should be, he hath forgotten to relate: and these papers came to my hand since his death, which otherwise in my often conferences I might haue learned. Perhaps he meaneth the *Pigmey Pongo* killers, mentioned.

What a pity Battell "forgot" to describe the "Engeco"! However, if the "Pongo" is the gorilla, as seems most probable, the "Engeco" is most likely the chimpanzee. We should note Battell's use of the word "monster." In keeping with the usage of the ancients and of Gesner, the word means weird manlike animals that are real, not imaginary. Like the reports of Hanno and Agatharchides, Battell's story made little or no impact on zoology: all were classed as mere "traveler's tales." But the truth was not far off.

It began with the work of the Dutch physician Nicolaas Tulp, a well-known and respected figure of his time, who is depicted in Rembrandt's famous painting "The Anatomy Lesson." Tulp appended to a medical treatise, published in 1641, a description of an ape from Angola, a part of Africa with which Holland was much engaged in trade at that time. This ape had been kept in the menagerie of Frederick-Henry, Prince of Orange, at his château of Honsholredijk, near The Hague.

Here is Tulp's account of the appearance of his specimen (translated from the Latin):

Satyrus indicus

Altho' outside the medical forum, I add nevertheless to this plan the Indian Satyr: brought, by our memory, from Angola; and given to Frederic Henry, Prince of Orange. This Satyr was a quadruped; but from the human face, which it bears, it is called by the Indians orang-outang; or man of the woods. Resembling in its height a boy of three years; as in thickness one of six years.

It was in body neither fat nor graceful, but robust: yet very nimble and very active. The joints are in truth so tight: and with vast muscles attached to them: so that he dares anything; and can accomplish it. In front it is everywhere smooth: but hairy behind, and covered with black hairs. The face counterfeits man: but the nostrils are flat and bent inward, like a wrinkled, and toothless old woman.

The ears in truth differ nothing from the human form. Nor the breast; furnished on both sides with rounded mammae (for the sex was feminine), the abdomen had a very deep umbilicus; and the limbs, both the superior and inferior ones so exact likeness to those of man: that you would scarcely see one egg more like another.

Nor were the joints required for lying down lacking; nor the order of fingers on the hands; nor the human shape of the thumb; or the calves of the legs; or the heel bones of the foot. Which, beautifully put together, and its members of such form, was the cause that it should walk much of the time erect: nor did it lift up any weight whatever, even of the heaviest burden with less difficulty or carry it less easily.

Judging from the ape's place of origin, Tulp's illustration of it (Plate 10), and his description, zoologists are agreed that this creature was in fact a chimpanzee. I should like to suggest that in all probability it was a pygmy chimpanzee, a distinct form that occurs south of the Congo River. There are three reasons for drawing this conclusion. First, pygmy chimpanzees normally attain, in the fully grown adult, a somewhat smaller size than their trans-Congo cousins. In his text, Tulp states that his specimen had the "height" (original Latin, *longitudine*) of a boy of three years, and the "thickness" (*crassitie*) of a boy of six. Not knowing exactly what dimensions he was referring to, we cannot be certain what size his animal was, but we can assume that it was a rather small chimpanzee. What age was it? The only indications we have are that it was an adult. Its breast was furnished with "rounded mammae," a feature of adult female chimpanzees but not of juveniles. The illustration confirms the description. It seems, therefore, that this was a small, but nevertheless adult, chimpanzee.

Second, pygmy chimpanzees often show webbing of the second and third toes of the foot (see page 61). Tulp's illustration shows a definite indication of webbing in exactly the right place.

Third, we know that Tulp's ape came from Angola. This Portuguese colony was temporarily under the control of Holland from 1640 to 1648. It lies almost wholly south of the Congo River (see Figure 1). According to a report dating from 1905, chimpanzees were still to be found in the forests south of the Congo and north of the Quanza River in the year 1882. This area is marked B on the map. There are no pygmy chimpanzees there today, distribution now being limited to the

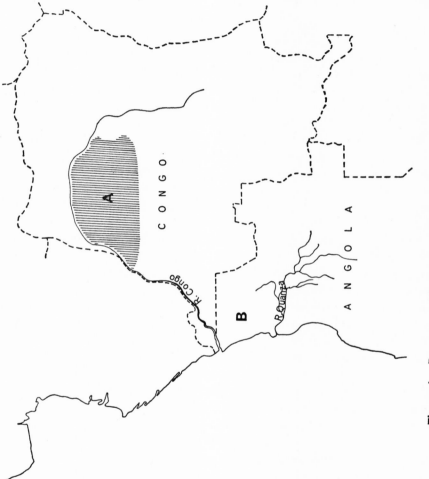

Figure 1. Present and former distribution of pygmy chimpanzees.

area marked A on the map. Although chimpanzees do occur north of the Congo, they cannot cross it; so the chimpanzees living last century between the Congo and the Quanza would probably be pygmy chimpanzees. They were living in an area where Tulp's specimen is very likely to have been caught, near the Angolan coast.

Therefore, Tulp's ape was, quite probably, a pygmy chimpanzee. However, since this form was not officially described until 1929, it is hardly surprising that Tulp did not know. After all, he had absolutely nothing but mythical creatures, monkeys, and a variety of freakish half-men to compare it with!

Tulp added to his firsthand description an account he had heard of the orangutan of Borneo from a traveler-friend of his called Blomartio. The king of that far-off land had told Blomartio tales of lustful and shameless male orangs who carried off women and girls to the woods, there to ravish them. Tulp firmly believed that the creature in his possession was the same as the Bornean orang and that both were the same as the original satyrs of India described by Pliny and others in ancient times, if one discounts "the ingenious figments of the Poets" that attributed horns and claws and pointed ears to the satyrs.

"If anything is a 'Satyr,'" he wrote, "the orang-outang is one." This approach was in strong contrast with that of Gesner. Tulp did not blindly accept what the classical authors wrote; he adopted a critical standpoint, attempting to distinguish fact from fancy. He ended his description by saying: "The appearance of this Indian Satyr, perchance becoming famous, may disperse this dense fog. It is difficult to please everyone." This was the essence of Renaissance empiricism.

However, Tulp did introduce considerable confusion over names. Though from Africa, he called his specimen "Satyrus Indicus," the Indian Satyr, after Pliny, and "Orang-outang," which means "Man of the Woods" in Bornean, and also, for good measure "Homo sylvestris," a Latin translation of "Man of the Woods."

Every subject boasts its "father" or "founder." In the case of primatology it is Edward Tyson. The most modest of men, heavy and serious in bearing, taciturn in company, Tyson can justly claim the following distinctions: he was the founder of the methods of comparative anatomy still used today; he was the first to study the detailed anatomy of an ape; he was the first to give evidence that man is closely related to the apes; and he was the first to make a comprehensive study of the previous references to and mythology of the apes.

Tyson was an English doctor who lived in London, and was a

Fellow of the Royal Society. He was born in 1650 and died in 1708. He made studies of the porpoise, rattlesnake, tapeworm, and opossum, besides his routine medical work. In early 1698, a live infant chimpanzee was brought to London from Angola, the first recorded occasion that an anthropoid ape had arrived in England. Tyson realized its extreme importance for science, and when the little creature died, in April, 1698, he took its body home to dissect it. An excellent anatomist and draughtsman named William Cowper helped him with the detailed description of the muscles and did numerous accurate drawings of the ape and the dissection (see Plates 11 and 12). On June 1, 1698, Tyson described his creature to the Royal Society, and gave the first scientific demonstration of man's relation to lower animals—a theory that was to wait almost two hundred years, until Darwin's *The Descent of Man* was published in 1871, before gaining acceptance. In June, 1699, Tyson's book was published in London. It was called *Orang-outang, sive Homo sylvestris: or, the Anatomy of a Pygmie Compared with that of a Monkey, an Ape, and a Man.* So excellent was this study that today it is no mere historical document; in the words of an eminent living authority on the primates, M. F. Ashley Montagu, "It will continue to serve as an inexhaustible storehouse of information as long as the study of the monkeys, apes, and man continues."

Tyson compared his specimen, point by point, at each stage of the anatomical dissection, with monkeys on the one hand, and with man on the other. In this way he drew up two lists. The first consisted of forty-seven characters in which his "Pygmie" resembled man more closely than it resembled any monkey, and the second consisted of thirty-four characters in which the "Pygmie" resembled a monkey more closely than it resembled man. He concluded that the "Pygmie" was an intermediate type, wholly distinct from both man and the monkeys. In his own words: "In this *Chain* of the *Creation*, as an intermediate link between an *Ape* [that is, monkey] and a *Man*, I would place our *Pygmie*." This was a "gradational" classification, not an evolutionary one. Tyson was a pious Anglican and, as such, a believer in the creation of all species by God. But his conception of the chimpanzee as a "link" between monkeys and man in the "chain of creation" was based on his belief that each group was related to each other group.

Tyson could not appreciate how young and how small his specimen was, compared with an adult chimpanzee. He had never seen an adult, and had nothing but the description and picture of Tulp (see Plate 10) to go on. As we have seen, Tulp's picture shows an adult, but his description states that it was the height of a three-year-old boy, probably because it was a pygmy chimpanzee. Tyson's specimen, judging from the detailed description and Cowper's illustrations, was probably the young of a common chimpanzee. Its height was twenty-six inches. If we accept that Tulp's specimen was in fact a pygmy chimpanzee, then Tyson was the first man to describe the common chimpanzee.

But how did Tyson come to call his chimpanzee by the name of "Pygmie," as well as the name "orang-outang" commonly applied to the various specimens of the manlike apes encountered by travelers and sailors of the times? Tyson had read Tulp's account of *his* "orang" and was excited by Tulp's theories that here he had discovered the satyrs of the ancient world. Tyson resolved to go back to all the ancient sources he could, and see what he could find. He was able to trace a reference to pygmies, meaning a race of tiny people, to a Greek historian, Ctesias, as far back as the fourth century B.C., and chiefly because the given stature of these pygmies agreed so closely with what he estimated for his own specimen, when adult, Tyson decided that in the Angolan "orang-outang" he had the source of all the tales of a pygmy race of men: "That the *Pygmies* of the Antients were a sort of *Apes,* and not of the *Humane Race,* I shall endeavour to prove in the following *Essay.* And if the *Pygmies* were only *Apes,* then in all probability our *Ape* may be a *Pygmie;* a sort of *Animal* so resembling *Man,* that both the Antients and the Moderns have reputed it to be a *Puny Race* of Mankind."

He did not think that Tulp's animal was exactly the same as his own, and realized that there were very likely different kinds of manlike creatures. For the group as a whole he retained the name "orang-outang."

As for the satyrs of India, which Tulp thought he had found, Tyson did not agree. He was of the considered opinion "that there were such *Animals* as the Antients called *Satyrs;* and that they were a sort of *Monkeys* or *Apes* with Tails."

Faced with a great confusion of fact and fancy through the ages on this subject, Tyson gave a commendable warning: "In the *History* of *Nature* we must not depend upon the Authority of the Number of those that only transcribe the same thing, without duly examining the matter themselves: For the Authority here wholly depends on the veracity of the first Relator."

Tyson's work was so good and so accurate that it is really a tragedy that his conclusion that he had discovered the "Pygmie" was wrong and that here, for once, the classical authors were right. Nearly two hundred years later, the discoveries of pygmy tribes in the Congo forests substantiated the accounts of the ancients, and proved Tyson wrong.

The whole of biology at this time was badly in need of reorganization. It needed someone with the right type of mind to categorize and classify all the known and described living things, and to give them names that could be scientifically and internationally viable. At the beginning of the eighteenth century Sweden produced Carl Linnaeus, a brilliant young botanist of peasant stock, whose formative years were spent cultivating as many remarkable plants as he could, in his father's garden. Though he was always short of funds during his studies in botany, and later in medicine, he possessed a lively and attractive personality that earned him patronage wherever he went. By the time he was twenty-five, he had already worked out principles of defining genera and species of plants and animals that even today form the very basis of our classifications. He published the first edition of his *Systema naturae* in 1735, and constantly revised it throughout his long life. Later editions of this work became more and more precise, and his tenth edition (1758) marks the starting point of modern taxonomy. Linnaeus was a pious man, with a pantheistic love of nature, in which he saw the reflection of God. He at first firmly believed that all the various species were created as such in the very beginning, and were immutable. "We count as many species as have been created from the beginning; the individual creatures are reproduced from eggs, and each egg produces a progeny in all respects like the parents." In his later years, however, he came to doubt whether all species were created as such. He himself was very successful in hybridizing plants in his own garden; and his studies had shown him how closely certain vegetable forms resembled each other, overlapping and merging. While he certainly never abandoned the theory of independent creation, he began to consider the possibility that it was the genera and only a few species that had been created, other species arising from the first ones. Here he was up against the problem that Darwin and Mendel between them were to solve. Linnaeus had no solution, but in the final edition of *Systema naturae* he omitted the assertion that no new species arise.

Linnaeus was the first to use the word "primates." In his 1758 edition, he used this name for a group of creatures comprising four genera: man (*Homo*), monkeys and apes (*Simia*), lemurs (*Lemur*) and bats (*Verspetilio*). With the exception of the bats, his thinking was fundamentally the same as that of modern taxonomists.

In the first genus, *Homo,* Linnaeus recognized two species, *Homo sapiens* (man) and *Homo troglodytes;* the latter was a creature described by Jacob Bontius, a doctor working in the Indies, who may have seen orangs in Borneo but who illustrated his account with a picture of a hairy woman. In the second genus, *Simia,* Linnaeus first placed the species *Simia satyrus,* the creature described by Tulp, that is, the chimpanzee. The other species were a variety of monkeys. Linnaeus seems to have known nothing of Tyson, for he never referred to him.

In 1760, a pupil of Linnaeus, C. E. Hoppius, reclassified the primates, but he too seemed unaware of Tyson's description of the Angolan chimpanzee. Hoppius used the term "Anthropomorpha" (which Linnaeus had used in 1735 but later dropped in favor of "Primates"), in a new and important way—to distinguish the apes from man on the one hand, and monkeys on the other. He thus progressed beyond Linnaeus, who had put monkeys and apes together in the same genus. Hoppius described four types of *Anthropomorpha* (see Plate 13):

> *Troglodyta,* derived from Bontius's dubious orang.
> *Lucifer,* derived from Aldrovandus, and imaginary.
> *Pygmaeus,* derived from G. Edwards, an eighteenth-century
>   naturalist, who drew an indeterminate type of ape
>   based partly on Tyson's work.
> *Satyrus,* derived from Tulp's chimpanzee.

Thus the apes had now been set apart as a separate group, even if extremely few people had so far been fortunate enough to see one. In 1738, however, a lively chimpanzee arrived in England and was put on show for all to see. The September issue of *The London Magazine* in that year reported:

A most surprizing Creature is brought over in the *Speaker,* just arrived from *Carolina,* that was taken in a Wood at *Guinea;* it is a Female about four Foot high, shaped in every Part like a Woman excepting its head, which nearly resembles the Ape: She walks upright naturally, sits down to her Food, which is chiefly Greens, and feeds herself with her Hands as a human Creature. She is very fond of a Boy on board, and is observed always sorrowful at his Absence. She is cloathed with a thin Silk Vestment, and shews a great Discontent at the opening of her Gown to discover her Sex. She is the Female of the Creature, which the *Angolans* call Chimpanzee, or the Mockman.

This, incidentally, was the first time the term "chimpanzee" was used. The name was probably derived from an African word. Apart from the usage in the quotation above, M. de la Brosse, also in 1738, referred to it as the "quimpézé." Both these names obviously have a common source in one of the central African languages, and a different one from the source language of the "Engeco" of Battel, which, as we shall see, came into popular use later as "Jocko."

Living at the same time as Linnaeus was a quite different kind of naturalist, a brilliant, aristocratic Frenchman Georges-Louis Leclerc, Count de Buffon, whose great *Natural History* was published in twenty volumes between 1749 and 1766. This was a description of the earth, its peoples and animals. In spite of the fact that Buffon had read every work he could find on natural history, geography, astronomy, and other subjects, and combined great knowledge from these fields, his writing was always lively, interesting, and easy to read. He tackled the problem of the manlike apes, drawing from more sources than the great Linnaeus, whose cold classifications of living things Buffon did not like. He realized that in Africa there must be two kinds of apes, one larger than the other, though he himself had seen only a chimpanzee. To the smaller one, which includes Tyson's "Pygmie," Tulp's "orang-outang," and Battel's "Engeco," Buffon gave the name of "Jocko." The larger one he termed "Pongo" after Battell's account, and included under this the various descriptions of the Bornean and Indian orangs. Both the "Jocko" and the "Pongo" were, he felt, no more than varieties of a single species, which he termed *Simia satyrus* or *Homo troglodytes*. In lumping them together, Buffon expressed regret that the information available to him was not better:

If these [the tales of travelers] were faithful, if they were not often ob-
scure, false, and exaggerated, we could not hesitate in pronouncing it [the
Pongo, or large type of ape] a different species from the jocko.

However, travelers' tales being what they were, Buffon decided to lump together both the Asian and African apes.

Buffon also described and illustrated the gibbon (Plate 14), and he was the first authority to use this name for it. He tells us in a footnote that he first heard the name from a M. Dupleix, but on reading Pliny, found that it was traceable back to antiquity, for Strabo used the word *keipon* for the *cephos*—a tailed monkey—and this *keipon* may be the name from which "gibbon" is descended (even though the gibbon has no tail). Buffon was the first man to establish the gibbon's existence in the popular mind, even though this creature, or the closely related siamang, had been previously described by Le Comte in 1697, and we can perhaps trace knowledge of it back to Pliny.

Buffon's description, in an English version of 1785, was as follows:

The Gibbon keeps himself always erect, even when he walks on four feet; because his arms are as long as both his body and legs. We have seen him alive. He exceeded not three feet in height; but he was young, and in captivity. Hence we may presume, that he had not acquired his full dimensions, and that, in a natural state, he might arrive at four feet. He has not the vestige of a tail. But he is distinguished from the other apes by the prodigious length of his arms: when standing erect on his hind feet, his hands touch the ground; and he can walk on his four feet without bending his body. . . .

Buffon describes the gibbon's face, and its "tranquil disposition," its delicate constitution, and he notes a fact that was to confuse later scholars: that "the gibbon varies in size and colour."

Buffon's work was really the first clear account, based on the most reliable sources, of the differences between the types of apes. Of the four kinds, the gorilla remained the least known, there being only Battell's account containing any detail, and thus it was easy for him to confuse it with the also little-known, but more often described, orangutan. The brilliant illustrator Jean-Baptiste Audebert included the gibbon (Plate 15), orang (Plate 16), and chimpanzee in his collection, published in 1802.

Buffon was also remarkable for some brilliant original ideas. Rejecting the biblical date of the earth's creation (six thousand years ago), he proposed instead that the earth was in fact the result of a collision between a comet and the sun and that the history of the earth's development, geologically and biologically, could be divided into seven periods, with animals appearing about the fifth period, and man not until the seventh. So, a century before other thinkers, he envisaged the birth of celestial bodies by natural means rather than by divine creation, and progressive changes in the animal and vegetable kingdoms from epoch to epoch rather than by divine creation of fully formed species.

After Buffon's account of the gibbon, several others appeared, under odd names such as the "Golok" and the "Wou-wou," a name obviously derived from the whooping calls gibbons make.

As for the misunderstood gorilla, the only extant report in the eighteenth century appears to be that of an unnamed sea captain (quoted by Monboddo in 1774) who had come across the "Impungu";

Of this animal there are three classes or species; the first and largest is, by the natives of Loango, Malemba, Cabenda, and Congo, called or named Impungu. This wonderful and frightful production of nature walks upright like man; is from 7 to 9 feet high, when at maturity, thick in proportion, and amazingly strong; covered with longish hair, jet black over the body, but longer on the head; the face more like the human than the Chimpenza, but the complexion black; and has no tail.

Although by now the history of scientific knowledge of our well-known and well-loved great apes seems hopelessly confused, it must be realized that only the chimpanzee had ever been brought alive or dead to Europe for the scientists to dissect and describe. The gorilla, the orang, the gibbon, all these were known of from the accounts of sailors and travelers abroad only, and these, of course, were not the accounts of specialists. There were no university primate expeditions of 1750, equipped with expert biologists and technical equipment.

The first record of an imported orang occurs in 1776 when a Dutchman named A. Vosmaer described a live female specimen from Borneo, which had been sent to William V by a merchant of the Indies Company. Vosmaer published a beautifully illustrated account of it in 1778 (see Plate 17). He did not distinguish his specimen clearly from the chimpanzee, however.

It was yet another Dutchman (Holland's shipping communications with the Indies were very extensive at this time), Pieter Camper, also a contemporary of Linnaeus and Buffon, who cleared away once for all much of the confusion surrounding the great apes. He managed to get a number of specimens of the orangutan, and dissected them. He also was able, in 1776, to study closely a live example at the menagerie known as Blaaw Jan, near Amsterdam. He came to the conclusion that he was dealing with a species distinct from that of Tyson's "Pygmie," and thus finally separated orang from chimpanzee.

But Camper's main contribution to the understanding of the apes was this. At the time, there were two great illusions current about orangs, and manlike apes in general, derived from the exaggerated tales and native folklore reported by travelers: first, that they walked upright like a man (often they were depicted leaning on a walking stick), and second, that, if they wished, they could speak.

In particular, Lord Monboddo, a Scottish judge, published in 1773–1792 *Of the Origin and Progress of Language,* in which, drawing from Tyson's work, he described the organs of speech in the ape as being almost identical to those in man, and he put forward the view that apes ought most certainly to be capable of language.

Camper undertook extremely detailed and careful investigations into the structure of the larynx, and made tests on his live orang, and concluded that it was incapable of articulate language. He also examined the musculature of the orang's limbs, and showed that it was in fact unable to walk completely upright as man does and that this was not its natural gait.

Thus by the end of the eighteenth century, the chimpanzee and the orang had both been examined and scientifically reported; the gibbon was known but had not been anatomically investigated, for no specimen had reached a European scientist. The gorilla was still only anecdotal. In 1819, T. E. Bowditch, in his *Narrative of a Mission from Cape Coast Castle to Ashantee,* contributed his share to gorilla lore. In the Gaboon, he heard of

the *ingena,* an animal like the orang-outang, but much exceeding it in size, being five feet high and four across the shoulders. Its paw was said to be even more disproportioned than its breadth, and one blow of it to be fatal. It is seen commonly by them when they travel to Kaybe, lurking in the bush to destroy passengers, and feeding principally on wild honey, which abounds. Among other of their actions . . . is that of building a house in rude imitation of the natives, and sleeping outside on the roof of it.

Finally, in 1847, the gorilla was discovered by science, and first described. At this time the commonest Latin name for the chimpanzee was *Troglodytes niger,* and Dr. Thomas S. Savage, who found the original gorilla skull, and Dr. Jeffries Wyman, who first described its skeleton, called their new creature *Troglodytes gorilla,* in memory of Hanno's "gorillas."

Savage and Wyman, the former an American missionary and the latter an American anatomist, had collaborated early in the 1840's to produce a complete description of the chimpanzee—its "external characters and habits . . . and organization." This was published in 1844, and confirmed the fact that the adult chimpanzee was a large animal with a markedly different appearance from the young one, the source of much confusion until then. Knowing the chimpanzee so well,

Dr. Savage was able to realize the importance of his new find. I quote the story of the discovery from T. H. Huxley:

Being unexpectedly detained at the Gaboon river, he [Savage] saw in the house of the Rev. Mr. Wilson, a missionary resident there, "a skull represented by the natives to be a monkey-like animal, remarkable for its size, ferocity, and habits." From the contour of the skull, and the information derived from several intelligent natives, "I was induced," says Dr. Savage, (using the term Orang in its old general sense) "to believe that it belonged to a new species of Orang. I expressed this opinion to Mr. Wilson, with a desire for further investigation; and, if possible, to decide the point by the inspection of a specimen, alive or dead."

Between them, Savage and Wilson obtained much information about the gorilla, and some specimens for Dr. Wyman to describe. Whether this new "gorilla" and the creatures Hanno's men named "gorillas" were one and the same species, no one can be sure, but Savage *was* sure that his gorilla was the "Pongo" of Battell, and here he was undoubtedly right. The "Pongo" thus became scientifically acceptable, more than two hundred years after Battell's death.

The discovery of the gorilla made an enormous impact on both public and scientists, in Europe and in the United States, much more than the discovery of the other apes, and perhaps more than the discovery of any other animal. There were several reasons for this. First, the discovery came *late*, when the era of modern science was already well under way, so that the techniques already existed for evaluating the new find and placing it among the apes, as a close relative of man. Second, the huge gorilla had "monster appeal" for an imaginative public. Here was a new monster, and one the scientists approved of! We shall see in Chapter 10 how things developed. Third, although the gorilla was described before the publication of Darwin's works, these, and the furious "Am I ape or man?" argument they triggered off (see Plate 18), helped to keep the gorilla in the forefront of people's minds. Today the gorilla certainly still ranks as the most fascinating of the apes even if, as a survey has shown, we are far more fond of the young chimpanzee.

The story of Charles Robert Darwin (1809–1882) is well known. His five-year voyage on the *Beagle* led him to doubt that each species was immutable and specially created in its present form. While he never abandoned the idea of a first "Creator," he doubted that a Creator would have found it necessary to make all the slightly differentiated and narrowly distributed species he observed around the world. From Malthus he gained the idea that, in every species, too many offspring are produced for all to survive. His studies of dogs and pigeons, made after returning to England, taught him that these offspring always vary from each other. He concluded that in the struggle for survival, those best fitted to the environment would survive and breed, and so they would pass on their particular variations to the next generation. This process he called "natural selection," and its result was the production, over time, of new species.

The year 1859 saw the publication of Darwin's *On the Origin of Species; The Descent of Man* followed in 1871. The theory it propounded was clear as daylight and easy to grasp: Man himself shared his origins with monkeys and apes. To most good Christians this was a blasphemous idea, and they would have nothing to do with it. Today the theory of evolution is universally accepted by scientists, and old bones dug up by archaeologists in Africa and Asia and Europe offer mute proof that apes and men have common ancestors.

From being man's closest relatives, as Tyson had said they were, the apes now came to be looked on as the closest living representatives of his actual forebears. A whole new range of concepts was born. If people in one part of the world looked more like apes than the white man, they must be backward. And if species evolved from each other, so did forms of social organization. Anthropologists and others busily graded races and societies according to their position in the scale. The white man and his society invariably came out on top.

The interest in gorillas caused an immediate demand for specimens. Expeditions were mounted by hunters for museums, universities, and zoos, and the peace of the African jungle was frequently shattered. Replication of the same wants in museum after museum, zoo after zoo, university after university, led to the arrival in Europe of a vast number of specimens, nearly all of them dead. One reason why the hunt was so successful was the habit of big males of charging the foe, the charge ending in a display in which the "old bull" stood upright, facing his enemy, and beat his chest. Alas, he made himself the easiest target the white hunters had ever known. But the gorilla was not quickly incorporated into the natural histories of the mid-nineteenth century (see Plate 19).

Just after the turn of the century, interest in the gorilla received a new impetus. Until this time, all known specimens had come from West Africa. To the east, in central and eastern Congo, no gorillas had been found. But on October 17, 1902, a German army officer, Captain Oskar von Beringe, and a friend, Dr. England, while traveling through central Africa, attempted to climb one of the volcanoes in what is today the southwest corner of Uganda, on the border with Ruanda. They had camped on a ridge at 3,100 meters, and then:

We spotted from our camp a group of black, large apes, which attempted to climb to the highest peak of the volcano. Of these apes we managed to shoot two, which fell with much noise into a canyon opening to the northeast of us. After five hours of hard work we managed to haul up one of these animals with ropes. It was a large, man-like ape, a male, about 1½ m. high and weighing over 200 pounds. The chest without hair, the hands and feet of huge size. I could unfortunately not determine the genus of the ape. He was for a chimpanzee of a previously unknown size, and the presence of gorillas in the Lake region has as yet not been determined.

"The genus of the ape" was not, in fact, hard to determine: Matschie, in 1903, showed it to be the gorilla of West Africa. But, in recognition of its hairier body, and other minor differences, he considered it to be a new species, which he called, after its discoverer, *Gorilla beringei*. Today this form has been thoroughly studied, morphologically, by a number of European and American scientists, and is considered to be no more than a subspecies of gorilla.

Meanwhile, a new kind of gibbon had been described by T. S. Raffles in 1821. This one was larger than the previously known gibbons, and was all black. It had certain peculiarities, such as the joining of the index and middle fingers of the foot by a web of skin, and an inflatable neck pouch, which it could blow up with air, perhaps to increase the volume of its vocalizations (ordinary gibbons, however, are tremendously noisy with no pouch). This new type became known as the siamang (see Plate 20).

About a century later, in 1929, it was established that the chimpanzees living to the south of the great Congo River were a much smaller race and had other anatomical differences, including recognizably distinct vocalizations, from the common chimpanzees of the broad belt of rain forest running west to east across Africa north of the Congo River. Sometimes called "bonobo" or, more often, pygmy chimpanzee, to distinguish it from the larger common chimpanzee, this type has probably been isolated for a long time by the uncrossable river, for apes are not known to swim. Mention has already been made of the pygmy chimpanzee on page 44, in connection with the specimen described by Nicolaas Tulp. That was the first ape ever to be clearly illustrated, and, as I have shown, it was probably the last variety to be scientifically described. But only probably. There may be another apelike creature which, so far, has eluded science—the yeti of the Himalayas.

Knowledge of the yeti has been at the "traveler's tale" stage since 1899, when a Major Waddell reported how, in the high peaks of Tibet, he found large footprints in the snow. The Tibetans told him that hairy wild men lived up among the eternal snows.

The Everest expedition of 1921 sighted dark-colored creatures moving over the snow well above the snowline, and much later, when the expedition reached the place, they found gigantic footprints, which the Tibetan porters all agreed belonged to the *metoh kanmi,* or abominable snowman.

Belief in these human-like creatures exists all over the Himalayan range, in Burma, Tibet, Nepal, Sikkim, Bhutan, and Assam. They have occasionally been sighted by climbers and travelers whose independent reports usually agree to a great extent. But it is over the footprints, seen by dozens of witnesses in the high snows, that the biggest controversies rage. The authenticity of these reports, which come from, among others, Eric Shipton, the mountaineer, in 1951, the *Daily Mail* expedition of 1954, and an RAF mountaineering group in 1955, cannot be disputed, and indeed are corroborated by photographs showing what could be anthropoid footmarks, with bipedal progression. Excrement has also been examined, showing an omnivorous diet. When the fauna of these regions is more exhaustively known than it is today, we shall probably have the answer. Until then, the possibility remains that the yeti is a so-far uncaptured and largely unknown type of ape.

CHAPTER 3

The Apes: Their Basic Structure and Behavior

THE NAMES FOR the members of the ape group are given in Table 1, page 60. There is not unanimous agreement about the table, chiefly because of lack of precise information. The three chimpanzee subspecies *troglodytes, verus* and *schweinfurthii* are thought by some authorities to be no more than a single subspecies; recent evidence showing differences between their blood-group frequencies has yet to be assessed. *Paniscus,* the pygmy chimpanzee, is considered by some authorities to be a full species. It has been suggested that there may be two subspecies of orangutan: the Bornean and the Sumatran. Some authorities recognize more gibbon species than I have listed, others less, and there is no precise information about the number of gibbon subspecies. *Syndactylus,* the siamang, is regarded by some authorities as no more than another species of gibbon, *Hylobates syndactylus,* and some would assign gorillas to the genus *Pan,* a view that is not subscribed by many authorities. The Eastern lowland gorilla is a newly recognized subspecies, described by Colin Groves in 1967.

[[59

TABLE 1. APE TYPES

Chimpanzee	Gorilla	Orangutan	Gibbon
1 genus: *Pan*	1 genus: *Gorilla*	1 genus: *Pongo*	2 genera: *Hylobates* and *Symphalangus*
1 species, 4 subspecies:	1 species, 3 subspecies:	1 species:	7 species:
1. *Pan troglodytes troglodytes,* central chimpanzee.	1. *Gorilla gorilla gorilla,* western lowland gorilla	1. *Pongo pygmaeus,* orangutan.	1. *Hylobates lar,* white-handed gibbon.
2. *Pan t. verus,* western chimpanzee.	2. *Gorilla gorilla manyema,* eastern lowland gorilla.		2. *H. agilis,* agile gibbon, or dark-handed gibbon.
3. *Pan t. schweinfurthii,* eastern chimpanzee.	3. *Gorilla gorilla beringei,* mountain gorilla.		3. *H. moloch,* wau-wau, or Sunda Island gibbon.
4. *Pan t. paniscus,* pygmy chimpanzee.			4. *H. concolor,* black, or Bornean gibbon.
			5. *H. hoolock,* hoolock.
			6. *H. Klossii,* Kloss's gibbon or pygmy gibbon.
			7. *Symphalangus syndactylus,* siamang.

Why is there all this confusion? There are two main reasons. First, all ape individuals are extremely variable in their body proportions and some even in their coat color, making it difficult to distinguish one form from another. Second, we are sadly lacking in information about the distribution of the various forms of chimpanzees and gibbons. Some of these merge into each other, while others do not.

The appearance of the four ape types is, in general, very well known. The chimpanzee (Plates 21 and 22) is black-haired, its skin pigment being black, blotchy, or light. Youngsters have a white tuft of hair on the rump above the anus, and have light-colored skin on the face (except in the case of the pygmy chimpanzee). Chimpanzees' ears are large—extraordinarily so in the case of youngsters—and tend to stick out, cauliflower style, from the head. The irises of the eyes are brown, as in all the apes. In their prime, chimpanzees, especially the males, are fine, active animals with plenty of hair. As they grow older they tend to become bald and may develop gray hair on the back and rump. Some chimpanzees are skinny, others sturdily built—in the wild and in captivity there is great variation among individuals. Occasionally a ginger-haired chimpanzee occurs, with sandy-colored skin.

Pygmy chimpanzees (*paniscus*) start life with a darker face than the other kinds, although it is not always jet black. Their lips are pink. They are, on average, somewhat smaller than other chimpanzees, have a rounder head, blacker and finer body hair, whiskers sticking out at the side of the face, and a higher-pitched voice. A frequent feature of the pigmy chimpanzee is that its second and third toes are joined by partial "webbing" (see Plate 23).

Gorillas (Plate 24) are black-haired and black-skinned. The males in particular, but also the females, are larger than chimpanzees. The male gorilla develops a "sagittal crest"—a ridge of bone on top of its head that makes it appear much larger than its brain requires. Mature and old males have a silver back, while females do not. An albino lowland gorilla (the first of its kind ever seen in captivity) is on exhibition at the Barcelona zoo at the time of writing. Mountain gorillas are somewhat longer-haired than lowland gorillas.

Orangutans (see Plate 25) are reddish-brown-haired with gray or sandy-colored skin. Their hair is often rather sparse on the head, but may be very long on the shoulders and back. Their heads are more rounded and less prognathous in the adult than those of African apes, and some individuals have a moustache and/or a beard. Alone among the apes, adult male orangs often exhibit cheek flaps—protrusions of fatty tissue sticking out from the sides of the face and making it look very wide. They may also have a throat pouch. This feature occurs in some adult males and is usually less marked in females, and can reach enormous proportions in old males. Its function is completely unknown. A throat pouch also occurs in the siamang, and small ones sometimes occur in gorillas and chimpanzees. Among gibbons, males of *H. concolor* have throat pouches.

Gibbons are very different in general appearance from the larger apes. They are smaller, with extremely long arms, and long hands and feet. They occur in a variety of colors. The white-handed gibbon has white hair around the face, and on the hands and feet. The rest of its body hair is either brown or black, going through color phases in the life span of the individual (see Plate 26). The skin of its face, hands, and feet is dark brown or black. The agile gibbon has white hair around the face, but not on the hands and feet. The rest of its hair is brown or black. The wau-wau has silvery-gray hair all over, sometimes black on top of the head. Its skin is black where exposed—on the face, hands, and feet. The Bornean gibbon is black in the adult male, with white or buff cheeks in some races. The female is pale buff with a dark cap. The hoolock has a band of white hair across the forehead, but is otherwise black or brown, going through color phases like the white-handed and agile gibbons. The dwarf gibbon is black all over, and the siamang (Plate 27) too, is black all over, coat and exposed skin. Siamangs are larger than the other gibbons, but share the same build. Gibbons and siamangs normally have ischial callosities, or sitting pads—a monkey-like feature—although in gibbons these pads develop later than in monkeys, at birth, or after, not at the embryonic stage. Most orangs, chimpanzees, and gorillas lack these pads, though a few do have them.

As we noted earlier, our information on the distribution of the various forms of chimpanzees and gibbons is not all that it might be. However, from the data available, distribution maps have been drawn up. See Figures 2, 3, 4, 5, 6, 7, 8, and 9.

We can make a slightly closer examination of this distribution by considering the habitat of the apes (Table 2).

Tropical rain forest is evergreen or semi-evergreen, that is, the forest *as a whole* remains green all year round, while individual trees shed their leaves at different times of the year. There may be a dry season, but if so it is short and not severe. Montane forest is semi-evergreen on

TABLE 2. APE ECOLOGY

	Chimpanzee	Gorilla	Orangutan	Gibbon
Habitat	Tropical rain forest Montane forest Tropical wood-land	Tropical rain forest Montane forest, including bamboo zone	Tropical rain forest	Tropical rain forest
Niche	Arboreal and terrestrial	Terrestrial and limited arboreal	Arboreal	Arboreal
Diet	1. Fruit 2. Pith, leaves, bark 3. Insects 4. (Meat)	1. Pith, vines, leaves 2. Fruit	1. Fruit 2. Bark, leaves 3. Insects, birds' eggs	1. Fruit 2. Pith, leaves 3. Insects, birds' eggs, nestlings

mountain slopes at altitudes up to about 10,000 feet. Tropical woodland is less dense than forest, with dense grass growth between the
scattered trees, and there may be a pronounced wet-season–dry-season
cycle, but the trees are never all bare of leaves at the same time. Apes
cannot survive where a seasonal cold period (winter) produces general leaf fall or special cold-resistant leaves (such as conifers possess).

Within these habitats, the apes differ from each other with regard to
the amount of time spent in the trees or on the ground, that is, they
exploit these "niches" in various ways (Table 2).

Adult gorillas rarely, if ever, climb trees, but young ones can and do
climb readily, for example, to feed or sleep aloft. Gorillas do, however,
spend most of their time on the ground. In contrast, chimpanzees
spend a large proportion of their time—about half of each day and all
the night—in the trees. Here the actual amounts vary a good deal
according to habitat, with more daytime spent on the ground in open
conditions than in forest. However, even in dense rain forest a period
of each day is normally spent on the ground below the trees. Neither
orangutans nor gibbons normally spend more than a small fraction of
their time on the ground. All the apes spend their night sleeping, and
all except the gibbon make nests for comfort and security. Nests are
made both on the ground and in trees, and are made for night use
primarily, but may be used for resting by day. The apes are all, primarily, vegetarians. Their basic dietary items are as indicated in
Table 2.

In this table, the foods are listed in order of the frequency with
which they are eaten. This varies from area to area, and from time to
time within an area. Meat eating by chimpanzees probably does not
occur among forest-living chimpanzees, whereas it does occur in more
open country. In gorillas, great variation occurs from one area to
another among the species of plants consumed, even when the same
plants are available in each area. This could imply that "traditional" or
"cultural" factors play a role in determining the diet accepted by
gorilla groups. Doubtless, too, individual choice and individual prefer-
ences play a part. A varied diet is normal—in contrast, for example,
with ungulates, but in common with monkeys and man. Food is taken
with the hands and transferred to the mouth, or bitten off by the
mouth direct. Water is rarely consumed by any of the apes. When they
do drink, they may put their lips to the water and suck, or utilize a
strange and unique method common to all four ape types but unknown
in other animals. This method is to dip one hand into the water and

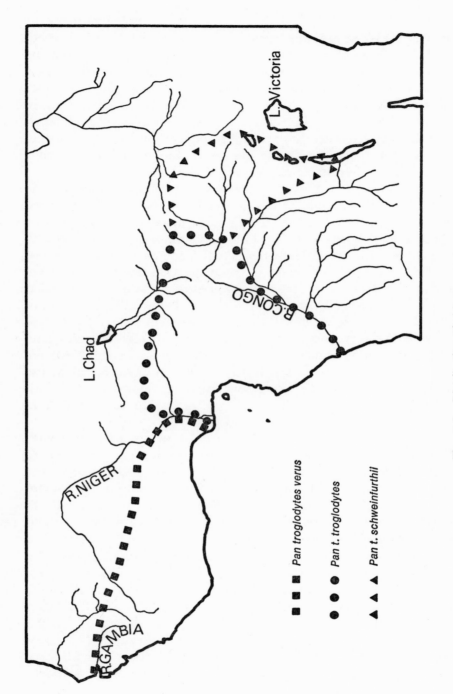

Figure 2. Distribution of chimpanzees.

Pan troglodytes verus

Pan t. troglodytes

Pan t. schweinfurthii

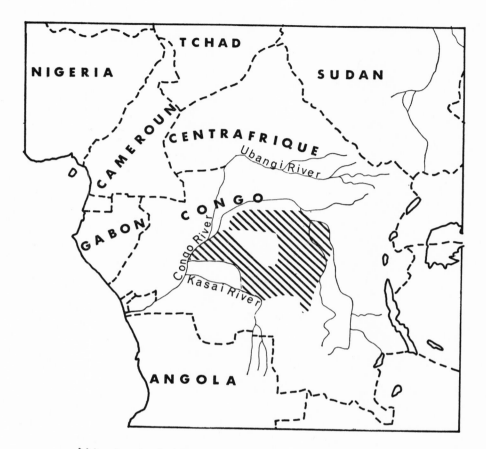

\\\ *Pan troglodytes paniscus*

Figure 3.   Distribution of pygmy chimpanzees.

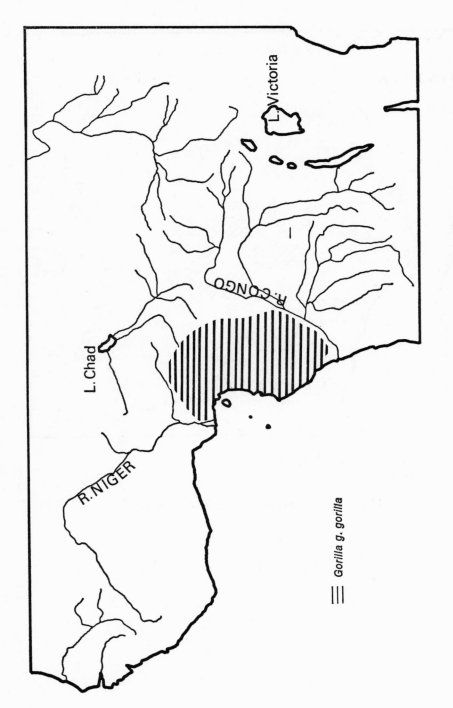

Figure 4. Distribution of western lowland gorillas.

≡ Gorilla g. gorilla

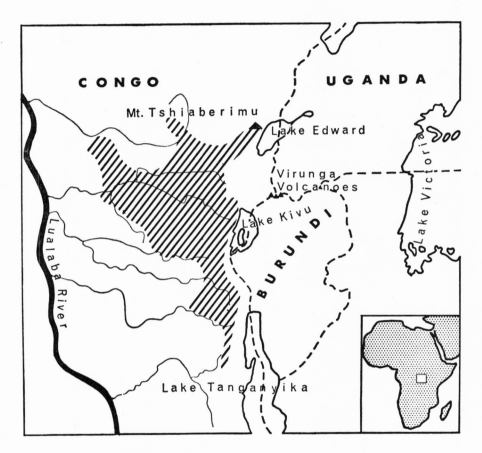

///   *Gorilla g. beringei*

Figure 5. Distribution of mountain and eastern lowland gorillas.

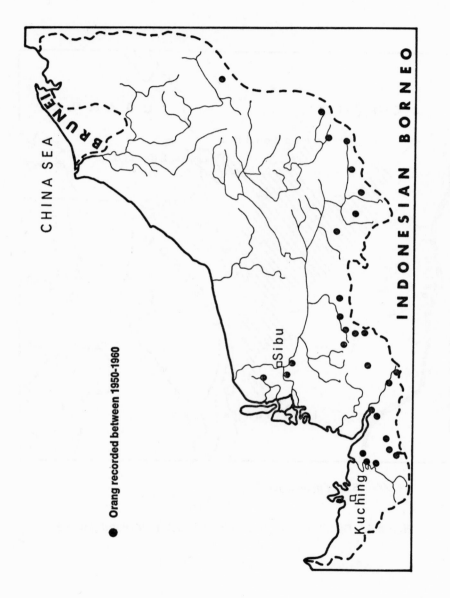

● Orang recorded between 1950-1960

Figure 6.   Distribution of orangutans in Sarawak.

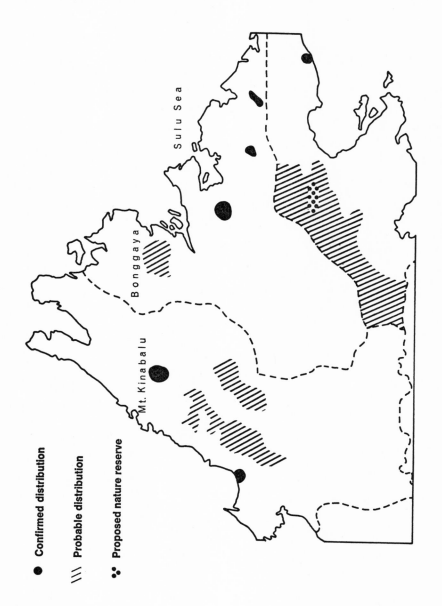

Figure 7. Distribution of orangutans in Sabah.

● Confirmed distribution

\\\ Probable distribution

∴ Proposed nature reserve

S u l u   S e a

B o n g g a y a

Mt. Kinabalu

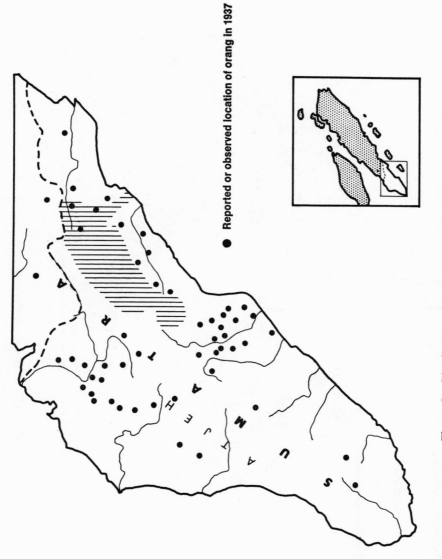

● Reported or observed location of orang in 1937

Figure 8. Distribution of orangutans in Sumatra.

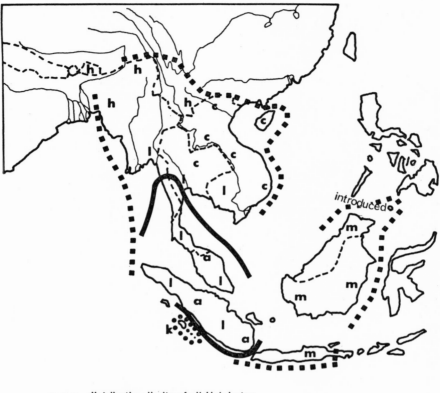

■ ■ ■ distribution limits of all *Hylobates*

▬▬▬▬ distribution limits of *Symphalangus*

k ••• *Hylobates klossii* **h** *H. hoolock* **c** *H. concolor*

l *H. lar* **a** *H. agilis* **m** *H. moloch*

Figure 9. Distribution of gibbons and siamangs.

then raise the hand quickly over the face, allowing the water to drip off into the mouth. This behavior, which could be called "finger-drop drinking," is as diagnostic of the apes as any other character, physical or behavioral.

In their habits of excretion, the apes have not developed specific patterns of behavior. They have no defecating areas, and no set times for defecation. This is typical of primates. Man learns the place to defecate; but wild apes do not, and apes raised in captivity mostly do not either. Wild chimpanzees avoid contact with their feces, while gorillas do not.

At birth, man is considerably heavier than any of the apes (Table 3). After birth, weight (naturally) increases, and the rate at which it does so has been measured in captive apes. When the data are plotted on a graph, they provide a growth curve (see Figure 10).

In the case of orangs and gorillas, captive adults tend to become obese and overheavy, so figures for specimens shot in the wild are of greater value. In chimpanzees and gibbons obesity is less common and so captive specimens are more representative. Some figures for average adult weights are given in Table 3. In siamangs, these weights are: male 11.1 kg., female 10.2 kg.

The differences in locomotor development among the apes have never been systematically studied, but data are available concerning the chimpanzee, gorilla, and man in this respect, that is, concerning the rates at which they learn to move about, and the differences in their actual patterns of moving. Figure 11 can serve to show the basic differences of shape in the infants of man and the chimpanzee. During the first year, chimpanzees are in advance of man in their postural development. The graphs of Figure 12 show the times at which baby chimps and baby humans start to walk with, and without, support.

In the gorilla, studies have been made on two babies, "Goma" and "Colo." The age of first appearance of various behavior patterns in these gorillas, chimpanzees, and man, are as shown in Table 4, page 77.

For the orangutan and gibbon, no such accurate developmental data exist, as far as I know.

One point in the life cycle that is of particular importance is the age of sexual maturity. As far as is known, this age is as shown in Table 3. "Sexual maturity" is here defined as onset of menstruation in females, and onset of sperm production in males. In male apes, as in man, potency, once achieved, is continuous until it is lost through disease or

TABLE 3 · APE DEVELOPMENT

	CHIMPANZEE	GORILLA	ORANGUTAN	GIBBON	MAN
Average newborn weight	1.58 kg.	1.92 kg.	1.48 kg.	0.40 kg.	3.29 kg.
Average adult weight					
male	45 kg.	175 kg.	75 kg.	5.7 kg.	65 kg.
female	40 kg.	85 kg.	37 kg.	5.3 kg.	58 kg.
Average age at sexual maturity					
male	7–8 yrs.	7–8 yrs.	} 6–8 yrs.	} 5–8 yrs.	c. 14 yrs.
female	7–10¾ yrs.	6–7 yrs.			12–14 yrs.
Average menstrual cycle length	36–37 days	30–31 days	29–32 days	30 days	28 days
Average gestation period (conception to birth)	242 days	265 days	233 days	210 days	275 days
Average cranial capacity of adults					
male	396 cc.	535 cc.	424 cc.	104 cc.	1400 cc.
female	355 cc.	458 cc.	366 cc.	101 cc.	1300 cc.
Period when deciduous dentition erupts	2½–14½ months	Complete early in second year	4–12 months	1–6 months	6–30 months
Period when permanent dentition erupts	3–10 years	Fully erupted in 11th year	3½–10 years	2½–8 years	6–19½ years

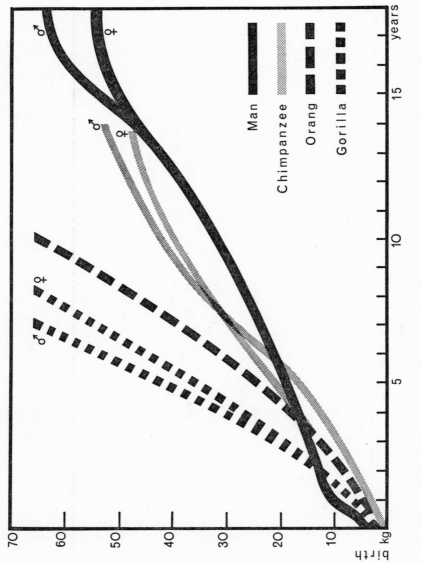

Figure 10. Weight curves for the large apes and man. Vertical axis: weight in kg. Horizontal axis: age in years. The data for orang are poorer than for the other species.

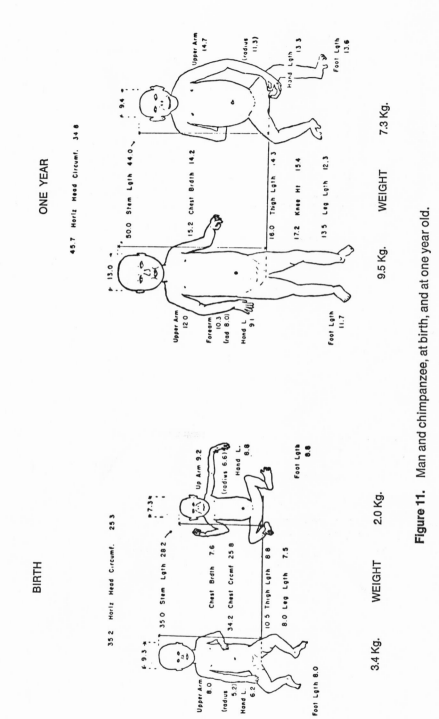

Figure 11. Man and chimpanzee, at birth, and at one year old.

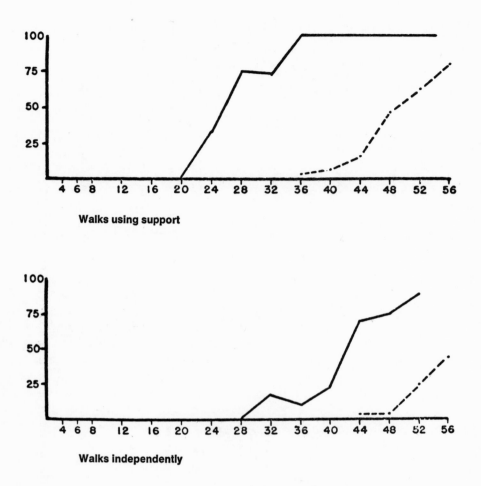

Figure 12. Graphs comparing the ages at which chimpanzees (continuous line) and humans (interrupted line) succeed in walking with and without support. Vertical axis: % successful; horizontal axis: age in weeks.

TABLE 4. ASPECTS OF POSTURAL DEVELOPMENT IN GORILLA, CHIMPANZEE, AND MAN

	Age of Appearance (in weeks)		
BEHAVIOR PATTERN	Gorilla	Chimpanzee	Man
Raises head briefly from supine position	2.5	4	28
Turns from supine to prone position	10	11	24
Crawls pushing with feet	10	14	36
Stands bipedally using support for hands	14	22	32
Sits steady indefinitely	20–22	20	40

senescence. In female apes, there is a menstrual cycle, of the human type. The average length of this cycle is given in Table 3.

In female chimpanzees there is a physical change at puberty not found in any of the other apes. Around the time of first menstruation (but not at exactly the same time) the female chimpanzee begins to exhibit sexual swellings at the time of ovulation, when she is most fertile. At first small, these swellings around her rear end become, in the course of years, quite large and prominent: the pink skin of the sexual swelling contrasts vividly with the black hair of the animal. The function of the bright sexual swelling is probably to attract males in the conditions of poor visibility in the forest where a female with a swelling is much more conspicuous than she is without one. Studies in captivity have shown that males are attracted sexually by the swellings, for they prefer to mate with a female during her swelling phase, and especially at its peak. They have also shown that the swelling is caused by the female hormone; injections of oestrogen cause immediate sexual swelling, even at a quiescent phase of the cycle.

Some female gorillas and orangs in the wild exhibit sexual swelling. In the case of orangs, the swellings occur only during pregnancy.

Sexual behavior is very variable in apes, especially in captivity, where it is often more intense than in the wild, especially in the chimpanzee and gorilla. In the wild, copulation in both chimpanzees and gorillas is normally dorso-ventral; in captivity both dorso-ventral and ventro-ventral copulations occur. I do not know of any reports of copulatory behavior in wild orangutans or gibbons, but in captivity both copulate dorso-ventrally or ventro-ventrally, and in both the act can be accomplished even while the pair are hanging from an overhead support.

In the wild, sexual behavior of any sort is rather infrequent in the apes; it is a daytime activity, and true homosexual and autoerotic behavior are not known. In captivity, the amount of sexual behavior is often great in the large apes, and both homosexual and autoerotic behaviors occur. Unfortunately, increased sexuality in captive apes does not lead to increased copulation leading to pregnancy. Many factors have to be present before apes will breed happily and continuously in captivity; most often, in the past, such factors have been missing, and so the sexual energy has been wasted in nonreproductive activities. What these factors are will be discussed in Chapter 11.

The average gestation period in apes is given in Table 3. No special behavior seems to be associated with pregnancy. In chimpanzees, although ovulation has stopped, sexual swellings continue to occur during pregnancy, as we know from the fact that numerous females with fetuses have had such swellings when they were "collected" (shot). This is known also to be true of the pygmy chimpanzee, for a pregnant female studied by Coolidge had such a swelling.

Chimpanzee births in captivity have been observed ever since the time of Mme. Rosalia Abreu's pioneering colony in Cuba, early in the present century (see Plate 104). And twins, while unusual, do occur in chimpanzees (Plate 28), at least four cases being on record. Recently the *Stuttgarter Zeitung* reported the birth of gorilla twins to the female Makula at the Frankfurt Zoo. Their father, Abraham, had died in January, 1967. The mother did not care for her youngsters, and they are being reared by the apes' keeper and his wife. In gibbons and orangs, I know of no cases of twins, but far fewer births have been observed than in chimpanzees. Infant apes soon show a strong clinging response toward the mother, although this response seems to be weaker in gorillas than in the other apes. Perhaps the mother's breast is too wide to allow a firm grip; at any rate, the wild gorilla mother normally cradles her infant with one arm when on the move, while in wild chimpanzees and gibbons this is not necessarily so, although it is done on occasion. After it is a year or more old, the baby chimpanzee or gorilla often rides on its mother's back rather than clinging to her belly or side, but this is done only when she is walking on the ground, not when she is in the trees. Orangs and gibbons do not carry their young on their backs, so presumably this is not suitable in the trees. Chimpanzee mothers quite often carry an older and a younger baby in the wild, one on their back and the other under their belly.

A behavior aberration frequently met with in zoos is that a mother will not care for her baby. This happened, for instance, with Colo, the first baby gorilla born in captivity, at the Columbus zoo in 1956, and with Goma, the first baby gorilla born at the Basel Zoo, as well as with the gorilla twins mentioned above. Studies of monkeys have shown that this can be a result of social deprivation and restricted learning opportunities in early life, and this may be true in the cases concerning apes. In all the large apes, the period of infantile dependence is very long—up to five years, for example, in chimpanzees. Captive specimens are normally caught and sent to zoos long before their period of dependence is over, and as a result they either will not breed or, if they do, they may fail to look after the baby. Bringing them up with other young apes in zoos helps to normalize them. And the fact that Goma's mother, Achilla, did look after her next two babies proves that the condition need not be permanent.

A question that is often asked is: How long do apes live? All our information on this point comes from captive specimens. There are many factors affecting an ape's life span in captivity, as opposed to its life span in the wild. In the wild, apes must find their food, and be fit enough to do so, or they die. In captivity, animals, well or sick, are given their food. Veterinary surgeons and animal hospitals can prolong life in captivity; isolation and poor diet can shorten it. Chimpanzees and gorillas probably live some twenty-five to thirty years in the wild.

In captivity, apes *may* live longer. A female chimpanzee at the Yerkes Laboratories was still alive in 1966 at the age of forty-five years, and another had recently died aged forty-six years. The male gorilla "Bamboo" died at the Philadelphia zoo after thirty-three and one-half years in the zoo, when he was perhaps a year older than this. Again at the Philadelphia zoo, the two orangutans "Guas" and "Guarina," a male and a female, were still living in 1963 after thirty-two years in the zoo. Prior to their arrival at the zoo, they had already been an unknown time in Mme. Abreu's ape station in Cuba. A white-handed gibbon, again at the Philadelphia zoo, died in 1938 after thirty-one and one-half years at the zoo. The above are *record* longevities, and the Philadelphia zoo can claim three out of four—an extremely fine achievement. *Average* longevities in captivity are, sadly, much lower, although some zoos, such as Chicago (Lincoln Park) and New York (Bronx) have very good longevity records, showing that all the apes can live over twenty years in captivity, if received as youngsters. Where they die before this, their deaths must be considered premature.

In all the apes, the head undergoes certain changes of shape during development. The jaws, from lying largely below the braincase at birth, grow forward to jut out in adult life. In chimpanzees and gorillas especially, the orbits of the eyes also move forward from beneath to in front of the brain. Even more than in man, there is a great deal of variation from one ape skull to another, even if the two animals are of the same type, age, and sex, and live in the same locality. I have seen hundreds of chimpanzees in the Budongo Forest, and have often been surprised at the obvious differences in proportions of the head from one animal to another. Some of these differences are superficial, but others involve differences in the underlying skull shape. Perhaps the function of this variability is to assist with recognition of individuals. It is greater, I suspect, in the large apes than in the gibbons. Schultz has photographed three skulls of wild male chimpanzees from West Africa showing just how marked the differences may be (see Plate 29).

One of the most interesting aspects of skull shape is the size of the brain cavity (and hence of the brain), usually measured in cubic centimeters. This volume is called the "cranial capacity," and one of the outstanding characteristics of man is that, on average, he has a large absolute and relative cranial capacity; that is, it is large both in comparison with other brains, and relatively to his body size. Cranial capacities for the apes and man are given in Table 3. Absolute brain size is thus much smaller in the apes than in man. It is possible to calculate relative brain size, by calculating the percentage of total body volume made up by the brain. This gives the following result in males: gorilla 0.3 percent, orang 0.6 percent, chimpanzee 0.9 percent, gibbon 1.9 percent (and man 2.1 percent). Here the high figure for the gibbon probably reflects its small body volume rather than anything else. The figures for the three large apes make a more meaningful comparison with those for man.

The dentitions of the apes all have the basic formula of Old World primates in general, that is (in the adult) two incisors, one canine, two premolars, and three molars in each quarter of the mouth, making a total of thirty-two. This is the permanent dentition. Before it there is a deciduous dentition consisting of two incisors, one canine, and two molars in each quarter, a total of twenty teeth. The time during which the deciduous and permanent teeth erupt is as shown in Table 3.

In later life the teeth wear out, or are attacked by diseases. Plate 30 shows a series of pathological conditions found in wild-shot apes. Such a series of disorders is truly shocking, and many apes must suffer agonies with toothache. Caries, the curse of teeth in modern man, is less common in apes. The frequency with which it occurs in old apes shot in the wild is shown in Table 5.

The fruit-eating chimpanzee is obviously much more prone to caries than its pith-and-stem-eating relative, the gorilla. Alveolar abscesses are another curse of the teeth in apes, as in man. Frequencies of abscesses for the same individuals described above for caries are given in Table 5.

All in all, it is a sad story. Dental trouble affects the lives of more than half the apes. They live only half as long as we do, so no wonder we need false teeth!

Apes have evolved a variety of methods of communicating with one another, but before discussing these we should pause to consider their ears. The ears of the apes vary widely in their relative size, that is, their size in proportion to the size of the head (Table 6).

The relative ear size of man is 4.9. We can see, among the apes, two clear groups. The chimpanzee and gibbon are large-eared, the gorilla and orang (like man) are small-eared. This is particularly interesting, because both the chimpanzee and gibbon have developed loud hooting calls in chorus for long-distance communication, while the gorilla and orang have not. Man, too, cannot communicate by voice over very large distances. So, relative ear size may possibly reflect dependence on long-distance hearing in social life. The ears of the apes are illustrated in Plate 31.

The most reduced ear is found in the orang. The orang and gibbon both lack earlobes, whereas the chimpanzee and gorilla, like man, have quite well-developed earlobes. In their vocalizations, as stated, the apes fall into two groups—those that chorus and those that do not.

TABLE 5.   APE PATHOLOGY

	Chimpanzee	Gorilla	Orangutan	Gibbon
Frequency of old apes with one or more carious teeth	30.6%	2.8%	13.0%	8.7%
Frequency of old apes with abscesses	59.6%	59.7%	60.8%	38.5%
Frequency of healed fractures	18.0%	21.0%	34.0%	33.0%

TABLE 6. APE COMMUNICATION

	Chimpanzee	Gorilla	Orangutan	Gibbon
Relative Ear Size (Ear: Head)	16.6	3.8	2.7	13.3
Occurrence of chorusing	Yes	No	No	Yes
Nonvocal noise production	Drumming on tree buttresses	Chest beating	Laryngeal sac	Laryngeal sac (siamang only)
Displays	Hooting Drumming (rapid locomotion) Throwing and shaking things	Hooting Chest beating (rapid locomotion) Throwing and shaking things	Throwing things Sudden falling forward	Hooting (rapid locomotion)

All the apes except the nonsiamang gibbons have additional, nonvocal ways of producing noise. These also are shown in Table 6. Finally, we can compare the displays of one sort or another that occur in the behavior of all the apes, especially the males (Table 6).

The auditory acuity of one type of ape—the chimpanzee—has been investigated experimentally, but not that of the others. The way in which this was done was as follows: Three young apes were given a warning light, and then a note was either played or not played. If the apes could hear it, they had to press a lever. If a note was played and they pressed the button, they received a reward. If no note was played and they pressed the button, or if a note was played and they did not press, they received no reward and might receive punishment instead. In this way, it was possible to determine the lowest intensity (quietest) sound audible to a chimpanzee. Sounds of a great variety of wavelengths were used. The conclusion was that throughout the range, the acuity of the young chimpanzees was the same as that of young humans. Our hearing ability, and the chimp's, are very similar.

Another experiment has tested the visual acuity of two chimpanzees, two human adults, and a five-year-old human child. Each had to choose a box associated with a circular field of light containing black lines, in preference to a box associated with a clear field of light without lines but of the same brightness. The box associated with lines contained food; the other was empty. As the test proceeded, the lines were made narrower and narrower until the subjects could no longer see them. The two apes differed from each other. One had better acuity than the other. The better one's acuity was as good as that of the human adults, whose acuity was better than that of the child. The second chimpanzee had poorer acuity than the human adults or child. In general, however, the study showed that the vision of chimpanzees is about as sharp as that of man. Other experiments have shown that chimpanzees and gorillas discriminate colors *as well as humans* can do, and a tendency toward myopia (shortsightedness) has been confirmed for laboratory-living chimpanzees.

Another experiment, again using chimpanzees only, has tested the reaction time of chimpanzees and humans. Four young chimpanzees, two human children, and six human adults were used. Various kinds of stimuli, visual, tactile, and auditory, were shown, and the subjects had to press a button immediately upon noticing the stimulus, in order to get a reward. The results indicated that there were no consistent differences between the three groups in regard to reaction time. In all groups, reactions to the visual stimulus were slower than to the auditory and tactile. We can conclude, in general terms, that chimpanzees are just as quick to notice things as we are. It would be interesting to do this test with the orangutan, which is often regarded as being slower off the mark than the chimpanzee.

The ability to discriminate between tastes of different sorts has never been thoroughly tested in any of the apes, but we know something about the subject from observations in captivity and in the wild. An early study showed that a chimpanzee in a cage, given a considerable variety of different foods on a plate, eats them in a certain fairly predictable order, thus proving that it can distinguish between their tastes. This study also showed that the order can be changed by satiating one taste preference or another with abundance of that food. All this is just the same as in man (we all know the results of eating too much chocolate).

Studies of wild apes have indicated that, in the African bush, chimpanzees and gorillas choose foods (especially fruits) that are highly astringent (bitter) to ourselves—so much so that we automatically spit them out. In captivity, they are very happy with sweet fruits, such as bananas, grapes, and apples. Meat eating, rare in the wild and unknown among wild gorillas, is very common in captivity. Wild chimpanzees chew tree bark and rattan creeper that, to humans, are virtually tasteless. Clearly, the subject of taste is a very complicated one.

Studies of the hands and feet of primates have suggested that the ability to grasp, common to nearly all of them but not present in their ancestral form, the insectivores is a response to increasing size. Lower primates (lemurs) and monkeys can maneuver and leap among the branches by grasping them, without danger of slipping off. In the big, heavy apes, this is no longer possible except on the biggest branches, and so they have become adapted for hanging from the smaller branches where the food grows, using both hands and feet to do so. This applies most of all to the orangutan, less so to the chimpanzee and gibbon, which rely mainly on their hands and less on their feet, and least of all to the gorilla, which (in the adult) is rather too big for arboreal life. All the apes use their hands for manipulating objects as well as hanging. None of them, however, has been able to abandon the locomotor function of the hands and use them for manipulation only, as man does. As a result, the hands of apes all show a mixture of the characteristics for hanging and locomotion—sturdy, tough fingers—with those of manipulation—a flexible, opposable thumb. This is relatively longer in the gorilla than in the other apes. In their feet, the opposite has happened. The apes have not specialized wholly for locomotion, as man has, and so their feet have kept greater flexibility and opposability of the big toe, while man's have rigidified and lost their former opposability. While man has divided up the functions of manipulation and locomotion, giving the former to his hands and the latter to his feet, the apes have not specialized in this way. Their hands and feet, and man's, are illustrated in Plates 32 and 33.

The gorilla, being the most terrestrial ape, has a foot more like man's than the other apes. The two most arboreal apes, the gibbon and orang, have each specialized their first toe, but in opposite directions from each other. In the gibbon foot, the first toe is the longest, strongest digit; in the orang foot it is insignificant, and in the majority of cases lacks its terminal phalanx and nail. Chimpanzee and gorilla first toes are intermediate between gibbon and orang.

In the hands, there are two main points of difference—the relative length of the thumb, which sets the gibbon apart from the rest, and the relative breadth of the palm, which is greatest in the gorilla, less in chimpanzee and orang, and least in gibbon.

A feature that distinguishes the hands of the African apes, and especially the gorilla, from the others is the development of thickened skin on the back of the second phalanges of the fingers. This is the surface on which the gorilla and chimpanzee rest the weight of the forepart of their bodies when walking along in their normal quadrupedal fashion, and so they have developed a typical walking "pad" for the purpose. This area has dermatoglyphics like the palms and soles.

G. B. Schaller's observations on wild gorillas suggest that they are somewhat right-handed: they started off their chest-beating displays with their right hand in 90 out of 110 observations recorded. G. Finch tested captive chimpanzees for handedness, and found, out of 30 subjects, that 14 were left-handed, 11 right-handed, and 5 ambidextrous. No data exist, as far as I know, for the other two apes.

Leaving the extremities and coming to the limbs, the big difference here is between the relative length of the arms in the gibbon and in the other apes. The extraordinary lengthening of the arm is the gibbon's outstanding specialization, underlying its special locomotor pattern—brachiation. Analysis of the arm shows that the forearm is the part that has become particularly elongated, the upper-arm length being comparable with that in the other apes. This specialization of the gibbon is really a specialized growth rate, as Professor A. H. Schultz has pointed out. Baby gibbons do not have such relatively long arms as adults. But during life, the gibbon arm grows faster than the leg.

In the orang, both limbs grow at the same rate, and in the gorilla and chimpanzee the leg grows faster than the arm. Nevertheless, in all the apes arm length exceeds leg length, in contrast with man, where the reverse is the case. The average lengths of limbs in adult apes are given in Table 7. These are absolute lengths. The average length of adult arms to legs can also be expressed as a proportion, as in Table 7. Here, if arm length equals leg length, the proportion is 100. It is perhaps surprising to find that the orang has proportionately longer arms, in relation to the length of its legs, than the gibbon. Probably, the orang's legs have become reduced, but orangs also have proportionately longer hands than gibbons, which helps to account for the overall difference. As we saw above, the orang's first toe is also very reduced. In the gibbon, leg length has not become so reduced, and the first toe has remained a most important grasping digit.

From the limbs we next come to the trunk itself. In the apes, as in man, the trunk is wider than it is deep. This is not so in monkeys and

TABLE 7. APE LOCOMOTION

	Chimpanzee	Gorilla	Orangutan	Gibbon	Man
Average lengths					
Arm	789 mm.	1086 mm.	924 mm.	661 mm.	773 mm.
Leg	577 mm.	787 mm.	545 mm.	402 mm.	882 mm.
Proportion arm length to leg length	136	138	172	165	88
Locomotion	1. Quadrupedal 2. Brachiation 3. Bipedal 4. Leaping	1. Quadrupedal 2. Bipedal	1. Quadrupedal 2. Brachiation	1. Brachiation 2. Bipedal 3. Leaping	Bipedal

the lower primates. Monkeys cannot extend their arms out sideways; apes and man can. The wide trunk goes together with emancipation of the arms from forward and backward movements only, that is, from typical quadrupedal running movements. With the specialization of the arms for hanging and swinging in the trees, the shoulder underwent extensive changes to allow a greater amount of arm rotation, and the whole upper trunk expanded sideways.

The absolute proportions of the trunk in the three large apes and man are shown in the beautiful drawing by Professor A. H. Schultz (Plate 34). This picture shows, from left to right, an adult orangutan, chimpanzee, gorilla, and man, all drawn exactly to the same scale. They are stripped of their hair; the limbs are stretched out; and the feet are extended sideways to facilitate comparison. Every measurement of the four individuals represented is exact, and the picture, at first glance an extraordinary one, is a faithful record of the facts. It summarizes volumes of information, and is a fascinating document from the age of science, just as the picture by Hoppius (Plate 13) is a fascinating one from the age of speculation.

The vertebral column of the apes follows a simple shallow curve, convex toward the back. It is a very variable part of the skeleton. For purposes of analysis it can be divided into five sections—cervical, thoracic, lumbar, sacral, and coccygeal—and the number of vertebrae in each section counted. This reveals, in the apes, an extraordinary amount of variation from one individual to another in the types studied—much more variation than is found in man. In the gibbon, the most frequent combination of vertebrae (vertebral formula) is 7–13–5–5–3, but even this is found in only 13 percent of cases. In a sample of chimpanzees, 21 percent had the "typical" vertebral formula; the rest were variants. We noted earlier that skull shape was very variable in apes and that the shape of the individual skull might serve to give each animal's head a distinctive appearance. Just why there should be so much variation in the apes' spines is not known. It is an unusual feature, for most animals are rather conservative in their bony skeleton, that is, there is little variation from one animal to another.

Having examined the limbs and trunk of apes, let us see briefly how they are used. The occurrence of the main locomotor patterns is given in Table 7. The locomotor patterns are listed in order of the frequency with which they occur. Brachiation (swinging along and between branches from the hands, with the body hanging free) is *typical* only in the gibbon; it is occasionally seen in orangs and chimpanzees, but not in gorillas. The commonest pattern in all the large apes is quadrupedal locomotion, which is not seen in the gibbon because its arms are twice as long as its legs. Many subdivisions of the locomotor patterns of the apes can be made, especially in the case of the adaptable chimpanzee.

Swimming ability is almost nil in the apes. A young gibbon that fell into a pond at a zoo drowned while its mother watched, too afraid to rescue it. No report of swimming by a gibbon exists, but several others confirm its inability to swim. Orangutans have never been observed swimming, and probably cannot. Gorillas, faced with the alternative of capture by man, dare not go into water more than two or three feet deep. They have never been observed to swim, and at least one mature male has drowned in a zoo water enclosure, sinking as soon as he fell in. Only in chimpanzees is there some evidence of swimming ability. A report from Spanish Guinea states that four chimpanzees were observed swimming across the 60 to 65-meter-wide Benito River. They made swimming motions like dogs. In captivity, attempts to teach chimpanzees to swim have met with failure, and deepwater barriers have often proved efficient in keeping apes on islands, as for example at the Paris (Vincennes) zoo. I am inclined to think that the "chimpanzees" seen swimming in the above report were some other species. The general response of chimpanzees to water is universally agreed to be one of avoidance and even fear. I have myself on two occasions helped to pull chimpanzees out of a water-filled moat in which they were quite clearly drowning, and I am convinced they cannot swim, although in their struggles as they flounder about they can sometimes make a little headway in the water.

Bone disease and injuries are very frequent in apes, judging from the skeletal material (see Plate 35). Repaired, fractured, and diseased bones are surprisingly common in adult, and especially old, chimpanzees. In the Budongo Forest I saw two chimpanzees fall out of trees—doubtless a common way of fracturing bones—and also saw a chimpanzee with a broken wrist, walking along holding one arm out in front of it with the hand hanging limply down. The frequency of healed bone fractures in a series of ape skeletons examined by Professor Adolph Schultz is given in Table 5. As Schultz points out, speed of locomotion and body size are not primary factors determining the frequency of fractures, as the orang and gibbon are almost equal. What seem to be more important factors are the degree of arboreality, and reliance on the arms in locomotion. Both the Asian apes share these features, while the African apes are more terrestrial and more quadrupedal. In all the apes, fractures are much more common in old age than in youth.

Another bone disease common in older apes (as in man) is arthritis. In a sample of 233 gibbons examined by Schultz, 40 had arthritic changes of skeletal parts (17 percent). When the 38 senile specimens in this sample were examined, 21 (55 percent) of them had arthritic changes. Orangs and gorillas get arthritis too, but in chimpanzees it is rare, only three cases being on record. In the search for a cure for arthritis in man, a close look at the chimpanzee might be rewarding.

Yaws, sinus diseases, abscesses, and other bone diseases are on record for wild apes, often in striking abundance. This has led Professor Schultz to write: "All these varied and amazingly common abnormal conditions in wild manlike apes combine to produce a mass of evidence which radically disagrees with the frequent assumption of prevalence of health and normality in nature." As he says, "Diseases, injuries and malformations must be recognized as being among the most significant selective factors in primate evolution."

Besides these natural bone diseases in the wild, there is a large number of diseases of the soft parts. I have observed bronchial and eye diseases in wild chimpanzees, and Schaller observed symptoms resembling the common cold, and found evidence of intestinal parasites in wild mountain gorillas. A whole variety of viral, bacterial, and larger parasitic infections has been recorded for wild apes.

Experimental medical research and accident have shown that the apes are susceptible, in captivity, to many diseases of man. These include paraplegia, tuberculosis, pneumonia, encephalitis, pericarditis, appendicitis, syphilis, typhoid fever, cholera, baccilary and amoebic dysenteries, exanthematous and recurrent typhus, yellow fever, pestilence, poliomyelitis, measles, scarlet fever, smallpox, trachoma, trypanosomiasis, leishmaniasis, influenza, whooping cough, and leprosy. No other group of animals is so close to man in this respect, and hence the great usefulness of the apes in medical research. As regards the degree to which each type of ape approaches man in its disease susceptibility, no clear answer can be given because most of the research to date has been done with chimpanzees, and we do not have comparable data for the other three types. On the basis of our knowledge of the structure of the apes' blood, however, it is probable that the chimpanzee's range of disease susceptibility is more like man's than that of the other apes.

The blood of apes has been subjected to close scrutiny in recent years in an attempt to find out how much individuals of one species vary from each other, how much the different species and types vary from one another, and how much the apes resemble and differ from man. This kind of work is important where ape blood is used in research on human disease problems.

The structure of blood is extremely complex, and this is not the place even to begin discussing it. Suffice it to say that tests that are used to determine the group to which a sample of human blood belongs have been applied to ape blood, revealing patterns of reactions characteristic of each type. One well-known set of blood groups is the A-B-O set. In man, individuals may have blood of any of the four groups O, A, B, or AB. In apes, the A-B-O blood groups so far found are given in Table 8.

Group A is itself a multiple group, consisting of three subgroups, A_1, $A_{1,2}$ and A_2, all three of which occur in man. Their occurrence in apes is also given in Table 8.

Other blood group sets exist in man, such as the MN group and the Rh (Rhesus) group. Studies of the apes have shown that each differs from the others for each set, and they all differ from man to a greater or lesser extent. If the results were easy to explain, I should tabulate them, but they are not.

TABLE 8. APE MICROSTRUCTURE

	Chimpanzee	Gorilla	Orangutan	Gibbon	Man
A-B-O blood groups	O, A	B *	A, B, AB	A, B, AB	O, A, B, AB
Subgroups of the A blood group	A_1, A_2		A_1		A_1, $A_{1,2}$, A_2
Number of Chromosomes	48	48	48	44 †	46

* For gorillas, groups O and A have also been reported, but at the time of writing further evidence is needed.

† Except the siamang, which has 50.

In the blood groups discussed so far, the part of the blood tested is the red cells, or hemoglobin, and it is these cells that react. A different advance in distinguishing ape bloods from one another has been made using the colorless part of the blood, or serum. This serum contains proteins, and by a process known as electrophoresis these proteins can be made to separate from each other, forming a pattern characteristic for the species. Thus we are not here concerned with the different groups that exist *within* a species, but with the differences between the protein structure of different species: chimpanzee, orang, gorilla, gibbon (and man). Plate 36 shows the different patterns for this group. Clearly the differences are not extreme, but they are constant. For present purposes, we do not need to know what each component on this figure represents except that it represents the final position reached by a moving component of serum protein.

A different, but not less recent, field of advance has been made in the isolation, counting, and analysis of somatic chromosomes. The number of chromosomes found in the apes is given in Table 8. The three large apes thus all have one pair of chromosomes more than man, while the gibbon has two pairs less (except the aberrant siamang). The chromosomes of man and the apes can be photographed by modern techniques, and laid out in a way that facilitates comparison (see Plate 37). In this plate, the X and Y (sex) chromosomes are in the second line of each set at the extreme right.

CHAPTER **4**

Evolution of the Apes

THE EVOLUTION OF life in various forms is a continuous and continuing process, and there is no point at which one can say "Apes began here." During the Mesozoic, the Age of Reptiles, which lasted 150 million years, the dinosaurs ruled the world, a world with many vast tropical jungles and swamps, with extensive warm and shallow seas, before the continents as we know them today had risen, and before the massive mountainous ranges that today define well-known geographical and national zones, had begun to build up. Among the enormous numbers of different species of reptiles evolving at this time were some that became warm-blooded and grew insulating coats of hair. It must be assumed that in some way these new characteristics enabled them to compete favorably in a particular environmental niche with other reptiles such as dinosaurs. Later in the Mesozoic Era, perhaps 150 million years ago, there is evidence that many species of very small *mammals* were living in the vast tropical undergrowth. They were the ancestors of the mammals that were to take over the world in later eras. Toward the end of the Mesozoic, there are

[[91

mammalian fossils clearly related to living primitive forms—on the one hand marsupials such as the opossum, and on the other, primitive insectivores such as shrews and hedgehogs. As long as the great dinosaurs dominated the earth, these ancestral mammals had to remain small and insignificant to survive, but when, about 70 million years ago, for reasons still completely unknown, all the dinosaurs and similar large reptiles became totally extinct, the mammals expanded explosively into thousands of different niches and forms.

Also at this time, toward the end of the Mesozoic Era, the face of the earth was itself changing. Gradually, over millions of years, the mountainous masses of the Alps and Himalayas were rising owing to forces inside the earth; new climatic zones came into existence, and temperatures began to fall. Plant life was revolutionized, and vegetation similar to that which we have today began to take over the earth. This process, however, was only started toward the latter part of the Age of Reptiles, and continued for many millions of years into the Cenozoic Era, the Age of Mammals. Certainly these topographical, vegetational, and climatic changes and the stratifications resulting must have been powerful forces favoring the differentiation and specialization of many different forms of mammals. In the very earliest fossil deposits of the Cenozoic Era we find very primitive primates, already distinguishable among groups of mammals. The Cenozoic began about 64 million years ago. It is divided into two epochs: the Tertiary, lasting until 2 to 3 million years ago, then the Quaternary, lasting until present times. The Tertiary epoch is the important time for the rise of the primates, as well as all the mammals, and it is itself divided into five periods:

the Paleocene	64–55	million years ago
the Eocene	55–36	million years ago
the Oligocene	36–26	million years ago
the Miocene	26–12	million years ago
the Pliocene	12–2+	million years ago

The earliest known fossil primates have been found in Paleocene deposits in Europe and North America only. They belong to the order of Prosimians, which means "before-monkeys," and at this time in the early Tertiary they included some sixty genera, in eight families, so that they were then more widespread and numerous than they are today. There are, however, three living families, the lemurs, the lorises and the tarsiers, which are living in much the same way as these earliest forerunners of apes and men. These primitive first primates were little climbing leaping creatures with simple reptile-like grasping hands and feet. This feature—the adaptation of climbing by grasping —then as now separated the primates from other mammals. This development enabled these early primates to occupy a particular niche in the primeval forests. Some of the families represented at this period had long front teeth adapted for chiseling and gnawing, but by the middle of the Eocene these families had become extinct, probably owing to the increasing number of small rodent species, better adapted for these particular niches.

The best known of the first fossil primates is named *Plesiadapis* (Plate 38), and examples have been found both in France and in North America, indicating a very wide distribution indeed. In fact this is the only primate genus, apart from man, known to have inhabited both the Old and the New World. *Plesiadapis* varied according to species from squirrel size to the size of a domestic cat, and probably looked more like a rodent than a primate.

Thirty million years of evolution take us to the middle of the Eocene period. Deposits of this age in North America, Europe, and in Asia have yielded various genera of prosimians more advanced than those of the Paleocene period. In particular, these animals had progressed in two typically primate characteristics: an enlargement of the forebrain, and a shifting of the positions of the eyes to face forward so that the visual fields overlap to give stereoscopic vision. Examples of these types of early prosimians are, in North America, *Notharctus* and *Smilodectes* (Plate 39), and in Europe, *Adapis* and *Necrolemur*. However, interesting though these fossils are, all the American and European finds so far are of fossil prosimians belonging to genera that have either died out or have close affinities with the lines leading to present-day lemurs and tarsiers. There must have existed, at the same period, a prosimian stock that was capable of evolving into the Old World monkeys and apes. The only fossils we have that could possibly fit into this category are a few jaw and tooth fragments from Burma, which, while they retain the primitive dental formula of the lemurs and the New World monkeys (thirty-six teeth), also show more advanced characteristics in the shape of the jaw and patterns of the teeth. These two fragmentary fossils, which may in fact lie on the line of evolution from prosimian to Old World monkey, are named *Amphipithecus* (Plate 40) and *Pondaungia*.

The strange fact is that as yet we have no Paleocene or Eocene fossil primates from the *African* continent. Indeed, we have no fossil deposits from central or southern Africa preceding the Miocene. It remains a great void. But it may be presumed that prosimians did in fact inhabit the African continent during Paleocene and Eocene times. During the Eocene a great sea advanced, called the Tethys Sea, which covered all of southern Europe and part of Asia, joining the Atlantic to the Indian Ocean. It enveloped also the top third of Africa, thus isolating the central and southern part of the continent for millions of years in the Eocene; then it withdrew again toward the end of that epoch.

Our information about climate during the Tertiary comes largely from the study of fossil floras. Fallen leaves, embedded in rocks or other deposits, tell paleobotanists about the type of forest that grew in a given area at a given time. By comparing these ancient forest types with modern ones, we can get a good idea of the prevailing temperatures at the ancient sites. When data from all over the world are plotted on a map, we can see the climatic zones as they were in bygone times. Ralph W. Chaney, an American geologist, has illustrated in this way the climatic zones of the world during the Eocene (see Figure 13). They were parallel with today's zones but farther out from the Equator. This means that the climate at that time was warmer in any given spot than it is today. (And it also proves that the poles were in the same position at that time as they are today, thus eliminating a source of confusion that has bothered geologists in the past.)

Let us take some examples to illustrate world climate in the Eocene. London, Paris, Kiev, Assam, and Wyoming had subtropical climates. Iceland, Spitzbergen, and Alaska were temperate. Novaya Semlya, Siberia, and Bathurst Island were cool-temperate.

With the closing of the Eocene period, 36 million years ago, the heyday of the prosimians passed. By the Oligocene period, most of the genera had become extinct, leaving only members of three families surviving, the lemurs, lorises, and tarsiers. Why such a profusion of species of one type of animal in one epoch, and so few remaining in the next? The answer must be simply that this is the way evolution has proceeded. At certain times, at certain stages of the earth's own development in terms of climate, vegetation, land masses, and so on, the development of certain types of animals seems to have been favored, as for example the dinosaurs that populated the earth for 150 million years. During such times, the forms of organisms that are favored proliferate into hundreds of species, exploiting every new

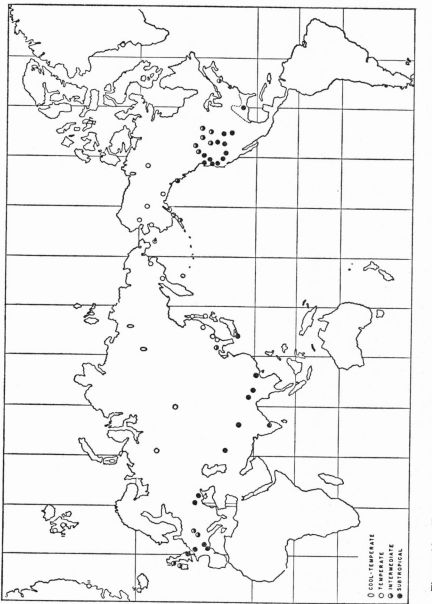

Figure 13. Eocene climate, as indicated by the study of fossil floras in specific localities (after Chaney).

niche, every new environment into which they can spread and fit. *Most* of these species, however, become overspecialized to suit a particular set of circumstances, and are destined to become extinct as soon as the environment changes or a new type of organism evolves with superior adaptations with which they cannot compete. Some of the species survive simply because they happen to inhabit an area that is not affected by environmental changes elsewhere or because the land they occupy is isolated and immune from advancing competitors. This is what saved the lemurs on the island of Madagascar. A very few species survive major environmental changes because in some way they had become "preadapted" to the changed circumstances in advance. For example, in human evolution, hands and arms originally adapted for locomotion in the trees were "preadapted" to develop other manipulative skills when this became an advantage.

Most types of early prosimians had become extinct by the start of the Oligocene period. At this distance in time, one can only speculate as to some of the reasons. One argument is that this was due to competition from the rapidly developing, more specialized rodents, carnivores, and higher primates.

The story of the further evolution of the primates is not known for several million years until the middle of the Oligocene period, and then it is taken up in Africa. In the Fayum in Egypt, sixty miles south of Cairo, and another site in the Libyan Desert, along what used to be the forest-fringed shores of a tropical sea (for during the Oligocene, the Tethys Sea rose once more), various primate forms have been found, over 30 million years old. From them we can deduce, in the lack of direct knowledge, that during the Paleocene and Eocene periods, primitive prosimians of the kind found in North America and Europe had indeed reached the land mass of Africa. In that favorable and relatively stable environment, during many millions of years of diversification, speciation, and selection, some had begun to evolve along lines leading eventually to monkeys, and others into the lines that later became apes. However, it must be stressed that the Oligocene primates were all very small generalized arboreal primates looking nothing like any monkeys or apes we know today. At the Fayum site have been found (along with insectivores, bats, rodents, giant hyraxes, birds, crocodiles, and fish) several different types of small primate: *Oligopithecus,* which from the nature of its teeth may be an early forerunner of the Old World monkeys; *Aeolopithecus,* which might be a very primitive gibbon ancestor; *Propliopithecus* (Plate 41),

Plate 1. The monolith of Shalmaneser II, King of Assyria, shows monkeys brought in tribute (ninth century B.C.).

Plate 2. Several *Cercopithecus* monkeys and a hamadryas baboon appear in this scene from the tomb of Rekhmara at Thebes.

Plate 4. A Cypriot kylix modeled into the face of a monkey (750–500 B.C.).

Plate 3. Terra-cotta of a climbing monkey, from Mohenjo-Daro (*ca.* 2500 B.C.).

Plate 5 Illustration of a creature which, it has been suggested, may be an ape, on a silver bowl from Praeneste, seventh century B.C.

ac die p singlas horas grens escā qm pdidit.
Neqʒ H rugit onager n qndo escam s grit.
sic dicit iacob. Nuqd sine causa clamabit o
nager agstis n pabulū desiderans? Similt
ter cʒ apls pet? de diabolo dicit. Aduisari
nr circuit qrens sit leo quē deuoret. Onager
interptat̄ asinus fer? onon gppe gn asinū
uocant. Agrian ferꝝ. Hos affrica ht mag
nos cʒ indomitos. cʒ in deserto uagantes.
Singli au seminarū gnibʒ psūt. Nascentibʒ
masclis zelant. cʒ testiclos morsibʒ detrūcāt
Qd cauentē matꝝ eos in secretis occultant.

Plate 6. The tale of a mother monkey and her two offspring, illustrated in an
English bestiary dated *ca.* A.D. 1170.

Plate 7. The Fall, according to Ludwig Krug. A monkey features in the scene in the Garden.

¶Raphaël Volaterranus mantichoram quoq; & crocutam ſimiarum genera eſſe putat, nullo authore, nullis argumentis: quanquam Albertus quoq; alicubi maricomorion(corrupto uocabulo mantichoræ)ſimiarum generis eſſe ſcribit, Ego ſententiam meam de duabus iſtis beſtijs, ſtatim poſt Hyænam ſupra expoſui.

DE CERCOPITHECO.

A.

his uerbis deſcribit:In Praſijs Indis ſimiarum genus eſſe ſe yrcanorum canū: tum earum comam etſi naturalem, ar uideri, tum barbam ipſarum ſpeciem ſatyricæ ſimilitudi ſpectari: reliquo corpore albas, capite & extrema cauda e & genere ipſo ſyleſtres ſint (montanis enim rebus & mò natura eicures, ad ſuburbium Latagis urbis frequen. ex comedendam obijcit,ae quotidie cibaria eis proijciun a moderatione redire,neq obuium quicquam lædere di a quoq; caudatum eſſe retulimus,& faciem ſatyro ſimilem m eſſe probabile fuerit. Huc pertinet etiam ille cerco Oceaneæ decadis tertiæ his uerbis deſerſbit. Animalia us: ſed unum reperere natu. o par, cauda longiore proce. terq; ſeſe deuoluens capien. e ſeſe proijcit in arborem, ac ſi confixit. Vulneratus ſeſe deſi rabidus adoritur. Stricto enſe eo abſcidit, cepitq; mancum . manſueuit inter homines pa. eruarent, è littoris trahunt pa. o aper & ipſe ferox oſtenditur: s furibundus ſalit, cauda cir. ictore ſuo lacerto, guttur apro lle. gnitudine & forma hominis: s hominē agreſtem, quia totus plus ſtando illo, homine ſolo is ac homines ſuæ regionis,co. is concumbere, quod nos uti. ed talis induſtriæ, ut homines quidem è noſtris ſed barbaris, ut Aethiopes Numidæq; qui. rorum etiam & quos piloſos libidinem commemorabi. ius imaginem hic adiecimus, Terræ ſanctæ mutuati,

DE

exemplo ſimia reperiatur,cynocephalum, ſtitutos ad mare deſcendēs,cum a ed piperis arbores uiderat,(de q ſtratus.)Erant enim nigræ uilloſ natura ancipite,partim homin Ariſtoteles. Et rurſus,Cynoce ſ nino ſpecies ſimiæ,ſed minor,A d hæc moribus ferocioribus eſt gum reliquum corpus canino m longiores,Albertus. Corporis nocephalo ſimile,Aelianus:atq lo & cani non conuenit. Sed St Cynocephali ſupercilijs aſpectu Fœminis ſua natura accidit,u Diodorus Sic. Plura de quibuſ

quinoctijs duodecies per diem, Vocem imitantur humanar. nar,ſed ululant,Aelianus. ¶S ygdala,glandes, nuces,excernu. ireijcioportere, Vini item potior etur,& his quidem recte & ſua gratæ elixis ualde offenduntur,a m ſint,ideo facile comprehendi m ſolem membratim conciſas c Aegyptiorum ſapientes ſacrificu ium abhorreat.(hic Græce addit ſiercerus uertit:quem tametſi pil non eſt,ſicut & externi (extri medit:& uerbum ἰχθυαζειν,non s gignitur,quam quidem circū. ndem ſedentem pingunt æquir n die per ſingulas nimirum hora:

Plate 8. *Above:* Cercopithecus monkeys were familiar in Gesner's day. **Plate 9.** *Left:* more manlike creatures were still largely mythological (from Gesner).

Tab. XIII

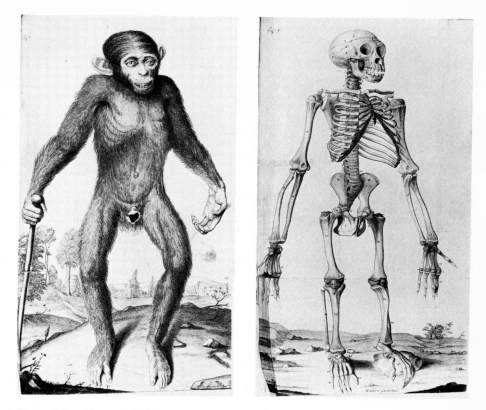

Plate 11. *Above left:* The chimpanzee described by Tyson in 1699. **Plate 12.** *Above right:* Its skeleton.

◀ **Plate 10.** Tulp's illustration of the ape he described in 1641.

Plate 13. The "anthropomorpha," according to Hoppius (1760).

1. *TROGLODYTA* Bontii   2. *LUCIFER* Aldrovandi   3. *SATYRUS* Tulpii   4. *PYGMÆUS* Edwardi

Plate 14. Buffon's illustration (1766) of a gibbon. The feet have claws instead of nails.

Plate 15.   Audebert's gibbon (1802).

Plate 16.   Audebert's orangutan,
or "jocko" (1802).

Plate 17. Orangutans reached Holland from the East Indies. These were drawn by Vosmaer in 1778.

Plate 18. Ape regarding the human skull, by Hugo Rheinhold, from the time of the Darwin controversy.

Plate 19. Gorillas were the last to appear. In this German natural history of 1886, they were not included.

Plate 20. St. Hilaire and Cuvier's siamang (1824–1857).

Plate 21. Portrait of a chimpanzee: face at rest.

Plate 22. Portrait of a chimpanzee: fear grimace.

Plate 23. Webbing of the foot in a pygmy chimpanzee.

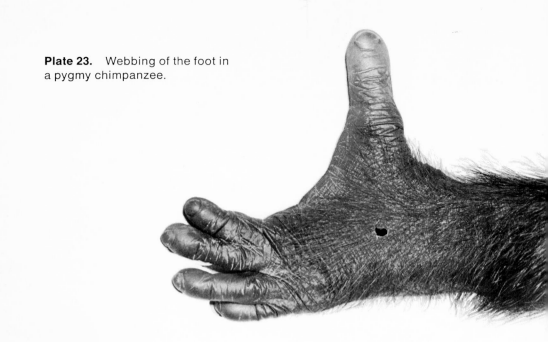

Plate 24. Portrait of a gorilla.

of which the significance is controversial. It is customary to assume that it is an unspecialized forerunner of the gibbons, but recently E. L. Simons has suggested that it is generalized enough to be related to later, larger apelike forms; the possibility even exists, put forward by Simons and D. R. Pilbeam, that *Propliopithecus* could lie close to the branching off of the line leading eventually to man. A recent and exciting find, made by Professor Simons at the Fayum site, was of *Aegyptopithecus*, a monkey-sized primate that, he says, is "the oldest undoubted great ape."

Thus, although the evidence from the Oligocene comes from only one site, and is based only on a few fragments of bone, teeth, and skulls, there is enough to show that already, over 30 million years ago, the higher primates had differentiated into a number of forms that later gave rise to monkeys, apes, and man himself.

There was also yet another type of primate found at the Fayum site, named *Apidium*, but this fossil is generally regarded as being on a line not related to any existing genus.

How is it that paleontologists are able to diagnose relationships from so many millions of years ago? For often enough they have only a few fragments of bones to go on; only very rarely, in quite exceptional circumstances, are complete skeletons preserved. Luckily, teeth are often the parts preserved, owing to the hardness of their enamel covering, and it is from the dentition that the experts can unravel affinities. Any schoolchild knows that the back teeth of a herbivore, such as a cow, look broad and flattened, while those of a carnivore, such as a domestic dog or cat, are sharp and pointed, with, farther forward, long, pointed "eyeteeth" or "canines" adapted to the tearing apart of their prey. But to the zoologist and anthropologist, teeth tell far more than whether the animal chews grass or tears meat. Using such parameters as shape of the jaw, the arch of the palate, the size of the canines, the numbers of incisors, premolars and molars, in particular the minute details of the pattern of the cusps on each tooth and the shape of the valleys between them, the paleontologist can tell not only what group the fossil belongs to but also how primitive or advanced it is along the line of evolution of that group.

By the time of the Oligocene and the Fayum fossils, the typical Old World monkey and ape dentition had developed, and *Oligopithecus, Propliopithecus,* and *Aegyptopithecus* had the Old World formula of (in each quarter) two incisors, one canine, two premolars, and three molars, making thirty-two teeth in all. They had lost along the way, since the earliest primates, one incisor and two premolars in each quarter. To return from this dental digression to the primate fossil *Apidium* found in the Fayum Oligocene site, it is because the teeth pattern of this fossil does not conform to the typical Old World dentition that had already developed by then that we know that it is on an aberrant line that became extinct.

Once more, and for the last time, the great Tethys Sea rose and fell at the end of the Oligocene, and a new period of the earth's history began. The Miocene period began 26 million years ago. Together with the Pliocene period, which started 12 million years ago and lasted until 3 million years ago, we could call this "The Age of the Apes."

It was an exciting time in the earth's development. Way back at the end of the Age of Reptiles, great forces had begun within the earth's crust that gradually were changing its surface from flat land masses covered with jungles and surrounded by shallow tropical seas. The continents began to rise from the oceans, and the great mountain ranges of the Himalayas, Andes, Alps, and Rockies began to build up. By Miocene-Pliocene times the great mountain ranges were completely made, and the continents had risen. Africa was joined to Eurasia, for the Red Sea rift had not opened. Then the African continent, which had until now remained stable, began to change. Until this stage, Africa had been a land of plateaus and gentle basins into which numbers of rivers drained. There were very few mountain massifs. Tropical forests covered most of the land. Then, during the Tertiary epoch, volcanic mountains began to rise in East Africa, changing the topography, and also incidentally improving the chances of fossilization of the species around them: volcanic lava is a very good preservative of bones. And also during the Miocene there began a series of disturbances within the earth that later caused the opening up of the two great rift valleys in East Africa, and the rise of the Ruwenzori Mountains.

And now the climate of the earth was gradually cooling, though still during the Miocene and Pliocene warmer tropical conditions were more widespread than at the present day. But with this cooling, the great forests began to shrink, and temperate conditions, with grassy plains, seasonal woodlands, and deserts began to spread southward over Europe, following the subtropical band. This of course was a slow process, which we can only recognize now it is past, lasting tens of millions of years, and leading ultimately to the period of the Pleistocene Ice Age when man was already inhabiting the earth. But the Age of the Apes dawned in the Miocene, still sunny, warm, and mostly forested over Africa, Europe, and Asia, 26 million years ago.

In East Africa at this time there is evidence that there were dense forests along the slopes of the rising volcanoes, many small lakes, rivers with gallery forests along them, and some open grassland. This setting was inhabited by apes, not just one species but several, and now that the continent of Africa was again joined to Arabia, these apes proliferated and dispersed toward Europe, India, and China. During the millions of years since the middle of the Oligocene period when three known types of small generalized ape forerunners lived in North Africa, the ape stock had been evolving in the particularly favorable conditions of Africa. If it were not for the volcanic eruptions going on at this period of the earth's history, the fossils of these apes might never have been preserved for us today, for it is a fact that the majority of Tertiary sites are within ten or twelve miles of a volcanic center. The lesson from this is that although most of our evidence of the whereabouts of the Miocene apes comes from volcanic East Africa, this may only reflect the fact that conditions there were suitable for the preservation of fossils. Many other parts of Africa almost certainly supported populations of apes at this period, but because they died in the lowland forests where the acid soil quickly obliterated all trace of them, nothing has been preserved for observation by us many million years later. Besides volcanic deposits, lakeside silt deposits have preserved some primate fossils.

In a deposit on Rusinga Island, in Lake Victoria, dating according to potassium-argon tests to between 15 and 22 million years ago, about eleven miles from the Rwanga volcano, have been found five or six different kinds of apes, all living contemporaneously, as well as lemurs (*Progalago*), and monkeys (*Victoriapithecus*). We know them to be apes because of the nature of their teeth (the monkeys have first and second molar teeth with four cusps, one at each corner, while all apes and man himself have molars with five cusps, which give the teeth a bumpy, irregular shape) and by the general morphology of the skulls and limb bones found. But none of these apes was recognizable as any of the apes we have today, because they were more primitive and had not yet evolved the particular specializations that characterize present-day apes—such as long, flexible, powerful arms. These early apes were of a variety of types and sizes. Two were variations of a genus called *Pliopithecus,* believed to be ancestral to the gibbons, on the basis of its skull and teeth characteristics. Its significance is now in doubt, however, as finds of *Pliopithecus* dating from later in the Miocene have been found in Europe (as well as Asia), producing skeletal remains as well. From these it appears that this primitive "gibbon" had many odd structural characteristics linking it rather with the New World monkeys and prosimians than with gibbons, and in addition it possessed a long tail! It is therefore possible that *Pliopithecus* represents a form of small primate destined for extinction, which nevertheless lay somewhere near the gibbon line.

But the most interesting and well-known of the East African Miocene apes have been called *Proconsul* (Plate 42), an odd name, meaning "before Consul." Consul was a famous English chimpanzee who used to perform in the music halls. One of the best known of these fossil ape remains was discovered by the wife of the anthropologist Dr. L. S. B. Leakey in 1948. As more specimens became available, it was found that related types of *Proconsul* apes came in three sizes: *Proconsul africanus* was about the size of a large monkey; *Proconsul nyanzae* was much the same size as a modern chimpanzee, and *Proconsul major* was an ape of about the same body size as a present-day gorilla. However, these early Miocene apes did not look recognizably like modern apes, for they had not developed the structural specializations we think of as being typical of apes. For example, they lacked heavy brow ridges. In brain size they were comparable to modern apes of similar size, but showed differences in dentition, having smaller incisors. The biggest differences, however, were in the structure of the limbs. Dr. J. Napier of London has studied in detail the anatomical structure of *Proconsul africanus,* for which skeletal material is available, and concluded that it was quadrupedal; probably its arms and legs were of approximately equal length. However, though it was therefore not specialized as a brachiator, there was some evidence that its arms were flexible and free-swinging, rather like present-day Colobus monkeys, so that it could have been well adapted to reaching, hanging, and breaking a fall after leaping, by using the arms extended above the head.

The *Proconsul* finds are immensely exciting. However, it must not be thought that they were the first primitive ape fossils to be discovered. Far from it. As far back as 1856 the French paleontologist Édouard Lartet reported finding in a Miocene site in France a lower jaw of a primitive ape, which he named *Dryopithecus*. Over the last hundred years, scores of apelike fossils of Miocene and Pliocene age have been discovered all over Europe, across to Russia, and also in China. Almost as many different names as there are paleontologists finding them have been given to these finds. And also in India, from the Siwalik Hills, have come numerous fossil apes, of the Pliocene Age this time, the first to be discovered being named *Sivapithecus* by G. E. Pilgrim in 1910.

Recently, two paleontologists, E. L. Simons, an American, and D. R. Pilbeam, an Englishman, examined all these Miocene-Pliocene apelike fossils, and recorded detailed measurements. They concluded that with three exceptions, to be mentioned shortly, *all* the fossils from Europe, Asia, and Africa could be placed in a single genus, containing only seven species. They called the genus *Dryopithecus*. The African *Proconsul* species were therefore renamed to become *Dryopithecus africanus, D. nyanzae,* and *D. major*. These species are of the early Miocene Age, from 18 to 23 million years ago, and thus antedate by several million years any of the European or Asian types yet discovered. It can therefore be presumed that the Dryopithecine primitive apes evolved within Africa, and spread out during Miocene and Pliocene times throughout the whole of the tropical forest belt that then covered most of Europe and central Asia. This view is supported by the fact that the European and Asian species of Dryopithecines also contain small, medium, and large species, which appear to be closely related, with some differences, to the three African forms. Thus in Europe and India there was a small ape, *Dryopithecus laietanus,* comparable in size to *Dryopithecus (Proconsul) africanus*. *Dryopithecus fontani,* widespread in Miocene-Pliocene Europe, between 10 and 17 million years old, and *Dryopithecus sivalensis* from India are chimpanzee-sized apes, similar in most measurements to *Dryopithecus (Proconsul) nyanzae* from earlier Miocene East Africa. Finally, just as we had a large gorilla-sized ape living in Africa in the early Miocene, *Dryopithecus (Proconsul) major,* so from East Europe, India, and China there is a similarly sized form, *Dryopithecus indicus*. The distribution of *Dryopithecus* is shown in Plate 43.

As we have seen, nearly all the scores of fossil apes discovered throughout the Old World, and dating from between 10 to 23 million years ago, belonged to one vigorous genus, *Dryopithecus,* which spread from Africa in the earliest Miocene Era, over the forested regions of Europe and Asia. These Dryopithecine apes are the substance of our story, but mention must be made of three types of apelike fossils of this period believed to be rather less closely related to the main tide of ape evolution. First, a giant species of apelike creature, dating from Pliocene and the even later Pleistocene periods, occurred in parts of southern China. It has been named *Gigantopithecus,* and is obviously related to the Dryopithecines, and probably descended from them, but is larger even than a gorilla. It is believed to have become extinct, but I like to speculate that the elusive "yeti" may prove to be a remnant population of this giant ape, still existing in the Himalayas.

Another rather puzzling ape, named *Oreopithecus,* has been found in lignite mines in central Italy, in deposits dating from the early Pliocene. This ape probably brachiated, might have walked erect, and was about four feet high. But because its teeth are very atypical of the main ape (or human) line of evolution, *Oreopithecus* is believed to have become extinct. It was possibly related to the unusual Oligocene primate *Apidium,* previously discussed, of which the teeth also were aberrant in a similar way. If this is indeed the case, then the existence of *Oreopithecus* illustrates an important feature of evolutionary progress: that the same or parallel line of adaptation and development can occur several times over in the evolution of a group, such as the primates, all sharing a common structural basis, and behavioral adaptations. Thus *Oreopithecus,* over 20 million years from the Oligocene *Apidium,* paralleled to a large extent the structural evolution of man himself, in that the body size increased, the face flattened, and he became capable of walking erect. In the same way, of course, the ability to brachiate has undoubtedly evolved several times over in the history of the apes and monkeys; for example in gibbons, in the larger apes, and to some degree in the South American spider monkey.

Finally, before returning to the Dryopithecines and the story of ape evolution, mention must be made of perhaps the most important ape of all. In the Siwalik Hills, in 1934, a paleontologist named G. E. Lewis found an ape fossil with some peculiarly human characteristics, dating from the early Pliocene. He called it *Ramapithecus.* Then in 1962, the anthropologist Dr. L. S. B. Leakey, working at the Fort Ternan site in Kenya, discovered the jaws of a similar creature, which he named *Kenyapithecus wickeri.* This fossil has been dated by potassium-argon tests to about 14 million years ago, that is, late Miocene times. Simons and Pilbeam include Dr. Leakey's find in the same genus and species as the Indian *Ramapithecus,* of rather later date. Despite their wide geographical separation, both fossils share the same essentially human-like developments—a rounded, manlike mandible rather than U-shaped mandible typical of the fossil apes; indications of a flatter, foreshortened face; and a small canine tooth. In their recent revision, Simons and Pilbeam have included under *Ramapithecus* one or two other fossil fragments, from Europe and from China, which had previously been assigned to the Dryopithecines. It is now believed, therefore, that *Ramapithecus* (Plate 44), while still very much an ape, represents an early stage of human evolution, some time after the line leading to man had diverged from that leading to present-day apes. This view is given added support by the very recent claim by Dr. Leakey to have identified a much earlier form of *Kenyapithecus*, living at the time of the early *Proconsuls* in the first part of the Miocene. He has named this fossil, of which there are only a few jaw and tooth fragments, *Kenyapithecus africanus*, and believes it is on the hominid line.

But what does all this add up to? Have we discovered enough of the fossil record to be able to postulate the probable times of divergence and lines of development of present-day apes and man? The answer is No. The fossil record alone permits of several different interpretations.

The following is just one possible theory of the chronology of the evolution of the apes and men; many anthropologists would not agree, others would declare that in the present state of the fossil record it is premature to speculate; but it is based on the recent survey of the Dryopithecine material by Simons and Pilbeam, taken together with other sources of relevant information from related sciences.

It seems a reasonable assumption now, on the basis of skull and dentition, that *Dryopithecus* (*Proconsul*) *major* is ancestral to the gorilla and that *D.* (*Proconsul*) *nyanzae* was a forerunner of the chimpanzee. Thus it appears that at least as long ago as 18 million years, chimpanzees and gorillas were specifically distinct. If this is taken to be the case, then it is extremely likely that the line leading to man was already distinct, though of course at that time no more than an apelike stock closely related to the Proconsuls. This would make the probable time of divergence of the ancestral human line from the line leading to the three great apes somewhere about the Oligocene-Miocene boundary, 26 million years ago (though the first recognized hominid fossil is 14 million years ago—*Ramapithecus*), and the divergence of chimpanzee and gorilla stock somewhat later, in the very early Miocene. The common stock of the large apes and man may in fact be represented by the Oligocene pongid *Aegyptopithecus* (although, as was mentioned previously, Simons and Pilbeam have recently suggested the possibility that the human line goes back even further, to *Propliopithecus* and beyond). Ancestral gibbons and siamangs were almost certainly distinct from the other apes already in the Oligocene, and may have evolved from *Aeolopithecus* (or *Propliopithecus*) through the Miocene *Pliopithecus*, though owing to the nature of the latter's postcranial material it now seems less likely. *D. (Proconsul) africanus* may be an early Miocene species that became extinct, or it is quite possible that it represents an earlier form of the other two larger Proconsuls.

As the early Miocene forms of Dryopithecine ape spread out from Africa into Europe and Asia where they are found in strata 17 to 10 million years old, they adapted to new conditions and evolved into new species. The medium-sized progressive Proconsul, *D. nyanzae*, is the species most likely to have given rise to *D. (Sivapithecus) sivalensis* in India, and also to the larger form, *D. indicus,* which, according to Pilbeam, may well be a fossil orang. This suggested chronology of the evolution of the known species of apes and man takes into account certain other bodies of facts. First, the work of A. H. Schultz and his colleagues in Zurich on the comparative anatomy of primates has shown that the three large apes share innumerable structural and ontogenetic similarities that set them apart from man on the one hand, and the gibbons on the other. This definitely indicates that the divergence of the lines leading to gibbons, and to man, occurred before the speciation of the three large apes from one another.

Another approach to the study of hominoid relationships is through the electrophoretic and immunological analysis of serum proteins and the analysis of hemoglobins (see Chapter 3). The results of this approach are leading to the development of theories about phylogenetic relationships. Some of these are at variance with those of the comparative anatomists. Immunological analysis of at least fourteen serum proteins as well as the fingerprints of hemoglobins have indicated that there is a closer genetic correspondence between chimpanzee and gorilla to man than between any of these three to the orang. Further work in this field may or may not confirm this. If it does, students of evolution will have to decide whether the new data imply that the orang left the common line some time before the chimpanzee, gorilla, and man, or whether the new findings are reflections of the greater genetic divergence between the orang and the other big apes owing to geographic dispersion. The gibbon, as was expected, has shown itself to be markedly distinct from the other apes and man at the genetic level.

Another source of evidence supporting the suggested chronology is what we know of the behavior, individual and social, of the apes and man; for behavior, too, is subject to evolution, and can develop changes only on the basis of what went before. Gibbon development and potential is more like that of monkeys than of the other apes and man (see Chapter 9); and its social organization of territorial monogamous families (see Chapter 7) is very unusual among apes; its locomotion is a unique specialization, for it brachiates quite differently from the other apes; it rarely comes down to the ground in the wild; it alone of the other apes and man does not make a nest (or bed) to sleep in. These facts clearly argue for an early separation of the gibbon line from the rest of the hominoid stock.

The three large apes and humans all share a number of typical behavior patterns in common, and ontogenetically for the first years of life show remarkable parallelisms (see Chapter 8). Humans differ most, of course, having developed bipedalism, and having taken to terrestrial savannah-living and carnivorous diet; ontogenetically the various stages of the life cycle have been prolonged in man, allowing, with the concomitant extreme development of the brain, for complex learning processes; culture and technology have resulted from this. Thus the line leading to man is very likely, on the basis of behavioral comparisons, to have diverged next after the gibbons. Let us now examine the common stock that led to the large apes and man, on the threshold of the Miocene, and try to imagine what they might have been like and how they came to differentiate.

This progressive proto-ape, somewhere between *Aegyptopithecus* and *D.* (*Proconsul*) *africanus* must have been gibbon-sized, with a shorter, flatter face than is typical of the present-day large apes. This was correlated with a tendency to erect trunk posture in the trees, which had most likely been a characteristic of the ancestral tree-clinging primitive prosimians from which it was descended. This erect body posture had also allowed the development of strong, flexible arms, hands, and fingers, able to swing, hang, reach, and break the fall after a leap, though the specialized forelimb structure for this was not yet evolved, and the arms were roughly equal in length to the legs. But this progressive species owed its success to its great *behavioral* adaptability. It had a well-developed brain for its size, for ever since the earliest prosimians there had been a selective advantage for visual acuity and an expansion of those parts of the brain, chiefly the cortex, that control the responses of the muscles to things seen, heard, felt, and remembered. It had developed the habit of flinging down broken branches at predator-enemies or other disturbing animals on the forest floor. And it used its hands and arms to weave springy nests of branches and leaves to sleep in at night. This particular behavior pattern evolved in part because of the gradual increase in size of this progressive pongid species; for increased body weight meant the need for more body support when sleeping. Being behaviorally exceptionally varied and adaptable (for in this lay the secret of its success and later expansion over three continents), our proto-ape began to come down more frequently to the forest floor to exploit the roots and stalks and lower-story fruits, in addition to treetop vegetation. It had often walked bipedally in the trees, holding onto the branches above for support, and now, when it started to come down to the ground, it also walked bipedally some of the time. On the forest floor it was more vulnerable to predator attack, but our proto-ape was able to defend itself. It had exceptionally good eyesight, hearing, memory, and learning power, and was very quickly able to identify signs of danger. Not only could it rapidly shin up any tree trunk by grasping the trunk with its strong arms and pulling itself up, but it was also able to adapt to good advantage its arboreal habit of branch breaking and throwing, causing such a disturbance that any would-be predator was scared away, if not directly hit. With all levels of the forest to exploit, and with arms and hands flexible and free from being necessary to locomotion, our proto-ape began to develop skills requiring greater coordination and manipulation, such as grabbing a small bird or animal that came its way, and using sticks and stones as tools to dig in the earth or crack open nuts.

We can guess that the proto-apes may have had a loose social organization, of small fluctuating groups, based on maternal and sibling relationship and age-mate friendship, living within a familiar range of forest. For in their evolutionary history up to the late Oligocene, they had been small, intelligent, agile arboreal primates, with little to fear from predators, and therefore there had been no selection pressures toward closed territorial groups ruled by large aggressive adult males specialized for defense of the group. They lived chiefly on vegetable foods, experiencing no shortages but preferring fruits to all else, and at times when a favorite fruit was in season in their part of the forest, all the groups inhabiting the area would join to feast together. At such times, there was much social excitement, shouting and calling, and the adult males would drum on tree trunks and bang the ground; others would rock rhythmically from foot to foot or round and round on the ground or in the trees. Sexual liaisons were frequent at such gatherings of all the inhabitants of an area, encouraged by the social excitement.

Such, perhaps, was the behavior and way of life of the small, wiry, intelligent little proto-ape at the end of the Oligocene, 26 or more million years ago. It seemed to be perfectly adapted to maximum exploitation and enjoyment of its tropical forest environment, but there was another world waiting to be conquered, outside the forest, and no one more suited physically or behaviorally than it was to conquer it. Consider for a moment the *edges* of the forest, where there are trees dotted around in woodland and, beyond, grassy plains with grazing ungulates. It was entirely natural that an inquisitive arbo-terrestrial proto-ape, which could shin up a tree to get a long view or peer over the tall grass to see ahead, should make excursions out of the forest from time to time. It was unafraid, for it was alert, and could run fast or it could leap into a tree and swing away; it could even break off a sapling and swish it in display and self-defense. And as visual conditions were better out of the forest, it was easier to catch and eat small mammals. Over millions of years a species (*Rama-pithecus-Kenyapithecus*) evolved that took to living by preference on the fringes of the forests, returning to a clump of trees at night or constructing simple woven shelters of branches and grass. From the generalized structure of the arm-swinging, erect-postured, mainly arboreal proto-ape, there were two likely lines of evolutionary de-velopment—one toward increased power and flexibility of the arms (as in the large apes), and the other toward erect terrestrial bipedalism. The proto-ape species that was eventually to become man took the latter course; as it became more efficient in killing small mammals for meat, it left the forests for the savannahs, where under the influence of quite different selection pressures from those of the forest, it developed its inherited behavior patterns of incipient tool and weapon use, flexible social grouping, and community festivals, into human tech-nology and culture. But that process took millions of years, and is another story.

Our main interest is in the proto-ape stock that remained within the forest. The main trend was toward increased body size (which was paralleled also in the species that led to man). Second, the arms, which were so important in reaching, hanging, swinging, holding, and climbing, became structurally longer and more powerful, a tendency that was to continue in all the large apes, in parallel with their less closely related cousins the gibbons, from the early Miocene onward. In earliest Miocene times, another species of proto-ape, *Dryopithecus (Proconsul) major*, began to differentiate, which became more and more terrestrial, and began to specialize on forest-floor vegetable foods such as roots, piths, stems, and canes. This ancestral gorilla in many ways took a rather sad and backward evolutionary step. For as it became big and heavy, it lost the arbo-terrestrial adaptability that had been the main reason for success in the Oligocene proto-ape species. When it became an habitual ground dweller, it became more vulnerable to surprise and attack by predators. This selected for increased mass and strength, and produced sexual dimorphism, with the male growing noticeably more massive and ferocious-looking (though remaining unaggressive in nature) than the female. At the same time, gorilla groups tended to become more stable, gathered round one or more adult males, who, with their formidable chest drumming, barking, and tearing of saplings and vegetation when excited, were more than a match for most would-be attackers. Preoccupied with poking around the vegetation to get enough to fill their massive bodies and vast energy requirements, gorillas became morose, persistent, and phlegmatic in temperament, but they retained the ancestral proto-ape characteristics of being friends with neighbors, not having territories, joining up with other groups, having a flexible group membership, and not being possessive in sexual relationships. Correlated with its becoming a ground forager, the gorilla developed specialized knuckle pads on its hands for walking, and a longer, more prognathous face. These were secondary specializations for quadrupedal gait and ground-living habits, but even today the gorilla walks and runs bipedally in its display, and juvenile gorillas brachiate and do bipedal walking quite spontaneously.

The ancestral proto-ape stock, which retained its behavioral and locomotor plasticity, spread far and wide in the early and middle Miocene, across to Europe and Asia, throughout the broad belt of tropical forest. It increased in body size, too, and continued to develop longer, stronger arms. It thus became structurally as well as behaviorally a brachiator. The proto-ape evolved into new species as it adapted to new habitats that became separated from the old. From this stock is most probably descended the African chimpanzee through *D. (Proconsul) nyanzae*, and the Asian orangutan through *D. (Sivapithecus) indicus*. The European species must have slowly become extinct with the Miocene-Pliocene shrinking of the tropical forested belt.

Behaviorally these two types have more in common than either has with any other ape or man. The main difference is the greater degree of arboreality of the orang. This is presumably due to its adaptation to the Asian type of swampy river-ridden forest. The orang was probably already a fairly large ape when it reached Asia, and took to an increasingly exclusive arboreal life. It has thus evolved unique structures of the limb joints and musculature that enabled it effortlessly to hang from branches in any position. The chimpanzee, on the other hand, as its body size increased, in a quite different type of forest environment, became less rather than more arboreal; as its food needs increased it had to travel longer and longer distances through the forest, and this it did on the forest floor, through a network of tracks. It also developed knuckle pads for walking on its hands, and a more prognathous face, both again secondary specializations.

Socially, however, both chimpanzees and orangs have no fixed groups; they meet up or part from others at will. Both are predominantly fruit eaters, and therefore seasonal nomads. Both are known to use sticks as tools to dig out insects, and use branches as weapons of intimidation and attack, though only the chimpanzee has been observed actually to kill and eat another mammal. In juvenile development (see Chapter 8) their progress, abilities, and natural skills are identical. In intelligence tests (see Chapter 9) their performances are similar, and at variance with results on the gorilla. One feature of chimpanzee life in the wild, the use of drumming and calling as long-distance communication between members, is lacking in recent field reports of the orang. However, earlier accounts from last century, when orangs were very much more numerous than nowadays, refer to "singing" by the wild men of the woods, and I wonder if it is not just underpopulation, through the drastic shooting of orangs, that has reduced social communication and social motivation in this species.

More recently, probably during Pleistocene times, the gorilla and chimpanzee have undergone subdivision. The gorilla has divided into a western and an eastern population, while the chimpanzee has divided into a common and a "pygmy" type.

In the case of the gorilla, the two groups are currently separated by some 650 miles, occurring on the west and east sides of the Congo

Forest. Why this separation? Schaller has speculated that in the past the gorilla population may have been continuous along a belt north of the present limit of the rain forest (see Figure 14) and that during a dry period this population died out. We know that Africa has been subject to wetter and drier periods, and it appears that gorillas can survive only in humid forests, and not in areas with a pronounced dry season. As the northern gorilla belt became drier, the gorillas would have to retreat southward in order to survive. But here were great obstacles—the Ubangi and Uele rivers, and after them the Congo. Gorillas cannot cross such deep, wide rivers. They therefore either died out or migrated east or west and then south, back with the humid forest. An interesting find of three gorilla skulls at Bondo, between the two areas today occupied by gorillas, suggests that once gorillas did live there. The separation may have occurred during the latter half of the Pleistocene—there is evidence that the Lake Chad region of West Africa was very much wetter in the late Pleistocene than it is now. The two groups differ physically from each other only in minor respects, indicating that they have not been isolated for long.

In the chimpanzees, separation of the "pygmy" form from the other forms is ensured by the Congo River, which is an uncrossable barrier. It is possible that the separation of the chimpanzee into two types dates from the time of the formation of the Congo River on its present course across Africa from east to west. For until the end of the Tertiary, when the great rift valley systems were formed, none of the hundreds of small rivers draining into the central Congo basin would have constituted such a continuous barrier. The pygmy chimpanzees may in fact represent the original chimpanzee stock more closely than does the larger, commoner type now. For their smaller average size indicates that they have lived longer and more completely inside the forest than their larger relatives.

In a way, the story of the evolution of the apes is a sad one. From being progressive, dynamic, and successful, in the Miocene, the lines leading to the chimpanzees, gorillas, and orangs became more restricted, confined on the one hand by the decreasing extent of the forests, and on the other by the onslaughts of their terrible cousin—man. If I were asked which of all the existing apes is most like the common ancestor of apes and man, I would say the chimpanzee—for the following reasons: first, it has remained within the African tropical forested belt in which the evolution of man and all the apes first took place; thus it lacks specializations of behavior or structure attributable

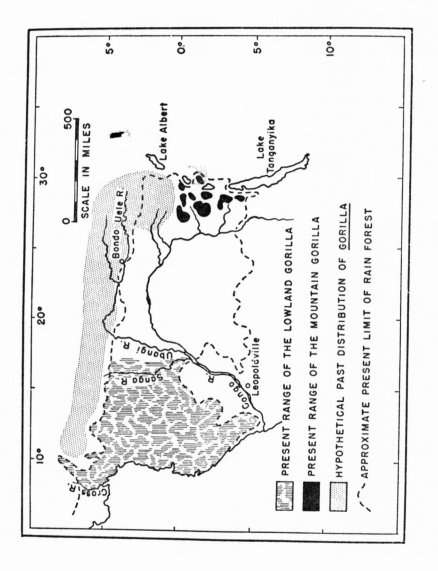

Figure 14. The present and hypothetical past distribution of the genus *Gorilla* (after Schaller).

to changes in habitat; second, of all the apes it has remained the least specialized in its feeding habits, its locomotion, its behavior, and its body structure, all of which characteristics must have been present in the proto-ape to account for its success and colonization of other areas; third, it has retained those behavior patterns of the opportunistic proto-ape which *preadapted* man, on leaving the forests, to evolve culturally and technologically. Thus the chimpanzee shares with humans the ability to use sticks and stones as tools and even weapons, to kill and eat animals and even share the meat, to dance, to drum, to roister, and to celebrate abundance of good food with community gathering and sexual activity.

CHAPTER **5**

The Natural Life of Chimpanzees

THE STUDY OF WILD chimpanzees really began with the zoologist R. L. Garner, a collector who also decided to watch apes in the jungle, and find out how they lived. This was at the very end of the nineteenth century. For his study area he chose the forests of Gabon, West Africa, where chimpanzees and gorillas were known to live. And inside the forest he built a big cage, not for any apes he hoped to catch, but for himself (see Plate 45).

This cage speaks eloquently of the climate of opinion concerning the great African rain forest in Garner's day. Paul du Chaillu's book *Explorations and Adventures in Equatorial Africa* had been out for over thirty years by then, describing in dramatic detail the ferocious charge of the gorilla, the violence of its roar, the awe of the natives before it. Du Chaillu was a naturalist, but also a great romancer; we shall look at his contribution in the next chapter, as it chiefly concerned the gorilla. Henry M. Stanley's books on "darkest Africa" were also vivid in people's minds, and, tinged as they were with bold strokes of drama, they were enough to put the idea of a trip to the forests of that country out of most sane men's minds.

So Garner armed himself, and built a big cage, and sat in it. In fact he spent most of the day and all night in it for 112 successive days and nights, waiting and sleeping. But it was too much to expect apes simply to come into view. If they saw cage, clearing, or any signs of foreign intrusion, they would be more likely to stop and peer cautiously from a protective screen of bushes than to expose themselves.

A few times Robert Garner saw a single chimpanzee or gorilla wander up to him and then move quickly away—a small return for his investment. But his achievement was a greater one than the collection of new raw data: he insisted on the observational approach to ape studies. In this he was out of his time, the prophet of a later generation. Garner did not return to America with notebooks full of data, but he did get some information concerning the fantastic shouting, hooting, screaming, and drumming of the apes, which he frequently heard. At first he thought this noise was produced by gorillas, but later concluded it must be chimpanzees. Never having seen the chimpanzees in action, he was led to accept native information to supplement his own ideas, and one result is the following delightful mix-up of fact and fantasy:

One of the most remarkable of all the social habits of the chimpanzee, is the *kanjo,* as it is called in the native tongue. The word does not mean "dance" in the sense of saltatory gyrations, but implies more the idea of "carnival." It is believed that more than one family takes part in these festivities.

Here and there in the jungle is found a small spot of sonorous earth. It is irregular in shape, but is about two feet across. The surface is of clay, and is artificial. It is superimposed upon a kind of peat bed, which, being very porous, acts as a resonance cavity, and intensifies the sound. This constitutes a kind of drum. It yields rather a dead sound, but of considerable volume.

This queer drum is made by chimpanzees, who secure the clay along the bank of some stream in the vicinity. They carry it by hand, and deposit it while in a plastic state, spread it over the place selected, and let it dry. I have, in my possession, a part of one that I brought home with me from the Nkhami forest. It shows the finger-prints of the apes, which were impressed in it while the mud was yet soft.

After the drum is quite dry, the chimpanzees assemble by night in great numbers, and the carnival begins. One or two will beat violently on this dry clay, while others jump up and down in a wild and grotesque manner. Some of them utter long, rolling sounds, as if trying to sing. When one tires of beating the drum, another relieves him, and the festivities continue in this fashion for hours.

This was a different story from the one the young explorer Winwood Reade had brought back with him in 1863:

> He [an African informant] took me into the wood, and showed me a large tree called *oreva*. It was hollow, for I could see where a porcupine had burrowed in it. This was the chimpanzee's drum, he said; and catching hold of two young trees, he swung himself in the air, and beat with the soles of his feet against the tree. I must confess, that I heard no sound like that of a drum; but he told me that the chimpanzee did it so "strong-strong-strong" that one could hear a booming noise ever so far away.

Both stories were, as we shall see, rather wide of the mark.

It was fully thirty years after Garner's pioneering study that the next attempt to get to grips with wild apes was made. During those years, chimpanzees had found their way into captive colonies here and there in the civilized world, for example in Mme. Rosalia Abreu's colony at Havana. The first collection of chimpanzees for scientific study was that of Robert Yerkes, in Orange Park, Florida. Yerkes, a highly original thinker, realized the need for scientific data concerning wild apes as well as the obvious need for apes themselves, to use in his laboratories. So he decided to send out two expeditions, one to central Africa to study the mountain gorilla, and one to West Africa to study the chimpanzee. Spearhead of the chimpanzee wing was Henry Nissen, who based himself at Pastoria, the laboratory of the Pasteur Institute in hot, dry western Guinea. His aims were twofold—to watch wild chimpanzees and find out how they lived, and to capture some of them alive for shipment to the laboratory in the United States, where their behavior could be further studied.

Nissen worked in the dry season. The habitat was fairly open, hilly country with tree-lined creeks and streams in the valleys. On the hills the trees were stunted and sparse, and the grass everywhere was five to ten feet high. During the first half of 1930, he spent a total of sixty-four days of full time fieldwork in the bush, taking copious notes as he traveled around, on foot with his crowd of native guides and porters, in search of chimpanzees. And during this time he learned many hitherto unknown facts about the behavior of wild chimpanzees.

It was too hot for comfort, and he was burdened by too much native "help"; yet, by dropping his men behind when chimpanzees were located, Nissen managed to make observations on forty-nine days, keeping his presence a secret. What he saw led him to question whether chimpanzees did in fact live in "families," an idea widely accepted at the time, and dating back a good many centuries. My favorite version of the family hypothesis is the statement from Livingstone's *Last Journals,* published in 1874, that chimpanzees "live in communities of about ten, each having his own female . . . if one tries to seize the female of another, he is caught on the ground, and all unite in boxing and biting the offender."

Nissen wondered whether there was any truth in this idea, and whether particular males kept with one or more particular females. Certainly the chimpanzees were usually in bands, but Nissen doubted whether these consisted of a male, his "wives," and their offspring, even though the local Africans assured him that this was so. For in many bands he identified two or more mature adult males, and often groups appeared to join and merge. One group he saw contained ten animals with no infants at all. And later research has entirely confirmed his doubts: there are no human-type families.

Then there was the question of territory: Did a band have its own "home," and if so was this area exclusive to the one band only? And was it defended? He found that bands wandered around in the food quest, the whereabouts of food being an important factor in determining their movements. And he doubted that they migrated over vast distances. He saw no fighting between one group and another, and this, coupled with the meeting and mixing of groups, argued against fixed territories.

In their daily routines Nissen found the chimpanzees were early risers, up and doing before sunrise, most active during the early morning and again during the late afternoon, resting in the midday sun. At this hottest time of day they made "day beds" on the ground, and occasionally made shady roofs (sun umbrellas) for them by pulling young saplings over themselves to give shade. At night they slept in nests, constructed up in the trees at dusk; their nests were kept clean of excrement.

Nissen collected thirty-four different kinds of chimpanzee food plants, but without great benefit to science, for, in his own words, "a family of field rats made their home under the floor of the hut and . . . destroyed most of my specimens."

He described the terrifying choruses of shrieks and cries and drumming noises made by the chimpanzees, which when close made his native porters tremble with fear. He tried to distinguish the individual calls, and named them, such as the "panting cry," "scream," "bark," "whine," "snarl," and "muttering." The drumming noise was made, he thought, by the chimpanzees beating on hollow logs. He was the first to notice that wild chimpanzees may in fact use certain gestures as a means of communicating with one another. For example he saw a female pointing as though to indicate his presence to the others. On one occasion, some animals saw him, thudded the ground, and as though in response to this signal, others in the trees hurriedly descended and ran away. He also saw a mother, who was carrying a small baby clinging to the hair under her belly, gently tap it before making a tricky crossing on a log across a ravine, as though to warn it to hold on tight.

Nissen was familiar with the bored and listless apes he knew in captivity before he visited Africa—they sat motionless for hours or turned to perversions or stereotyped ritual movements—while the apes he now watched in their natural habitat were lively and contented. He watched young ones playing for twenty minutes in the trees, leaping one after the other onto a pile of leafy branches on the ground, then getting up to do it over again. He saw a mother teasing her infant by tickling it with a branch while it slept. He had a hair-raising moment one day as he saw a full-grown male charge straight toward him; when it was a few yards away it suddenly stopped, picked up a juvenile chimpanzee, and retreated fast. It was clear that the male had considered that the young one was in danger by being too close to a human, and had run to save it.

One thing puzzled Nissen. On the whole, the apes he watched led an easy, uncomplicated life. Being vegetarians, there seemed a plentiful supply of food, and with their ease of locomotion on the ground or in the trees, they had little to fear from predators. And yet Nissen knew from his studies at the Yerkes Laboratories of Primate Biology, then located at Orange Park, Florida, that chimpanzees possess a highly developed brain and a sensitive, emotional temperament similar to that of man. They show high intelligence (see Chapter 9), can imitate man's actions, solve problems such as building up boxes in order to reach a suspended banana, can open doors by using a key, and have a long and accurate memory. How had they evolved such abilities when their forest life seemed so undemanding? This is a problem that continues to puzzle scientists today. The truth, I suspect, is that their life in the wild is by no means so undemanding as it seems at first sight.

In 1960, Adriaan Kortlandt, a zoologist from Amsterdam, set out to

tour the African rain forest in search of a good place to study chimpanzees. After several months he found a suitable spot in East Africa—a
paw-paw plantation regularly raided by chimps, which the owner
tolerated and which were not molested by the local Africans. Here he
built blinds where he hid to watch the animals—the best method to
adopt if they are sure to return to a given spot, but useless when they
do not. One of the blinds he placed at the top of a tall tree overlook-
ing the plantation—it was over eighty feet up, and "on windy days
the tree swayed so much that I could not use my field glasses. When a
tropical thunderstorm came up unexpectedly, I could only pray that I
would not be electrocuted."

Kortlandt spent several seasons at this plantation, waiting and
watching and making notes on what he saw. At first there would be a
noise inside the forest, which came up to the edge of the plantation.
This would be the hooting and drumming of the approaching chimpanzees. Then they fell silent. Carefully, out into the clearing stepped
the first few chimps—adult males as a rule. Behind them followed the
females with their young. Once out in the open and certain they were
safe, the males often broke out into a wild and deafening display—
shrieking and screaming, stamping on the ground and smacking tree
trunks, pulling down saplings and brandishing branches. Then they all
fed on the melon-sized paw-paws, rather wastefully, returning to the
forest edge sometimes with a paw-paw under one arm and another in
one hand, so that they would make their way along like little men,
walking on their hind legs only. But they did not have to be carrying
pawpaws to walk upright like this; often they would simply do so by
preference; perhaps the extra height enabled them to see better over
the grass. Apart from their screaming displays, the chimpanzees were
quiet on the plantation. Youngsters played in silence; they begged for
food from their mothers by holding out a hand, and jumped obediently
onto mama's back when she looked them in the eye.

As for social organization, Kortlandt found no evidence of "family
groups" or "harems," but he did notice that mothers with their offspring tended to keep together in "nursery groups" (Plate 46)—a great
step forward in understanding chimpanzee society and how it compares with our own. For it does seem, and other studies have confirmed, that one of the principles of chimpanzee social structure is that
mothers with their young keep together, as distinct from the males and
childless females and adolescents. Kortlandt also distinguished what
he called the "sexual group," consisting of these adult males and child-

less females. The sexual groups he saw were generally larger than the nursery groups, the former type having over twenty members, the latter under fifteen, of which more than half were children. There was also a big difference in behavior—the sexual groups ranged over an area of several square miles of forest, and were noisy and brash; the nursery groups were very shy and far less mobile, keeping nearer to the plantation. My wife and I, on our later study of chimpanzees right inside the forest, found the same thing: noisy, mobile males, and quiet, slow mothers. And we believe this distinctive social pattern, first discovered by Kortlandt, lies at the very heart of any understanding of chimpanzee society.

But chimpanzee groups, sexual or nursery, should not be thought of as permanent in membership. Kortlandt wrote: "Individuals were free to join or leave a group at will, and the groups themselves often merged or split up." This finding has also been confirmed by later workers; while particular chimpanzees do tend to band up with each other, the bond keeping them together seems to be one of convenience or even "friendship," and there seems to be no concept of belonging to a specific group with which one will always stay: chimpanzees are remarkably independent-minded in this respect.

One advantage of Kortlandt's open plantation study area was that the regular appearances of chimpanzees at the same place, using the same pathways day after day, enabled him to devise and execute a unique experimental program of a kind hitherto presumed impossible on wild apes. He was able to present the chimpanzees with such things as live snakes (contrary to expectation, these apes just casually by-passed the snake, and did not show the "instinctive horror reaction" that has been described in zoo experiments), freshly killed or live goats, and even a stuffed leopard with a realistic twitching tail. Kortlandt was able to take a series of fantastic photographs showing a female chimpanzee brandishing a stick and throwing it in the direction of the leopard (see Plates 47 and 48). In addition, he has collected data from many people who have made observations on apes in the wild or in zoos, and has in this way been able to show that chimpanzees have certain behavior patterns that are often thought to have developed only with the emergence of man. For example, chimpanzees captured in savannah habitats throw and aim sticks at predators such as leopards in captivity. And other studies have shown that wild chimpanzees make and use simple tools, to obtain honey or insects to eat.

It is often assumed that when the first "ape-men" had left the forest and taken up a plains existence, the use of weapons in hunting game for food became necessary to ensure their survival, yet here are apes showing weapon and tool using, which are not demanded by their forest life. This is akin to the problem Nissen posed: Why have high intelligence and skills developed in forest-living apes that do not appear to need them? Kortlandt's explanation is that at some stage in our evolutionary past, the African apes and man lived in semiopen country outside the forest proper, and that man forced the apes to resume a forest existence because they were unable to compete with him in the savannahs and open woodlands. This is a most intriguing theory and Kortlandt has made many return visits to East and West Africa in search of new data. His research continues at the time of writing.

One of Kortlandt's conclusions is that chimpanzees are not primarily rain-forest animals, but are "eurytopic," that is, they live in a wide variety of habitats, including, besides forest, dry woodland and savanna zones. He has come to believe that in the past chimpanzees must have evolved in, and favored, a type of habitat in which large fruit trees stood well apart from one another. Monkeys would not be able to exploit such trees, being unable to climb smooth, thick tree trunks, and so the long-armed chimpanzees would have a secure niche.

In their original optimum habitat, with its tall, isolated trees, the ancestral chimpanzees developed their long arms as a climbing adaptation, while the ancestral hominids took the reverse course, and concentrated on hunting, according to Kortlandt. This was a game-rich area, and one of the chief reasons for the lack of understory, herbage, and lianas was the browsing and grazing activities of the game.

Since those far-off times, in Kortlandt's opinion, the evolution of hunting man has led to the elimination, almost everywhere, of this "original optimum habitat." The chief reason is fire. For many thousands of years man has burned the nonforest zones of Africa in his quest for game. This has resulted in the elimination of all nonfire-resistant tree species, and so the chimpanzees' food supplies have largely disappeared outside the humid forests, which will not burn. In addition, man has hunted the chimpanzee directly (Plate 54), and so, for both reasons, it has been forced back into the forest. Today, it is only where human competition and bush fires are absent that chimpanzees occur outside the forest, and in such areas they are plentiful.

Having to compete with monkeys for the available food has made chimpanzees, according to Kortlandt, adapt as long-distance walkers, this rapid and continuous travel being necessary for a large animal, whose numbers constitute a large "biomass."

Kortlandt rightly emphasizes the question of how chimpanzees succeed in evading predators. They live in leopard-ridden forests, and some in lion-ridden areas too, yet do not feature in the diet of these cats. Why not? Perhaps the simplest answer that comes to mind is that the cats find apes unpalatable, certainly less palatable than ungulates. But this would be difficult or impossible to prove. Kortlandt emphasizes the possibility that the big cats are actually afraid of chimpanzees. He stresses the enormous amount of noise they can produce, their wild displays, their black color, and their resemblance to man. Certainly, in the Budongo Forest, my wife and I and our tracker were frightened by the uproar of a group of chimpanzees, and Nissen's porters "trembled despite themselves" in the same circumstances. It is quite reasonable to assume that loud noise is as upsetting to a cat as to a human being.

Man, the chimpanzee's closest living relative, is also the mammal species it fears most. Kortlandt's unorthodox hypothesis is that as man developed the spear, so the chimpanzee took to hiding away in dense groves in the savannas; as man developed a bare skin to lose heat on the plains, so the chimpanzee developed a thick coat of hair for protection against thorns in the thickets. The thick coat is also an all-weather protection, against rain in particular; to avoid overheating, chimpanzees in all areas keep in shady spots under trees during the heat of the day.

Kortlandt was able, as I have described, to conduct a series of experiments with wild chimpanzees, and could prove that they were not interested in molesting live animals that he pegged out on their pathways. They ignored, or were frightened by, antelopes, goats, monkeys, and hens, among the many species tried. Likewise, in the Budongo Forest, chimpanzees seemed to be noncarnivorous (see page 129). On the other hand, as we know from Jane van Lawick-Goodall's study (see page 123) they can be meat eaters in the wild; and in captivity they very often develop a taste for meat. Kortlandt interprets this as signifying that their ancestors were, at some time, carnivorous, so that the tendency is latent in chimpanzees today, and will emerge under certain conditions. This, of course, ties in with his theory based on the attacks of wild-caught, captive chimpanzees on a stuffed leopard, which led him to the same conclusion.

However, although Kortlandt's theories are attractive in that they appear to account for the great mystery surrounding chimpanzees— why are they so adaptive and intelligent when their way of life seems to make no such demands on them—there are as yet no means of proving that such behavior patterns as tool using, weapon using, and meat eating are remnants of a previous stage of evolution as Kortlandt thinks. More likely they are just another example of the extreme adaptability to different conditions and of the variability of response that characterize all primates to some degree, and the apes and man most of all.

A very comprehensive field study of chimpanzees is being made, at the time of writing, by Jane van Lawick-Goodall, who went to Tanzania in 1960. Her study area is in the Gombe Stream Reserve, which borders Lake Tanganyika to the east of the lake. This area is mountainous, with forested valleys and more open, deciduous woodland on the slopes. There is a clear-cut dry season, with grass fires, and a wet season, from October to May, with heavy rain on most days.

Miss Goodall succeeded, after many months of trying, in habituating the chimpanzees to herself and her campsite. The first to become "tame" were three adult males. The first twenty-four months of her study will be chiefly reported on here.

These chimpanzees were nomadic, and sometimes left the reserve. Goodall estimated that 60 to 80 chimpanzees occupied the 22.5 habitable square miles of the reserve, giving a density of 3.3 per square mile.

Although the supply of individual food species varied from year to year, there was no "lean" time for the chimpanzees, which could adapt well to the variations seen. Some animals sneezed and coughed and one had a cold; some showed loss of hair, and a few had minor injuries of fingers or toes.

The pattern of food distribution had a marked effect on the movement patterns of the Gombe chimpanzees. The cycle of dry season and rainy season also affected them: in the rains they stayed in their nests longer at night, and did more arboreal traveling. These chimpanzees did not seem unduly disturbed by leopards, and had no other predators.

They normally moved around on the ground, helping themselves up steep slopes by hauling on tree trunks or low branches, as I have seen gorillas do on the Virunga volcanoes. They spent between 50 and 70 percent of the day in trees. Bipedal standing occurred when they wanted to look over grass, and bipedal walking and running also occurred, as during the branch-waving display and during greeting and courtship. Quadrupedal gait was the norm, however.

Between six and seven hours a day were spent feeding, and 90 percent of their food was found in the trees. These were vegetable foods. They also ate two types of gall, two species of ant, and termites. The latter, and the ants, were obtained by selecting a grass stalk, twig, or vine, shaping it and poking it into the ants' nest or termite heap. The insects would cling to the "intruder" by their jaws, and the chimpanzee could then pull them out and eat them. Meat was also eaten by the Gombe chimpanzees. Meat eating was seen nine times, and monkeys and young bushpigs were among the victims. One monkey, a red colobus, was observed as it was caught, killed, and eaten. An adolescent caught and killed it, but six other chimpanzees managed to grab bits of it. The meat was eaten slowly, with a mouthful of leaves between each bite. Goodall heard two reports of human infants being carried off and mauled by male chimpanzees. Chimpanzees were observed to drink from streams by sucking water with the lips, and more recently Goodall has reported that some chimpanzees fashion a sort of "cup" from leaves, which they use to scoop up the water and drink from. Leaves certainly seem to be useful to the chimpanzees, as she has even seen a chimpanzee using leaves for a most intimate toilet function!

Each chimpanzee built a new nest every night, except infants sleeping with their mothers. There were no ground nests, and the average height was thirty to forty feet up. Goodall observed the growth of a "fashion" for nesting in palm trees. In the rains, nests were frequently made for resting in during the daytime, but during the dry season the chimpanzees rested on the ground. There was a midday rest period every day, in which the chimpanzees took a nap.

Although young infants, pregnant females, and females in heat were seen at all times of the year, Goodall observed a high frequency of matings at times of the year when the chimpanzees were moving in large groups, as though the social excitement had a direct effect upon sexual activity. Sometimes a female in estrus actively solicited copulation. On other occasions, mating was initiated by a kind of courtship display on the part of the interested male. The male leaped into a tree, with his shoulder and head hair erect, and swung about purposefully. The female who was approached in this way then crouched, and the male came up, squatted behind her, with one hand on the female's back, and the other holding a branch above. The females were promiscuous; one allowed seven males to mate with her in quick succession. Often the female's young offspring would watch the mating procedure with evident interest.

Goodall, like other fieldworkers, found that chimpanzees had a loose social structure, with temporary groups, no sexual jealousies, no permanent leaders, and little fighting or aggressive behavior. However, when two individuals happened to meet, for example walking in opposite directions along a branch, one would tend to think of himself as subordinate, and either move away or make a greeting to the dominant animal by touching him on the lips, thighs, or genitals. When two groups met and joined, each containing a mature male, there was usually much noise and excitement, with the males drumming, slapping the ground, shaking branches, and hooting loudly. This sort of display was probably concerned with sorting out the dominance relationships between the males. Females and juveniles would rush out of the way, screaming.

Since the chimpanzees gradually got used to Goodall's camp, and would approach for bananas after a year or so, she was able to observe closely the behavior of known individuals. Her most interesting contribution is in her observations of mother-offspring interactions.

During the first six months of life, the mother keeps her infant within two feet of her body, enclosing it in her arms if any danger threatens, such as the approach of a hawk. Occasionally, an infant, though dependent on suckling for its chief nourishment, was seen to take chewed-up fruit out of its mother's mouth and eat it. The baby clings to its mother's belly when she travels.

Between six and eighteen months, the infant learns to ride piggyback on top of its mother, although if she has to move quickly, or push through difficult forest, she gives it a gentle push and it moves into the underneath position. By now the young chimpanzee is beginning to be a bit more adventurous, moves farther from its mother, and starts to interact with other infants in play. Although the developing youngster is fast learning to depend on solid foods, no mother was ever seen to reject a large infant that wished to suckle. As the infant becomes a juvenile, its interactions with other members of the chimpanzee community expand. Young chimpanzees often seek out the company of adult females other than their mother, and also play a lot with other juveniles and adolescents. Adolescents sometimes were seen to "mother" younger chimpanzees by carrying them about in play.

As the chimpanzees became more and more habituated to the presence of Jane Goodall and her camp's attractions for them, she was able to get to know certain frequent visitors very well. Among the most interesting characters was one old, rather homely female called Flo, and her offspring. This mother had a male infant and a female juvenile just growing into adolescence. The young female chimpanzee was obviously fascinated by the new baby and tried on many occasions to take it away from the mother and hold it herself, just as human children do. She also seemed to suffer some of the agonies of jealousy and rejection as she watched her mother busy with the younger sibling, and she would rock from side to side as she sat a little apart, her eyes fixed on the maternal pair. This mother-offspring unit was sometimes joined by an adolescent male, who was probably an older brother of the two others. It may be that, while chimpanzee society has no permanent groups, a permanent family tie remains between a mother and all her offspring even into their adulthood and that from time to time they meet and join up for a while, recognizing their close relationship. If this is so, it is clear that chimpanzees differ greatly from most other known primates, in that they are able to recognize and respond to relationships, while not maintaining a close or permanent spatial grouping.

With regard to the way chimpanzees express and communicate their moods and intentions, Goodall distinguished some twenty-three calls, including grunts, barks, and screams. Threat by a male was made by moving bipedally toward the opponent, giving high-pitched screams with exposed teeth and erect hair. Attacks were rare but did occur, the attacked animal rejoining the group afterward. A chimpanzee that had become aware of danger might run away silently, so that the others remained unaware.

Frustrated chimpanzees would yawn, rock, or scratch, or redirect their aggression at another chimpanzee. Threat displays included shaking branches, waving sticks, and running and roaring. Four times, six or more males joined in a branch-waving display, running down the mountainside.

Mutual grooming became progressively more frequent after adolescence, most (69 percent) involving one or two mature animals. Only 17 percent was mother-young grooming. Males mainly groomed males, females mainly females. Grooming sessions might last up to two hours, and grooming groups could number up to six.

There were several ways in which the Gombe Stream chimpanzees would "greet" each other. Most often, one would touch the other with the hand or fingers on the top of the head, shoulder, groin, thigh, or genital area. Or they might embrace each other. If submissive, a male chimpanzee might touch another while baring his lower teeth, and a female might "present." A chimpanzee that wanted to share another's food might "beg," holding out its hand palm uppermost. Goodall's work is remarkable in the extent to which her mother chimpanzees have allowed her to observe intimate details of social interaction, hitherto totally unknown. And her work is continuing at the present time.

In 1960 my wife and I planned a trip; we wanted to attempt what we were told was impossible—a study of chimpanzees actually inside their natural home, the tropical evergreen rain forest (see Plate 49). In 1962 this plan became a reality. We chose the Budongo Forest in Uganda because there were a few tracks running through it; a sawmill operated deep inside it, providing us with a communications center; and it was well mapped by the Forest Department (at two inches to the mile). It seemed to us to be a pleasant forest, not too hilly or too swampy, and last but not least we were assured that the forest contained a large number of vociferous chimpanzees.

We found that it was possible to follow chimpanzees in the forest with the aid of a panga (knife to cut the undergrowth). The maniacal calls of groups of chimpanzees could carry for two miles over the forest, and at dawn we set off when we heard the first calls, following a compass bearing we had taken on them. As we approached a group feeding in the trees, we crept and crawled silently along chimpanzee or buffalo tracks until we found a position behind a tree trunk or in some undergrowth on the forest floor, where we could watch them without their seeing us.

We soon realized that it was going to be impossible to habituate them to our presence. The reasons were that chimpanzee groups were constantly changing their membership and moving around over long distances across the forest, so that it was not possible to locate the same individuals on successive days. Also, inside the forest they seemed extremely shy of man, as though suspicious of his presence there, and so they all usually ran away when one of them spotted us. Occasionally, however, a whole group of ten or twenty would surround us, hooting and screaming, slapping tree trunks, and getting closer and closer in furious annoyance. Either way, things were not conducive to our making notes on their natural behavior, and so we learned to observe as much as possible undetected by them.

The chimpanzees we watched had a lovely life. In the cool mornings they would sit in the sunny treetops, near the nests in which they had just spent the night, helping themselves to handfuls of ripe fruit whenever they felt like it. As the day grew hotter, they would stay cool under the top canopy, sitting about on the shady branches, grooming each other, or dozing. Then they would move around, walking serenely even when they were 150 feet up on a swaying branch (see Plate 50), pulling themselves up or lowering themselves on their powerful arms. Then the call would come to move on. Hooting, slapping the ground, and occasionally pausing to eat an *Aframomum* (ginger) fruit on the forest floor, they would follow each other along one of their well-known trails between the trees.

Chimpanzees always keep an eye open for danger on the ground, and only rarely did we see them moving like dark shadows between the trees, as they usually spotted us first, and detoured. Sometimes they did walk right by us, though, silently, and once a female with a *toto* (baby) riding jockey-style on her back passed by me so close I was tempted to reach out and pluck the little one off. But I resisted, and they passed on; we wanted no pet chimpanzee babies, and we had no desire to cause unnecessary worry to a chimpanzee mother.

Some were dark-faced and others light. The babies were all light-faced, with black hair and a little white "tail tuft" at the rear. All, that is, except one, which was sandy brown on the face and hands and had orange-ginger-colored hair. Adults tended to have dark faces, but it was not a rule, and all shades from pink to shiny jet black occurred. Each face was distinctive, and yet we so rarely saw the same individuals two or more days running that we came to recognize only a few. For there were many chimpanzees in Budongo—some ten to the square mile—and in our selected study area alone we had over 150 of them. Our study area was a matter of convenience, for we simply could not tackle the whole forest, with its 170 square miles of trees. We focused on the area around our home, and here we found three separate "ranges," or areas within which chimpanzees could usually be found. These ranges overlapped each other, being some six to eight square miles in area, but each contained a year-round supply of food and probably had a fairly constant chimpanzee population, though many chimpanzees, especially active adult males, went off on trips to other areas.

The population of one such range numbered around seventy chimpanzees, including infants. These seventy were split up for most of the year in smaller or larger groups, which met up with each other or formed into smaller units every few hours or days. Only at one time of year did all seventy come fairly close together, and that was during the fruiting period of the *Maesopsis* tree, which occurred in July and August of 1962. (The fruiting times of tropical trees are not always annual, there being no clear-cut seasons.) And throughout the annual cycle the chorusing waxed and waned together with the food supply, helping foraging chimpanzees to find food as well as expressing delight on the part of those who had found it.

We also noticed "nursery groups," as Kortlandt had done, and we found bands of adult males. One such band came to be known to us as the "royal clan"—it consisted of four very relaxed males who seemed to have little or no fear of man and who strode about with great dignity and bearing, even to the extent of walking down the main road through the forest one day to have a good look at us and the camera (which, until the film ran out, was making a beautiful record of them). We confirmed Kortlandt's idea that mother bands were less mobile than the bands of adult males or males and childless females, and it occurred to us that it might well be these more mobile groups, traveling far and wide through the forest, that located new food sources and then, by their persistent loud chorusing, attracted the mothers to the new site. This would save the mothers, who had to carry their young, much time and energy. We tested this hypothesis on a number of occasions, and often found that after a large group of chimpanzees had been feeding daily on a particular tree or group of trees, gradually fewer and fewer would arrive as the fruits began to fail. A few mothers with their offspring were often the last to continue coming to the tree, while from far off, a mile or two away, each day the calls and drums and excitement grew louder. Then the mothers would leave the tree and go toward the noise, to feed there for several days. When large numbers were congregated in a good feeding area, we often noticed small bands of males or single males leave the main feeding area and go bounding and hooting off, slapping the ground as they left, to another place, to return later in the day. These males were exploring, and it would be to the places they visited daily that the others, in twos and

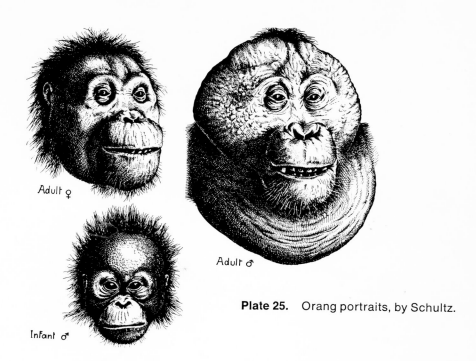

Adult ♀

Adult ♂

Infant ♂

Plate 25. Orang portraits, by Schultz.

Plate 26. Two color phases in the gibbon, *Hylobates lar*.

Plate 27. Portrait of a
siamang.

Plate 28. Chimpanzee twins,
Tom and Helene.

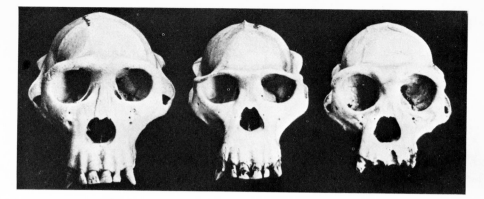

Plate 29. Identical views of three wild adult male chimpanzee skulls from West Africa, showing the great variability found in apes.

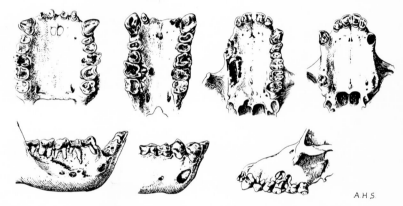

A.H.S

Plate 30. Loss of teeth, caries, and abscesses in wild-shot apes.

Plate 31. Ears of man and the apes. All are right ears, drawn to scale except in the case of the gibbon, which is 50 percent larger than the rest.

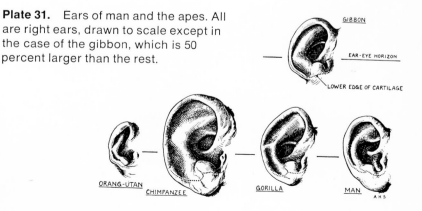

GIBBON

EAR-EYE HORIZON

LOWER EDGE OF CARTILAGE

ORANG-UTAN
CHIMPANZEE
GORILLA
MAN
A.H.S

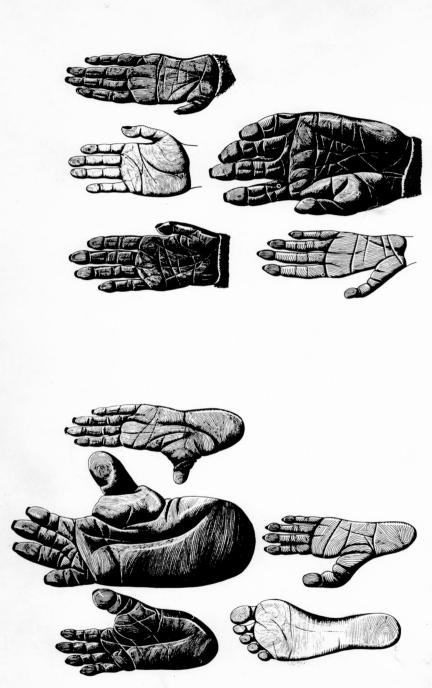

Plate 33. Hands of man and the apes. Top *(left to right)*: chimpanzee, man, orangutan. Bottom *(left to right)*: siamang, gorilla.

Plate 32. Feet of man and the apes. Top *(left to right)*: Chimpanzee, gorilla, orangutan. Bottom *(left to right)*: man, siamang.

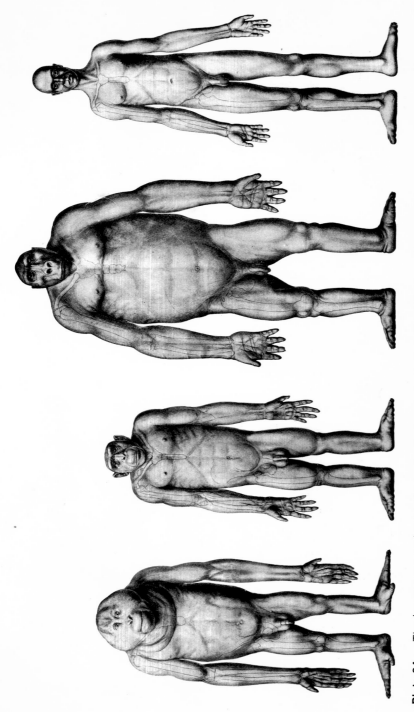

Plate 34. The large apes and man, drawn by Professor A. H. Schultz. All are to the same scale. The hair has been omitted, the legs straightened, and the feet placed sideways to facilitate comparison. *Left to right:* orangutan, chimpanzee, gorilla, man.

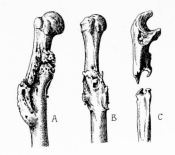

Plate 35. Examples of badly repaired fractures in wild apes. *A* and *B:* adult orangutan humeri; *C:* ulna of adult gorilla (after Schultz).

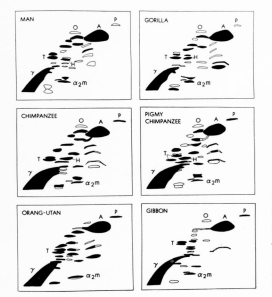

Plate 36. Serum protein electrophoresis patterns of man and the apes: P = prealbumin; A = albumin; O = orosomucoid; T = transferrin; H = haptoglobin; y = gamma globulin (after Goodman).

Plate 37. Chromosomes of man and the apes. *Top to bottom:* man, chimpanzee, pygmy chimpanzee, gorilla, orangutan, gibbon. All male (after Klinger *et al*).

Plate 38. *Above:* Known remains and reconstruction of the Paleocene prosimian *Plesiadapis* (after Simons). **Plate 39.** *Below:* Known remains and reconstruction of the Eocene prosimian *Smilodectes* (after Simons).

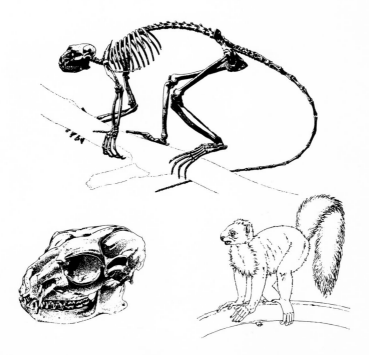

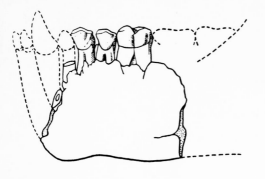

Plate 40. Mandibular fragment of *Amphipithecus,* an Upper Eocene fossil from Burma (after Colbert).

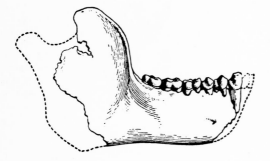

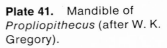

Plate 41. Mandible of *Propliopithecus* (after W. K. Gregory).

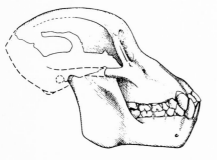

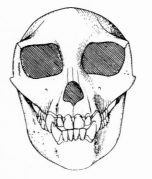

Plate 42. Skull of *Proconsul* (after J. T. Robinson).

Plate 43. Distribution of *Dryopithecus.* Dots show sites where fossils of this genus have been found; crosses mark the advanced form, *Ramapithecus* or *Kenyapithecus* (after Simons).

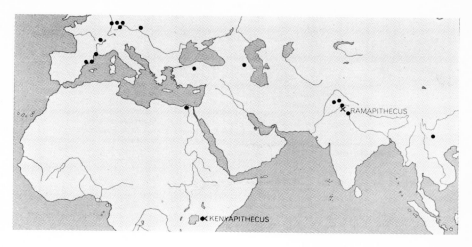

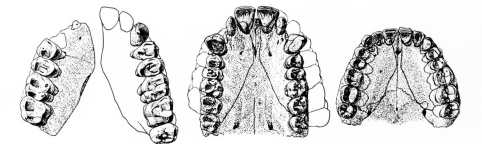

Plate 44. Upper jaw of *Ramapithecus (left),* compared with that of an orangutan *(center)* and a man *(right).* In each comparison, the jaws have been made the same size (after Simons).

Plate 45. R. L. Garner and his cage.

Plate 46. A "nursery group" of chimpanzee mothers with their offspring.

Plates 47 and 48. Chimpanzee mother using a stick as a weapon to attack a stuffed leopard with a baby chimpanzee doll in its paws.

Plate 49.   Chimpanzee habitat — the Budongo forest, Uganda.

Plates 50 and 51.   *Top:* Adult male chimpanzee walking quadrupedally on a high branch. *Bottom:* Chimpanzee picking ants off a tree trunk.

Plates 52 and 53. *Above:* Chimpanzee swinging from tree to tree. *Below:* Chimpanzee's nest.

Plate 54. Hunters of the Manyuema tribe, East Congo, killing chimpanzees (from D. Livingstone).

Plate 55. Chimpanzee drum.

Plate 56. A fearless old male chimpanzee in the Kalinzu forest, East Africa.

threes or in larger groups, would make their way over the next few days.

Aside from their social organization, which was our main interest, we made many other observations on these forest chimpanzees. On two occasions we were charged, once by an adult male and once by an adult female. Each time we were making our stealthy final approach, and each time the chimpanzee came pelting out of cover just ahead and made straight for us, turning back in response to our shouts when only a few feet away. We saw a chimpanzee drinking in a crotch high up in a tree; he was dipping his hand into a natural bowl and licking the drops off his hand, just as other apes do.

We found that these chimpanzees were primarily frugivorous, some 90 percent of the bulk of their diet consisting of fruits. In addition they ate leaves, bark, pith, and insects—these latter were ants crawling up and down tree trunks (see Plate 51). But we never saw them eating meat, and probably they do not do so in this forest environment. Their movements and distribution through the forest were very much affected by which trees were fruiting. The different species of fruit trees occurred in different types of forest, some in swamp forest, others in mixed forest, and others still in colonizing areas at the edge of the forest. The chimpanzees' chief task was to locate the best food sources. They spent from six to eight hours each day feeding and foraging, and when the food was scattered they had to travel several miles a day to fill their bellies; when it was concentrated, however, they stayed where they were.

We distinguished eleven different types of locomotion in these highly adaptable chimpanzees, which were equally at home on the ground or in the trees. They were: quadrupedal walk, quadrupedal run, rapid run, gallop, vertical climb, bipedal walk, bipedal walk on legs with use of arms, ground leap, vertical leap, swing, and brachiation. It is well known that chimpanzees walk on their "knuckles," and we found that this was true even high up on branches in the trees (Plate 50). On the ground, they walked in a lithe, agile way, looking around frequently. When running rapidly, their arms moved forward and backward together, while their legs moved alternately—a unique method of locomotion as far as I know. They could climb vertically up any tree trunk around which they could throw their long hands and arms sufficiently to obtain a grip to stop the body falling backward, and then their stubby legs literally walked them up the tree. They did not often walk bipedally, at most only a few paces, and then usually to see better. If they had to leap a ditch, they invariably swung their legs under their bodies and landed on their feet, not their hands—presumably their feet were better adapted to take the shock of landing than their hands with in-curled fingers. Their most spectacular acrobatics took place in the trees, for example, at "carnival" time, when they leaped huge distances downward from branch to branch, or swung across from one tree to the next, high up in the canopy (Plate 52). Brachiation, that is, moving along in the branches by hanging on with the hands, while common enough, was never the usual way of getting about, which was ordinary walking on all fours. When animals brachiated (and all age groups occasionally did so), it was usually in response to the specific arrangement of branches along which the chimpanzee wanted to move.

Between 6.30 P.M. and 7.15 P.M., as dusk fell over the forest, the chimpanzees made nests to sleep in (Plate 53). A few, probably, did not, but they were exceptional. The job was normally done in five minutes or less, branches being pulled in from all sides, and a layer of twigs and leaves placed on top. The commonest height was thirty to forty feet from the ground, in the understory, and 30 percent of all the nests we found were at this height. Two were found on the ground, and some 10 percent were over a hundred feet high. Sometimes nests were made in sunny spots during the daytime, and a chimpanzee would take a nap.

The chimpanzees tolerated light rain without changing their behavior, but if the rain was heavy they just sat still where they were in the branches, their heads resting on folded arms, face down, so the rain hit their backs. They never built "rain shelters" and never sought "dry spots," but in either case the chances of keeping dry in a really heavy downpour would be remote. They disliked swamp water and streams, using natural tree "bridges" if possible, or keeping high up in the trees.

These Budongo chimpanzees were, we found, untroubled by predators of any kind. Leopards and pythons, both common, preferred to eat duikers (small antelopes). Man, who is the chimpanzee's major enemy in parts of the Congo (see Plate 54) and West Africa, was no trouble here—there were no poaching of chimpanzees for trading purposes, no eating of chimpanzees, and no tradition of keeping them as pets. Relations between the chimpanzees and three of the four common monkey species in Budongo were neutral. With the fourth, baboons, there was an avoidance reaction—even adult male chimpanzees moved out of a tree when baboons moved in. I doubt that they were afraid; more likely they did not relish the baboons' company.

Our observations indicated that an adult female chimpanzee has, on average, a new infant every three to four years. Some breed faster than this, others slower. There were fifty-four occasions on which we saw a mother with more than one youngster. When both were small, one would cling beneath her belly while the second rode on her back. But usually one of the two was already semi-independent, and was jogging along behind the mother while the latest-born clung to her.

Chimpanzees, like humans, probably die more from diseases than from any other cause. We saw two accidents in which chimpanzees fell from trees because the branch they were resting on broke, but in neither case could we establish whether injury occurred. As formerly mentioned, we saw one chimpanzee with a broken wrist, but it could climb trees despite the fact that one hand was completely limp and out of action. One male had a whitish, glassy eye—probably blind through cataract. And one female coughed badly—a long, deep, prolonged cough—but we did not discover whether she ever shook off this bronchial ailment. Only a few times did we see really senile chimpanzees. One was an old, sunken-faced female who rested in nests during the daytime. She seemed really old and infirm. Normally, however, old chimpanzees appeared to be just as nimble as young ones, and probably it is not possible for a very infirm chimpanzee to survive long, as it could not reach the food at the treetops.

Our study, like Kortlandt's and Goodall's, showed that the Budongo chimpanzees did not have any permanent groups at all, certainly no "families." Males, having mated with females, left them, perhaps to meet again, perhaps not. Only the basic tie that runs throughout the mammals—the mother-young tie—was strong. This relationship lasted fully five years, if not more.

As I have said, two of the most striking things about the chimpanzees were the quantity and volume of their vocalizations. We distinguished twelve different kinds of calls, all of which merged into one another. During the average day, animals would frequently raise their voices in chorus to a crescendo that could carry over two miles. If they were on the ground, they would drum on the plank buttresses of the large ironwood trees (see Plate 55). This chorusing grew most wild and exciting, if not terrifying, at the chimpanzees' "carnivals," which occurred when a large number of animals met together. At carnival time the chimpanzees would fling themselves from branch to branch, climb rapidly up and down trees, shake branches and saplings, and hoot loudly. The best answer we could find as to why this occurred was that all this excitement was caused when groups of chimpanzees that normally had different ranges met in the same area. But it was not aggressive excitement, for there was no fighting; and in due course all the animals settled down together.

Normally, calling was less prolonged, but nonetheless very intense and quite intimidating if heard from close quarters. It probably served to communicate the whereabouts of one band to others in the surrounding forest, and to announce the whereabouts of good food, for calling was loudest when food was abundant, and there was little calling when food was scattered and scarce. Drumming served the same functions.

Dominance relations were not a major feature of chimpanzee life. Big males took precedence over smaller ones, for example in feeding situations, and males were dominant over females with one exception, when a female in estrus chased off a small male. Groups had leaders, and these were fully adult males, often with graying rumps. When they left trees in a purposeful manner, others feeding in the tree would follow them, hastened on by drumming from those below. Such mature males sometimes stayed behind when we had disturbed a group and the rest had fled. They watched us and barked, showing not a trace of fear (Plate 56). Twice such a rearguard male lay down at full length on a branch with his back to us, as if in open contempt.

During three hundred observation hours, we saw only seventeen quarrels, all brief. Usually there was just a brief scuffle and a chase, and then the quarrel ended. Grooming was frequent when there was ample food. After feeding intensively for a while, small groups would settle down for a grooming session in shady parts of the tree. Most grooming was between males and females, especially when the female was in estrus. In addition, mothers groomed their young, males groomed males, and females groomed females.

We saw many females in estrus, and half of them already had offspring. These latter, however, were mostly in the presence of males, and not in mother groups. Sometimes a particular male was in attendance, but only four times did we see copulation take place. Sometimes several males were interested in an estrous female, and followed her in single file, awaiting their turn. There was no sign of jealousy between them. Despite David Livingstone's affirmation to the contrary, we decided that chimpanzees were promiscuous.

So it is that the way of life of our closest animal relatives is being made known to us, and many unexpected facts are being discovered. Such facts, quite apart from their intrinsic interest, are of practical value, for they will enable laboratories and zoos that maintain chimpanzees to plan conditions that will suit their natural temperament and social behavior. This policy will in turn pay dividends, for happy chimpanzees are more likely to breed in captivity, to provide more lively entertainment for visitors, and to prove cooperative and useful subjects for experiments. Finally, detailed studies of the development of behavior in wild chimpanzees may help to shed light on problems of human behavior.

CHAPTER **6**

The Natural Life of Gorillas

AFTER THE DISCOVERY of the gorilla and its entry into the public mind, it became a focal point of interest both to zoologists and to the public at large. Naturally, people were curious to know more about this gigantic ape—in particular, about its way of life in the wild.

Paul du Chaillu set out to provide an answer. He was an American trader on the West African coast who turned zoologist-explorer. He set off to the inland forests of the Congo in search of new species—and in search of fame. Equatorial Africa was still enshrouded in mystery for the civilized world at this time. Who could say what he might find there?

It was undoubtedly the reports of the behavior of the gorilla that attracted him most. Apart from Andrew Battell's account, there were several new ones, all in substantial agreement. The American missionary Thomas Savage, in the original scientific description of the gorilla in the *Boston Journal of Natural History*, 1844, wrote:

The *enge-enas* (gorillas) are exceedingly ferocious, and always offensive in their habits, never running from man as does the chimpanzee. They are objects of terror to the natives, and are never encountered by them except on the defensive. . . . When the male is first seen he gives a terrific yell, that resounds far and wide through the forest. His under lip hangs over the chin, and his hairy ridge and scalp are contracted upon the brow, presenting an aspect of indescribable ferocity. He then approaches the hunter in great fury, pouring out his horrid cries in quick succession. The hunter waits until the animal grasps the barrel of his gun, and as he carries it to his mouth, he fires. Should the gun fail to go off, the barrel is crushed between the teeth, and the encounter soon proves fatal to the hunter [See Plate 57].

Another American missionary, Wilson, had written at about the same time as follows:

It is almost impossible to give a correct idea either of the hideousness of its looks, or the amazing muscular power which it possesses. Its intensely black face not only reveals features greatly exaggerated, but the whole countenance is but one expression of savage ferocity. Large eye-balls, a crest of long hair, which falls over the forehead when it is angry, a mouth of immense capacity, revealing a set of terrible teeth, and large protruding ears, altogether make it one of the most frightful animals in the world.

Some years later another American, named Henry A. Ford, added:

When he hears, sees or scents a man, he immediately utters his characteristic cry, prepares for an attack, and always acts on the offensive. . . . Instantly, unless he is disabled by a well-directed shot, he makes an onset, and, striking his antagonist with the palm of his hands, or seizing him with a grasp from which there is no escape, he dashes him upon the ground, and lacerates him with his tusks.

Without much hesitation, Du Chaillu set out. His aim was to obtain specimens of gorillas and chimpanzees and any other animals he could. What he actually did in Africa we do not know. As he would have us believe, in his own book written upon his return, he went deep into forest hitherto unexplored by the white man, spent months there tracking and catching animals of all sorts, hunted, and was the first white man to kill two new species of chimpanzee, a further sixteen species of mammals, and fifty species of birds hitherto unknown to science. And he claimed to have hunted and killed a full-grown male gorilla—the first white man to do so. Here is his description of the kill (see also Plate 58).

His eyes began to flash fire as we stood motionless on the defensive, and the crest of short hair which stands on his forehead began to twitch rapidly up and down, while his powerful fangs were shown as he again sent forth a thunderous roar. And now truly he reminded me of nothing but some hellish dream creature—a being of that hideous order, half-man half-beast, which we find pictured by old artists in some representations of the infernal regions. He advanced a few steps—then stopped to utter that hideous roar again—advanced again, and finally stopped when at a distance of about six yards from us. And here, just as he began another of his roars, beating his breast in rage, we fired and killed him.

With a groan which had something terribly human in it, and yet was full of brutishness, he fell forward on his face. The body shook convulsively for a few minutes, the limbs moved about in a struggling way, and then all was quiet—death had done its work, and I had leisure to examine the huge body. It proved to be five feet eight inches high, and the muscular development of the arms and breast showed what immense strength it had possessed.

After his trip, which lasted from 1856 to 1859, Du Chaillu returned to the United States, where he received widespread acclaim. He was invited to England by the Royal Geographical Society. His prestige grew. He was talked about in scientific circles, in high society, and the general public knew of him. Everyone was eager to learn about darkest Africa. Du Chaillu addressed a crowded audience of scientists in the Royal Geographical Society, and was given an ovation. He had stuffed specimens, pictures, skeletons of all his "new" species, and a sense of drama to enliven his descriptions.

His book told how "I travelled—always on foot, and unaccompanied by other white men—about 8,000 miles. I shot, stuffed, and brought home over 2,000 birds, of which more than 60 are new species."

Some of his descriptions were obviously from firsthand observations, such as the one of the first gorilla he obtained—a youngster two feet six inches long, and brought in alive by the hunters, who had shot its mother.

It was a young male gorilla, evidently not yet three years old, fully able to walk alone, and possessed, for its age, of most extraordinary strength and muscular development. Its greatest length proved to be, afterwards, two feet six inches. Its face and hands were very black, eyes not so much sunken as in the adult. The hair began just at the eyebrows and rose to the crown, where it was of a reddish-brown. It came down the sides of the face in lines to the lower jaw much as our beards grow. The upper lip was covered with short coarse hair; the lower lip had longer hair. The eyelids very slight and thin. Eyebrows straight, and three-quarters of an inch long.

This was actually the first account ever written of the appearance of a young gorilla.

Occasionally, however, Du Chaillu was obviously misled by false reports, which he accepted too readily. One day he saw a shelter built in a tree. One of his hunters, Okabi, told him it was made by an ape.

Okabi, who was an old and intelligent hunter, was able to tell me that the male and female together gather the material for their nests. This material consists of leafy branches with which to make the roof, and vines to tie the branches to the tree. The tying is done so neatly, and the roof is so well constructed, that until I saw the nchiego actually occupying his habitation, I could scarce persuade myself that human hands had not made it. It throws off rain perfectly, being neatly rounded at the top for this purpose.

Du Chaillu accepted this erroneous description of the nest-building behavior of the chimpanzee, and even illustrated it (see Plate 59) and created a special "new" type of ape as the creature responsible for it.

His book quickly gained popularity. But when zoologists had had time to assess his findings and study his specimens, their investigations raised grave doubts.

For a start, none of the specimens of "new" species he had exhibited at the Royal Geographical Society turned out to be in fact new. His picture of the skeleton of his gorilla was a copy of one in the British Museum, as a bone fracture showed. The frontispiece of his book was shown to be a copy of an illustration of the specimen in the Paris museum. So was his figure of one of the two "new" chimpanzee species (neither of which was new). All these points were made by John Edward Gray, in 1861, and acknowledged by Du Chaillu in the second edition of his book. Gray was a scientist, leveling valid objections at Du Chaillu. "It is evident," he wrote, "that we must make great allowance for the exaggeration some travellers seem to think it necessary to infuse into their narratives." Gray blamed the publisher, who, he believed, wrote Du Chaillu's book ("for it is generally allowed that M. du Chaillu did not write it"), and he blamed a credulous public, especially "the best educated classes of the public," who swallowed his tales.

Du Chaillu was overdramatic, and was unable to describe such a creature as the gorilla in purely objective terms. Like other travelers, he was caught up in a mainstream human response to this giant ape which he could not analyze but which, from the live experience of seeing it, led him to put down his excited, emotionally charged description. It is a process that goes on today, whenever ordinary men, Africans or white, come face to face with these giant apes—there is this instinctive response of emotional power.

One Englishman took the war against Du Chaillu to its logical extreme—he went out to West Africa to see for himself. This was Winwood Reade, a self-styled "young man about town" rather than a naturalist. The nearest he got to a gorilla was as follows:

We toiled along for some time, and in the afternoon we came suddenly upon the track again. . . . Etia and I crawled cautiously till we were very close to the gorilla, which was slowly retreating before us, breaking the branches as we went.

I was trembling all over, and I could feel my eyes dilating as if they would burst from my head. I grasped my gun tightly and clenched my teeth. At length I was to be rewarded for my five months' labours and disappointment.

But I happened to step on a dry branch, which broke (as it seemed to me) with a sound like thunder. The noise ahead of us ceased for a moment. Then there was a mighty rush, followed by infernal silence. *The gorilla had run away!"*

On the basis of his interviews with the local Africans, Reade concluded that Du Chaillu was all wrong.

After five months' careful investigation I found that the gorilla neither beats his breast like a drum, nor attacks man in the above manner; that M. Du Chaillu has written much of the gorilla which is true but which is not new, and a little which is new, but which is very far from being true. I am compelled to put aside as worthless the evidence of M. Du Chaillu; who has had better opportunities than any of us of learning the real nature of the animal, but who has unhappily, been induced to sacrifice truth to effect, and the esteem of scientific men for a short-lived popularity.

A few pages later, Reade wrote:

When the female is pregnant the male builds a rude nest, usually about fifteen or twenty feet from the ground. It is a mere layer of dry sticks and young branches, which he tears off the tree with his hands. Here the female is delivered and the nest is then abandoned. At the rutting season the males fight for their females.

The judgment of history is, I fear, harsher on some of Du Chaillu's critics than on the American explorer.

If we compare Winwood Reade's conclusions with Du Chaillu's, we see that the former denies what the latter asserts: the ferocious nature of the gorilla. Winwood Reade did not know about the bluffing charge and chest beating of the gorilla, and so passed it off as exaggeration. On the other hand, a whole series of field studies has shown that the general nature of the gorilla is peace-loving and even amiable.

The first of the true field studies was made by R. L. Garner, the zoologist with a determination to find out how the African apes lived in the wild. In the last chapter we saw how he caged himself up, and we discussed his findings on chimpanzees.

As for gorillas, Garner relied on native statements and the popular ideas of his day for information. He wrote:

It is certain that the gorilla is polygamous in habit, and it is probable that he has an incipient idea of government. . . . In the beginning of his career, in independent life, the gorilla selects a wife with whom he appears to sustain the conjugal relations thereafter, and preserves a certain degree of marital fidelity. From time to time he adopts a new wife, but does not discard the old one; in this manner he gathers around him a numerous family, consisting of his wives and their children.

Today we would not talk of "polygamy," "government," "wives," or "family" with regard to apes, for it has become plain that these terms are only applicable to man and his ways of life. But in Garner's day this was the Victorian way of seeing things (see Brehm's early illustration of a gorilla family, Plate 60).

Gorilla families, thought Garner, keep well apart from one another. They number ten or twelve animals, under the patriarchal father, who is leader on the march, selects the feeding and sleeping grounds, and decides when to break camp. Garner denied that gorillas make nests, for he never saw any. He believed that lone gorillas were young males in search of a wife. And he disputed Du Chaillu's claims of gorilla ferocity, stating that "he is shy and timid, and shrinks alike from man and other large animals."

The next big "gorilla man" was Carl Akeley. Although he was a hunter and collector, and made almost no significant discoveries concerning gorilla behavior, his exploits were so big and his death so tragic that his name is always remembered. Akeley began as a collector and taxidermist for the Museum of Natural History, New York. One does not think of taxidermists as impulsive, tough adventurers, but Akeley, on his first trip to Africa, hunted elephants and was charged and almost killed by a wounded bull, hunted lion, buffalo, rhinoceros, hippopotamus, and zebra, and actually fought and killed a full-grown leopard in single-handed, unarmed combat (he shoved his hand down its throat).

On his next expedition he went to gorilla country, to collect. He hunted and shot gorillas, five in all, for display in the museum back home. But in addition he took some three hundred feet of film of wild gorillas—the first ever made—and, with all the intensity of his nature, came to realize that this creature was exceptionally interesting and worthy of study and that if shooting went on unabated it might become extinct. In his own words: "In the midst of a forest, a land of beauty, we overlooked a scene incomparable, a scene of a world in the making, while our great primitive cousin, whose sanctuary we had invaded, lay dead at our feet. That was the sad note." He suggested that a gorilla sanctuary be set up, and a scientific study made of the giant ape. In this way not only could the species be preserved but also many of the problems of the gorilla's way of life could be solved by patient, undisturbed study. Garner had claimed that gorillas were polygamous. Since that time at least one person, a German named Edward Reichenow, had come up with an alternative theory—that gorillas are monogamous. Akeley himself saw a band with one adult male and several females. He says: "The extra females may have been spinster aunts of the family, but on the other hand, it might just as well have been a case of polygamy. The truth is that people know little about the habits of the gorilla." So he was noncommittal, and thereby showed the caution of a good scientist, who knows when he hasn't got enough facts to make a decision.

Unlike Garner, who had claimed gorillas make no nests, Akeley affirmed (correctly) that they did so, but (incorrectly) only on the ground. He thought that the gorilla has "nearly passed out of the arboreal phase of life and is perhaps entering the upright phase," for he saw these apes in trees only once. But he made few actual discoveries—his main contribution was the idea of the sanctuary: "As I travelled down from Mikeno toward the White Friars Mission the fascinating possibilities of the study of the gorilla and its immense scientific importance filled my mind along with the fear that his extinction would come before adequate study was made. These considerations materially led my mind to the idea of a gorilla sanctuary."

That was in 1921; in 1922 the Albert National Park was set up by Belgium, and in 1926 Akeley, accompanied by his wife this time, set off for the park to survey the newly created sanctuary and to make the first behavior study of mountain gorillas. They had been collecting in Kenya and Tanganyika for eight months before they set out for the mountains, and Carl had just got over an attack of fever. The climb to their gorilla camp at Kabara was made in two stages, the first up to base camp at Rweru, the second on up to Kabara, at 10,200 feet. It was a cold, miserable trip up the volcanic slopes; mist and rain swirled around the party. The porters shivered and huddled together for warmth. Carl and his wife, Mary, were alone here, away from all roads and any possible contact with white civilization, in the remote heart of central Africa. Mary tells her terrible story with moving simplicity:

I have said the Rweru camp was one of the strangest of all places. Over it soon fell the shadow of a great fear for here my husband had a recurrence of fever and my own anxiety became intense. Alternately walking and being carried in a hammock he courageously continued up the mountain-side, and we finally reached our Camp Kabara on the slopes of Mt Mikeno. . . . It was the beautiful land of my husband's dreams—the spot he had longed to reach.

. . . In this wildly beautiful spot, remote almost as on another planet, and with barely time to glimpse this realm of his heart's desire, my husband began another journey—the last long pilgrimage.

Mary buried her husband at Kabara, and his grave is there today. She took up his work before leaving; but the mountain is rugged, and the apes yielded her few secrets. With her husband's body, she left her heart in Africa, and the great wild country claimed her with its scars; she has written delightful books about it, and she has once returned to Kabara and stayed five days at that meadow of shattered hopes, and built a low wall round the gravestone to keep it clear.

In perspective, one of Akeley's greatest achievements, apart from the sanctuary, was his insistence that the gorilla was less savage than it was made out to be. He stated, as a kind of *credo,*

. . . that the gorilla is normally a perfectly amiable and decent creature. I believe that if he attacks man it is because he is being attacked or thinks he is being attacked. I believe that he will fight in self-defense and probably in defense of his family; that he will keep away from a fight until he is frightened or driven into it.

This was not a new idea, for Garner had expressed it years earlier. But in the intervening time the hunters had been at work shooting, and writing books, and Garner's small voice had been forgotten. Akeley gave the idea new impetus; his attitude was the same as that of George

Schaller, who forty years later took up the story where Akeley left off.

At the same time that Nissen was trailing chimpanzees in Guinea, the American naturalist Harold C. Bingham was scouring the slopes of Mount Karisimbi in the Congo, on the trail of the mountain gorilla for the Yerkes Primate Laboratory. His task was a tough one. Not only was the terrain mountainous, but the gorilla was still held in respect, if not fear. Garner had said that gorillas were "shy," but he had locked himself in a cage nonetheless. Akeley had stated his belief that gorillas were "amiable," but had not lived to prove it; his corpse lay buried near Bingham's Kabara camp. So it was that Bingham carried a rifle, his wife (who accompanied him in the fieldwork) a pistol, and his gunbearer a second rifle. Together with guides and porters, the party was unwieldy and unsuitable for the job.

However, Bingham did manage to observe some gorilla behavior. On the slopes of Mount Karisimbi he followed gorilla trails, once for a hundred hours in succession, and once for sixty hours. He observed, on the first occasion, a group of nine gorillas, led by a rather emaciated silver-backed, hollow-cheeked male who roared twice at Bingham's party. Later he observed a group of over twenty, and found a nest site where over thirty gorillas had slept side by side. In one group he saw four grayback males, who in turn "stood, barked, clapped their chests, and sat down again. This performance was imitated by two youngsters. . . ." He reported the odd popping sound made by the gorilla when he beats his chest. One large gorilla threw twigs and leaves in the air with exaggerated gestures.

Bingham attempted photography, but without much success. He crawled up to the gorillas with his head in a black bag. I think he must have lost good observations that way.

And then came drama. It was September 13, 1939. The party had been trailing a gorilla group, which seemed "on edge." Deciding to return to camp, Bingham ordered his men to retrace their steps. The guide was in the lead, followed by Mrs. Bingham, and then came Bingham himself. According to the report, which is laid out with scientific accuracy and attention to detail, a big male gorilla suddenly charged straight out of the undergrowth ahead of the party and made for the guide and Mrs. Bingham. She stepped aside and the guide fled, the gorilla giving chase. Bingham fired; the male turned, ran forty paces, and died. It was the old story, yet this time the story was coming from a scientist, not a hunter. Were there indeed brute gorillas, man-killers? Were Garner's and Akeley's beliefs dangerously misleading? Or had there been, this time, undue provocation by Bingham and his men? Going forward to the spot where the male fell, Bingham found evidence of recent feeding by other gorillas. That meant he had inadvertently been blundering straight into another gorilla group, whose presence neither he nor the guide had suspected. In these circumstances, a charge could well be expected. Now the crucial question is: Was the shot necessary to save Mrs. Bingham or the guide from attack? We cannot be sure. Only three paces separated the big male and Mrs. Bingham at the moment the shot was fired. And while most gorilla charges are merely bluff, this is not always so—sometimes they lead to attack.

Shortly after the incident, the field study was transferred to a new area, and on October 12th, after barely a month and a half in the field, it ended. Bingham was criticized for the shooting incident, but I do not blame him for that. I think he established a useful point—that a big party cannot successfully track gorillas. Later attempts would have to be on a much smaller, more intimate scale.

Several short studies of gorillas followed. During the thirties, the gamewarden Charles Pitman watched them feeding in trees in the Impenetrable Forest, Uganda, and found nests in trees, proving that this giant ape has not by any means lost all its arboreal faculties. On a later visit to this forest, Pitman was accompanied by the governor of Uganda, to whom he wished to show the apes. Having watched a group for some time, the party withdrew, but the gorillas were curious and followed them. Then a big male barked. Pitman describes his feelings: "For a game warden it was an unenviable position. On the one hand, the sacred person of the Governor, on the other the almost sacred and strictly protected gorilla . . ." However, all ended well, and there were no rash moves on either side.

Later, toward the end of the 1950's, two adventurous girls, Rosalie Osborn and Jill Donisthorpe, helped by Walter Baumgartel, made studies of the Virunga gorillas' way of life, obtaining information about their natural foods, their movements, and their behavior. Jill Donisthorpe once saw two groups pass within a hundred yards of each other without antagonism, making her skeptical of the popular idea of exclusively held gorilla territories. And she found that while tree nests were rare most of the time, there was one group, observed in September, that was at that time consistently building in the trees. So much for all-embracing theories!

Also at the end of the fifties came one of the very few reports on the lowland gorilla, when the naturalist Sabater Pi gave details on the stomach contents of five lowland gorillas collected in Spanish Guinea, showing that at certain times of the year their diet consists largely of banana pith, which they obtain by raiding native plantations, while at other times they eat almost nothing but forest fruits. He observed two groups in the wild: one consisted of a big male, three females, and a youngster; the other had eleven members. He saw young gorillas climb trees, but not fully grown ones. And nests were always either on or very near the ground, never high in the trees.

In central Africa and among the mountain gorillas, the end of the fifties witnessed a transformation that was to turn this species from the subject of little fact and much speculation into the most fully documented primate, and indeed one of the most completely described mammals in the world. This transformation was the result of the work of George Schaller.

Starting with a census to arrive at an approximate figure for the total population of the mountain gorilla, Schaller and his professor, John Emlen, had toured the known habitat in the Virunga volcanoes region, had sampled forest areas, and, after pushing the known range of mountain gorillas much farther westward than it was thought to extend, had arrived at an estimate that there were between 5,000 and 15,000 mountain gorillas in existence, living in about 35,000 square miles, three quarters of them, despite their name, in typical lowland forest. This population figure is low—not so low, happily, as that for the orang, but low enough to mean that protection from hunters must be enforced if the species is to be safe for the future.

Having made their census, Emlen returned to America, leaving Schaller (accompanied by his wife) to make a detailed behavior study. This he did, working mainly from his base at Kabara (Akeley's, then Bingham's old base), in the Virunga volcanoes area. Here he spent ten months, from August, 1959 to May, 1960, where in the *Hagenia* woodland zone, around 10,000 feet, he observed ten separate gorilla groups and got to know their 200-odd members so well that he could recognize most of them individually.

Schaller's favorite study method was to habituate the gorillas to his presence in the field by approaching them slowly, alone, and in full view. After a number of contacts most groups came to accept him as a harmless addition to the scenery, not even a very interesting one. Perhaps they accepted him as a wandering lone human male with no great love of his own kind, a hermit who had retreated to the hills. It would be natural for them to do so, for among the gorillas themselves, as Schaller found, lone males do exist.

Gorillas live in fairly stable groups, the average size of the groups around Kabara being seventeen, although groups of as few as two and as many as thirty gorillas were observed. Each group contained at least one dominant silver-backed adult male, sometimes two or three, and one or two younger and less dominant adult black-backed males (see Plates 61 and 62). In addition, each group included a number of females and their offspring of various ages. Some groups retained the same members over eighteen months of study, while other groups lost some and gained other members. On one occasion two new females and infants joined one group; but usually group membership changes were due to the coming and going of adult male gorillas, which seemed to be free to join or leave groups as they wished. The dominant leader male, however, was never observed to leave his group. When two groups of gorillas met, only rarely was there any hostility. Sometimes they seemed to be friendly neighbors, and might forage together for a short time before going their separate ways.

As had long been supposed, each group has a leader, a big silver-backed male, who determines the direction and speed of travel, resting and feeding places, time and place of nesting. He it is, too, who stays behind, roars at intruders, displays, and (if need be) charges. But in all his time with gorillas, at Kabara and elsewhere, Schaller was never attacked, indicating that, if not provoked, the gorilla is not aggressive. Garner and Akeley had both said the gorilla has a peaceful disposition; Schaller now proved it beyond question.

Each gorilla group had its own range, wandering over this area but not beyond. Most ranges were some ten to fifteen square miles in extent, and overlapped considerably with the ranges of neighboring groups: gorillas have no defended "territories." Unlike chimpanzees, gorillas do not "follow the food," for during most of the year there is the same amount of forage to be had almost everywhere within the range. The reason for this is perfectly simple—the gorilla eats plant stems, vines, and leaves more than fruits, and therefore, in the moist zones that it inhabits exclusively, there is never a time of scarcity. It does eat some fruits, but they are not of sufficient importance to determine its movements. As Schaller points out, the food quest alone cannot account for the gorilla's wanderings over its range; perhaps there is a desire for variety, a change of scene, or perhaps an instinctive urge to move on—how shall we ever know?

Gorillas are quiet most of the time. Postures, gestures, facial expressions, and vocalizations are all important in communication within the group, but there is no chorusing, perhaps because there is nothing to tell other groups about food. Only one or perhaps two sounds carry far enough to reach nearby groups—the great roar of the angry male, and the commoner chest-beating sound, a strange *plop-plop-plopping* that sounds more like cheek-slapping than like chest-beating, but which has a high carrying power in relation to its volume. This sound is part of an intimidating display that gorillas frequently give among themselves, a display that Schaller divided into nine acts—hooting, "symbolic feeding" in which the animal places a leaf between its lips, rising onto the hind legs, throwing vegetation into the air, beating the chest (the climax), leg-kicking, running sideways, slapping and tearing nearby vegetation, and finally thumping the ground. Many variations on this underlying pattern occur, and some acts may occur alone, but the big leader silver-backs often give the whole sequence, taking a full half minute to act it out.

The meaning of this ritual is not wholly clear. Schaller points out that it makes an individual conspicuous and that it tends to occur in disturbing situations when it could be interpreted as an intimidation display toward another gorilla or an intruding human being.

More ordinary behavior is typical of the gorilla, however. A rather lazy wanderer, it loves to doze or sunbathe in the midmorning rest period between bouts of feeding. Grooming is a favorite activity of females with their infants; unlike chimpanzees, adult male gorillas were *never* seen to groom each other or adult females. (Chimpanzee males frequently do so.)

The gorillas were normally quadrupedal and terrestrial, walking bipedally for short distances only. They climbed trees with ease to sit, feed, rest, and nest, but the bigger the animal, the less high it climbed. They never brachiated, contrary to common belief. Their food—vines, leaves, barks, roots, and fruits—was mainly collected on the ground, feeding in leisurely fashion as the group moved along, and selecting the "best" parts of each plant, rejecting the remainder. No food-sharing, tool-using, or feeding on animal matter was observed. In different areas, gorillas selectively fed on different plants, even though some of the same ones were available—that is, there were "cultural" differences in food habits. They were never seen to drink, and probably got adequate moisture from the succulent forage.

Gorillas made nests for resting at any time of day, but especially for nighttime sleeping. The nest was a roughly circular platform made by bending in branches from all sides and placing them under the body. Some gorillas scarcely built at all, sleeping on the ground. Others built good-sized, well-rimmed ground nests. In the Kabara woodland area, 97 percent of nests were on the ground. Elsewhere, tree nests were as common as, or commoner than, ground nests, especially in the lowland forest, where 38 percent of all nests were from twenty to sixty feet from the ground (see Plate 63).

In Schaller's study area the density of the population was 2.9 gorillas per square mile. In another area sampled by Schaller, the Kayonza Forest, Uganda, where Pitman had watched gorillas, there were 1.9 gorillas per square mile. Infants remained with their mothers for about three years, and the females gave birth, on the average, every 3½ to 4½ years. Mortality, as in chimpanzees, was due chiefly to diseases, respiratory and intestinal, with, in addition, injuries and occasional predation by man. Death probably occurred before thirty years of age, and was more frequent in the case of adult males than females, for the overall sex ratio of adult males to adult females was 1 male to 1½ females.

The young gorillas Schaller watched were playful animals. Often they played alone, swinging and sliding on branches and lianas, or, equally often, in twos or threes, wrestling and chasing. Sometimes they played "King of the Mountain"—a particularly appropriate game for this species! The ties between infants and their mothers remain close for about three years. By the age of seven or eight months, infants are on a diet consisting chiefly of forage, and they rarely suckle after one year of age. They are born, it appears, rather more helpless than other apes, for Schaller observed that they appeared to lack the strength to clasp the mother's hair securely during the first month of life, so that she had to support the newborn with one or both of her arms. By one month, infants clung unaided; by three months they rode on the mother's back; by four to five months they walked unaided; by six to seven months they climbed as well. But in an emergency, young up to three years old were still carried on their mothers' backs. Some youngsters developed strong attachments to females other than their mothers; and this we saw also in the wild chimpanzees.

Within any group Schaller watched, social interactions of any kind were quite rare; this seems to be a function of the introverted temperament typical of gorillas, and also their preoccupation with foraging for food most of the day. The adult males of the group had a hierarchy of dominance, which was occasionally manifested by one gorilla barging into another, and the lower-ranking one giving him room. Large silver-backed males were the most dominant animals, and on the move the leader of the group was at the front. Females did not have an obvious hierarchy among them. Sexual behavior among the gorillas Schaller watched for so long and so intimately was remarkably rare—in fact, he witnessed only two matings. In each case a female of a group was mounted by a male who was not the leader of the group, without any interference or aggression by the dominant male. However, most females had offspring with them, of various ages, indicating that there is no particular breeding season among gorillas.

Aggressive behavior was also very rare, and, usually, it did not go further than an irritable slap or threatening stare; no fights were seen.

The ferocious gorilla? Schaller did not find it. Perhaps the worst that can be said about the temperament of the wild gorilla is that it is morose and sullen; at best it is amiable, lovable, shy, and gentle.

CHAPTER **7**

The Natural Life of
Gibbons and Orangs

OUR KNOWLEDGE OF the natural ecology and behavior of the Asiatic apes has lagged behind that concerning their African cousins, even though an earlier start was made in Asia. This is primarily because of lack of data about the orangutan, which has not until recently been the subject of field studies. In the case of the gibbon, our information is somewhat more complete.

Scattered reports about the smallest of the apes—the gibbon—are found in the early literature. In 1903, a man called George Candler made it known that gibbons can walk upright, are unable to swim, "work their ground systematically," are extremely shy, and make amazing sounds—"Hooloo! Hooloo! Hooloo! with the accent on the Hoo . . . but it is really quite indescribable in writing." A previous writer, Lieutenant Colonel Tickell, had attempted to record the calls of the gibbon in musical notation. He wrote, in 1864, that "during these vocal efforts they appear to resort to the extreme tops of the loftiest trees, and to call to each other from distant parts of the jungle."

Early in this century, R. A. Spaeth made a study of the reproductive

[[151

habits of gibbons in Siam. Unfortunately, he died before publishing his findings, but he left his notes, from which his wife compiled a manuscript that is quoted by R. M. and A. W. Yerkes in their book *The Great Apes*. I shall repeat the quotation here, as it represents the valuable findings of the first field study of the gibbon:

Dr Spaeth found that the gibbons were for the most part in family groups. So far as he could ascertain, they have their young in the early summer and spring. . . . On one occasion he came upon a group of males alone in a tree early in the morning . . . and he concluded that it was some sort of bachelors' club gathering. But as a rule he found what appeared to be families. The gibbon has only one young a year and it takes three or four years for them to mature, so a family frequently consisted of two or more young ones in various stages of growth beside the father and mother. . . . They hang onto the mother with an extraordinarily strong grip as she swings thru the trees. She appears to be not in the least incommoded by the baby hanging to her and swings along as unconcernedly as tho she were alone.

Spaeth's report of seeing a group of males together may be questioned in view of recent field studies using systematic techniques of observation.

It was in 1937 that the first full-scale scientific expedition was mounted to subject the elusive gibbon to scrutiny. It was launched from Harvard and Columbia Universities and consisted of Harold Coolidge, Jr., Adolph Schultz, C. Ray Carpenter, Augustus Griswold, Sherwood Washburn, and two assistants. During the spring of 1937, these men spent about four months in the forests of northern Siam, looking for gibbons. Carpenter was in charge of the behavior studies, his brief: to make "a systematic naturalistic study by observational and recording methods of the ecology, behaviour and social relations of the gibbon, *Hylobates lar*, in its natural environment in Siam (more recently Thailand)."

Carpenter was already an experienced primate fieldworker when he set out to do the gibbon study, for he had twice been into tropical forests, the first time in quest of howler monkeys, the second in quest of spider monkeys. So he started off with an advantage possessed by neither Nissen nor Bingham—a basic knowledge of forest tracking techniques, and an appreciation of the advantages of working alone or in a very small party.

After a couple of weeks, he settled on an area called Doi Dao to do the major part of the study. Here gibbons were plentiful and, importantly, they were considered quasi-sacred by the local people, and shooting of them was not permitted. The forest was mountainous, and, being some 19 degrees north of the equator, was not true evergreen forest but somewhat deciduous, that is, monsoon forest. Trails made by elephants while logging helped Carpenter make his way between the trees.

Carpenter followed one group or another of the incredibly agile gibbons as they made their way through the treetops. After a period of calling early in the morning, he found that they fed, in desultory fashion at first, then more actively, took a noontime siesta of three hours or so, then fed again during the afternoon before finally going to sleep. All this time they remained aloft. Gibbons are, in fact, totally arboreal in their natural life. Carpenter also confirmed that gibbons make no nests. Here they differ from the other three apes and resemble the monkeys. Gibbons are, of course, monkey-sized, and so, like monkeys, can sleep in the treetops without building a supporting structure to prevent themselves falling in the night; but size is not the only factor that determines nest building, for some of the very small lower primates make them too.

Carpenter also confirmed that the locomotion of the gibbon is primarily of the type known as "brachiation," or swinging along by the arms. This way of moving through the trees is an arboreal specialization found chiefly in the apes. Orangs, which spend most of the time in the trees, brachiate more frequently than chimpanzees. Among gorillas, now a predominantly terrestrial species, only the young ones are seen to brachiate. Anyone who has watched gibbons swinging about in a zoo will know just how spectacular this form of locomotion is. In the wild it is more so, for the distance is not restricted, and leaps of twenty feet or more from one branch to another frequently come between the long-armed swings, so that the little ape appears literally to glide through the treetops without effort (see Plate 64). Such rapid movement is reserved for emergencies, however: normally progress of the gibbon group is leisurely and slow.

Mention of the word "group" brings us to another feature of gibbonness: the small-scale organization of society, the unit of which in this ape seems to merit the name "family." By carefully counting and identifying the groups he saw, Carpenter found, as Spaeth had done, that the average number of gibbons in a group was four and that, on average, these consisted of one adult male, one adult female, one juvenile, and one infant—a typical "monogamous family." In one instance, an old senile animal was seen in a group, but on only two occasions was there more than one adult male or female. The pattern of individual monogamous family groups was consistent over Carpenter's study area, but one thing called for explanation—what happened to the young males and females as they matured? Carpenter sometimes observed that young adult males were repulsed by older males; thus it seemed probable that on growing up, maturing males and even females left their family to form new pairs. There were occasions when neighboring groups would "intermingle for short periods of time"; and at such times new groups might be made.

Female gibbons, Carpenter found, were more emancipated than their chimpanzee or gorilla counterparts. He did not see any evidence that male gibbons were dominant over females, a feature of their behavior that ties up interestingly with the absence of a distinct difference in size between the sexes. In the large apes, the male is bigger than the female, and in these species, too, he dominates her.

The vocal efforts of the gibbon place it second only to the chimpanzee. Carpenter confirmed that early morning was the favorite time for calling. And he discovered that each gibbon family had a fairly clearcut territory, some thirty to one hundred acres in extent, within which it stayed at all times and which it actually defended against the encroachments of neighboring groups. The method of defense was, according to Carpenter's interpretation, a vocal display. Each group knew the borders of its territory, and if this area seemed in danger of being invaded, the group rushed to the spot, calling and shaking the branches until the trespassers retreated. In Carpenter's own words, "When a group of gibbons, e.g. Group 2 encroaches on the territory of Group 1, what the animals are observed to do is first to call, to answer call for call and then when rushed, to retreat toward the heart of their own territory, the less dominant Group 2 giving ground."

This territory ownership and the vocal fighting associated with it are found not only in the gibbon but also, for example, in the howler monkey; indeed, it somewhat resembles the situation found both in man (have you never been shouted off a farmer's fields?) and in many birds, which sing in pride of ownership and keep a beady eye on the position of neighboring songsters. But, among the apes, it is only the gibbon that behaves in this way, so far as is known.

Carpenter made many other observations on the gibbons' behavior. He described the play of the young, which included repetitive behavior, chasing, wrestling, and surprise attacks, much like the play of other apes and monkeys. He found that the gibbons were not troubled by predators. Their food was, he estimated, 80 percent fruits, 20 percent leaves, buds, and flowers.

In the social life of adults sexual behavior was infrequent, and only two copulations were observed. The nervous, excitable disposition of adult gibbons fitted them well for their sudden, agile movements in the trees, and for their displays, in which the calling rose to a pitch and ended up with wild leaps from branch to branch.

During the 1960's John Ellefson made a study of wild gibbons in the Johore region, Malaysia. He worked on *Hylobates lar,* which was the same species previously studied by Carpenter. This work is largely unpublished at the time of writing, but a preliminary report indicates that the small closed family groups, living in their own territories, and battling at the borders, are found in Malaya just as they were in Thailand. Ellefson calculated that the average size of the territory of a gibbon family was 250 acres, with a range of from 40 acres to over 300. This seems a remarkably small area to support four apes throughout the year. As group size increases, so must the territory, but where the adjacent forest is occupied, the growing subadults must leave the group. They probably in due course find mates and set up new territories elsewhere. Ellefson thinks that adult gibbons are intolerant of other adults, with the exception of their own mate, and that this is the way that territory ownership has been built into the species behaviorally.

Loud vocal choruses occurred mostly before 10:30 A.M. and were undoubtedly of vital importance in communicating the presence of one group to another and warning them off the territory; but Ellefson found that displays of branch-shaking, rushing, and chasing were more effective in actually intimidating intruders than were the calls.

Each group slept toward the center of its own territory. In the course of its daily foraging, it tended to be away from the middle and near the boundaries, where the chance of contact with a neighboring group was consequently high. Adult males did most of the battling, and Ellefson noted that they often fed for up to an hour longer than the rest of the group, probably as a result of the time and energy spent battling (see Plates 65 and 66).

In recent years, studies of the orangutan have been primarily concerned with conservation. It has not always been so. Alfred R. Wallace (who developed the theory of evolution with Darwin) and William T. Hornaday both shot orangs for sport, and then wrote notes on their habits. Other reports have come to us from collectors interested mainly in anatomical and embryological data. Conservation studies involve finding out *how many* orangs remain, and where they live. Carpenter was first in the census field, with his report on the status of orangs in Sumatra in 1938. Now, in the sixties, there is a whole burst of literature on the orang's declining numbers and the need for more stringent measures to protect the ape from poachers. Several articles on the subject have appeared in *Oryx*, the journal of the London-based Fauna Preservation Society. And, of course, there has been the untiring work of Tom and Barbara Harrisson, who have taken in and reared, in their Sarawak home, many pitiful baby orangs, confiscated by the Forest Department, which had been illegally captured for export by the shooting of their mothers, and kept in native huts until they could be sold to dealers. The orang trade is examined in more detail in Chapter 12.

Barbara Harrisson has described a trip into the forest in search of wild orangs. She managed to see a group of three young feeding and playing, then watched a solitary old male make his nest, fussing around for fifteen minutes, laying a cushion of leaves, and removing twigs that might poke into him during the night. Next morning, before dawn, she climbed into a tree near the place where the three youngsters had nested, and watched "the *Grande-Levée* of jungle man. He sat up, looked about, scratching his back. He lifted his elbows sidewards, fists rubbing the eyes; inhaled deeply, stretched his back straight and flung out wide, first one fist, then the other, to each side. Slumped back, exhaling. Sat, to look down over the nest. He scratched his back between the shoulder-blades, slowly but firmly, again and again. He stretched once more, this time bending and straightening his legs; sat for a while gazing, as if contemplating the new day. Then he started to poke around inside his nest." The other two had slept curled up together in the cold rain in another nest.

There followed the apes' breakfast, on big durian fruits, after which all went to sleep in the warm sunlight, the two friends cooperating to build a comfortable nest right at the top of a tree. She watched an orang drink from a natural tree-bowl by the time-honored ape method of dipping in a hand, pulling it out wet, and licking off the water.

The natives of Borneo will tell you that there are in fact three different kinds of orangs, small ones, medium ones, and big ones, and that they do not mix. Zoologically it is known only that orangs at different ages have different appearances. However, Barbara Harrisson's observation of three young orangs, apparently alone together, and the prevalence of this native belief, indicate, as she suggests, that "teenage groups . . . perhaps form regularly at a stage when the young leave their mothers to fend for themselves." A loose, unstable social organization is also indicated by the brief observations of orangs made by George Schaller in 1961. He too observed a pair of young orangs apparently all on their own, which supports the teen-age group theory above. On another occasion he watched a mother with an infant and a juvenile, who were accompanied by an adult male one day, but he left them the next.

This strange lackadaisical way of life, here today, gone tomorrow, with lone individuals, small bands of adolescents, tiny family units, wandering and roaming through the jungles of Borneo, meeting, mixing, splitting up, is quite different from the way of life of the gorilla or the gibbon. But not so different, as we have seen, from that of the chimpanzee.

Hornaday, in 1885, had noted seasonal movements by the orang population (see Plate 67). According to him, orangs were up on the hills during the fruit season, from January to May; then from May to July they retired to the depths of the forest, reappearing by the rivers during the rainy season, from August to November, when the forest was flooded. A. R. Wallace, five years later, described the orang as living in the canopy of low, swampy forests. Its movements as it walked through the trees and swung from tree to tree were deliberate and slow. It had no great fear of man and probably had no other predators. Both he and Hornaday were struck by its solitary nature.

G. B. Schaller had found that of the various forest types used by orangs in Sarawak, swamp forest was their favorite habitat, judging largely by the location of nests (Plates 68 and 69). This attachment to swamp forest is interesting because it suggests a very good reason for the orang's arboreal adaptations (it is almost as arboreal as the gibbon): its preferred foods, for part of the year at least, occur in areas where progress along the ground is very difficult, and probably unhealthy as well.

Following orangs as they fled, he found that they could keep up no more than three miles an hour or so in the treetops. Perhaps this is why they are so easily caught and nearly extinct as a result: they are too big to flee nimbly through the trees, as gibbons do, and they do not run off on all fours along the ground like chimpanzees and gorillas. They are the slowest of the apes, too big for their arboreal habits, too arboreal for their size.

The orang is not only the slowest but also the quietest ape. In fact, the chimpanzee and the gibbon are both very vocal, while the gorilla and orang are not. One female orang annoyed by George Schaller gave a kissing sound, a gulping sound, and a loud two-toned burp; Barbara Harrisson has reported on a whining sound, a kissing sound, and a grunt or bark. So while the orang certainly has its share of communicative noises, there seems to be nothing very spectacular about them. Some orangs, however, have developed the art of counterattack on troublesome humans more than other monkeys and apes have done—Schaller had thirty branches hurled at him in the space of fifteen minutes by one irate old lady; and, as he says, it "kept me effectively away from beneath the tree." A male bombarded him for over ten minutes, and one female urinated on him. These orangs certainly knew how to use the trees.

The only recent field study of orangs has been made by Richard Davenport of the Yerkes Primate Center, who went to the state of Sabah in Malaysia, remaining there for the dry season. Sabah is in what used to be British North Borneo and is 80 percent primary forest, transected by numerous rivers and few roads. The problems faced by Davenport were typical of those facing anyone attempting to study wild orangs: the necessity of traveling to orang habitats by jungle rivers; having to camp inside the forest for weeks at a time; and the great difficulty in locating any of these rare, silent, and often solitary animals. Davenport had with him six local men experienced in jungle work. Each day these men left the camp site in pairs and searched the surrounding forest, equipped with small transistor radios for communication. If they managed to locate an orang, they took Davenport to the spot for observations. Even with this degree of organization, he came in contact with only sixteen orangs in the seven months of his field study—more, however, than in any other previous field study (Plates 70 and 71). He was able to observe continuously for several hours, even days, many of these orangs, because, unlike chimpanzees, they do not flee at high speed on the forest floor if they smell danger, but remain in the treetops, traveling at a speed a human can keep up with. Thus Davenport observed behavior for 192 observation hours, and three of the orangs were followed or kept in contact for 48 hours. His information is therefore most valuable and the best we are likely to get for some time.

Davenport's data confirm the essential solitariness of this vanishing species, at least as it is in its present-day low-population state. He saw only one group, a "family" of an adult male, female, and an infant; three times he located a mother and infant on their own; and the other seven orangs he saw were completely alone, four being adult, three adolescent. From occasional observations of behavior, it would seem that this self-reliant, rather unsociable nature of the adult and adolescent orang may be voluntary and natural, for Davenport once watched two adolescents move within fifty yards of each other. One was apparently aware of the other's proximity, but silently watched it move away once more, with no attempt to join up. On another occasion, he was watching a mother and her juvenile offspring feeding in a nest. The juvenile noticed Davenport, and without any warning cry or gesture, rushed away into the jungle ahead. Nor did his mother appear surprised or worried at his sudden departure, if she even noticed it! However, twenty minutes later she too saw Davenport, and she immediately went off in the same direction. This observation indicates that orangs are very familiar with the areas of forest they frequent, however vast their range, and probably have well-known directions and routes of travel; distances within the forest undoubtedly seem far greater to us than to them, for it is their natural environment.

However, as Davenport himself points out, it may be that the scattered and solitary social organization of the orangs he encountered was typical only of that season of the year, and the availability and distribution of food. He was observing during the part of the year when there is no fruit in season in that area, and the orangs he saw were feeding only on leaves and shoots. The local natives told him that during the season of the large and succulent durian fruits, orangs congregated in the vicinity. In chimpanzees, as we have seen, fruiting seasons (which, however, are occurring in different species throughout the year) certainly affect the size of groups and scatter of the population; and social interactions are at their maximum frequency and intensity during the fruiting of their favorite foods.

Davenport distinguished four sounds in the repertoire of the wild orangs he met: a smacking of the lips; a low two-toned belch or grunt; the squeal of an infant; and a roar heard sometimes in the early morning, perhaps as a locating signal to other orangs in the area. (The roar was not heard by Harrisson and Schaller, and Harrisson describes a whining not heard by Davenport.) The lip smacking and belching often occurred as part of a threat pattern that consisted of the breaking off and dropping of branches onto the observer; this was sometimes accompanied by urination and defecation in his direction. Although he never observed this threatening behavior pattern applied to any other annoyance than himself, Davenport felt that the noise and commotion produced would be sufficiently intimidating to scare off natural predators. Interestingly, when he located the family group, the male alone descended the tree some way to threaten Davenport, while the female and infant climbed higher and remained silent.

Davenport observed another item of behavior that he thought might also be included in the threat pattern, and that seems to be a form of competitive intraspecific display, possibly normally occurring when two males meet: this was termed the "dive." The orang stood quadrupedally on a branch, then suddenly raised his hands and lunged forward, keeping hold of the branch with his feet, until he was hanging below the branch swinging upside down! The orangs seemed to be very agile in the trees, and able to use hands or feet in any combination to hang, reach, swing, locomote in any position above or below branches, up or down trunks. But they were nevertheless always careful, and normally kept at least two extremities gripping the branch.

Some interesting observations were made on the daily routine of orangs. Most of them got up rather lazily about 8:00 A.M., and one individual did not vacate his sleeping nest until after noon. They were usually settled for the night in their nests again by 6:30 P.M., having spent 60 percent of the daytime napping or resting! New nests were invariably made for nighttime sleeping, whereas old ones were commonly used for daytime naps.

Davenport was able to watch one particularly interesting item of behavior—an orang building an overhead shelter against the rain. He constructed it in the same way as a nest, but from underneath. This appears to be a remarkable adaptation of the nesting pattern peculiar to orangs—chimpanzees, very capable nest makers, simply endure the rain, sitting on their nests miserably hunched up, or nestless.

And that is all we know of the life of wild orangs.

A most interesting part of Barbara Harrisson's work on orangs has been her attempt to educate young orangs to live wild again in the jungle of Bako National Park. While not a true field study, the results of this project are worth recounting. After a period spent familiarizing themselves with trees in Barbara Harrisson's garden, a young trio, "Arthur, Cynthia, and George," was transferred to the jungle where a special enclosure had been built as a transition stage from human dependence to self-maintenance in the wild. After a few days in the enclosure the door was opened and the orangs were given an opportunity to explore further if they wished (Plates 72-74). At a later stage regular walks were taken with the oldest and most adventurous orang—a male named Arthur—in order that he might get a feeling of territory in the forest. For all the orangs were loath to lose sight of their human "mother," and kept returning to the enclosure.

As Arthur began to feel more at home in the jungle, his behavior started to provide information on the natural inclinations of orangs. After nine months' freedom, he roamed a territory of two miles radius from the enclosure. He drank at rocky pools by sucking with his lips or by scooping water over his face. He took to paddling in shallow water. One fascinating observation was when he explored a cave, and, collecting leaves, made himself a bed there and lay down.

By now Arthur was building nests at night in the forest, and he chose a place where he was within hearing distance of his two companions (who as yet were too timid to go wild). Another nest would be built for a siesta about midday—just as Barbara Harrisson had seen the three really wild young orangs do. One day Arthur was seen to hang *under* his nest in the rain, though, unlike the orang observed by Davenport, it was not a specially constructed shelter. The most fruitful observations were on the calls made by the orangs; because now that they were in natural surroundings and often split up by stretches of trees, the significance of the calls could be more clearly understood. For example, if Arthur heard his companions whining in the distance, he remained immobile watching, and then would go toward the enclosure where they were. This indicates that orangs may in fact keep in contact this way during their wide roamings through the jungle. Arthur also developed a way of greeting the others on his return by a loud "raspberry"-blowing.

All the orangs have been seen poking into termites' and ants' nests, sometimes with sticks, and consuming the contents, a behavior obviously natural to them, as they have had no opportunity to learn it in captivity. They investigate everything, and take eggs from nests.

Another observation concerns Arthur's reaction on meeting a snake in the forest. He took a stick from the forest floor and chased and hit the snake with the stick before it escaped down a hole. Cynthia, the younger female, however, fell out of a tree with shock on seeing a snake there.

Thus, slowly, we are building up a picture of the natural life of the orang, although little is yet known in comparison to the well-documented gibbons, gorillas, and chimpanzees. This situation is likely to remain, owing both to the exceptionally difficult conditions for field-work, and to the fact that the orang is becoming rarer and rarer. The illegal and unnecessary deaths of mothers and infants through poaching are a threat to the survival of this species, and may snuff out the flickering flame of orang survival before the end of the present century.

CHAPTER **8**

Living with Apes

SOME APES HAVE become famous and had books written
about them. In this chapter, I want to discuss just a few of the best-
documented and most scientifically valuable accounts of individual
apes, to see what can be learned about the typical development of the
young ape. The gibbon is not represented in this chapter, for although
many people have kept gibbons as pets, no one, as far as I know, has
written a book about one. Most of the information in this chapter has
been drawn from written accounts of chimpanzees, gorillas, or orangs
that have been brought up from infancy in a human household. Occasionally, extra material has been drawn from stories of caged apes.

For human "parents" there are more problems in raising an infant
ape than an infant human being. For one thing, the ape's rate of early
physical development is much faster than that of a human baby. By
the time it is six months old, it will no longer stay happily in basket or
playpen. It can walk and is starting to climb, and the foster parents are
looking for a carpenter to fix a strong barred roof over the top of the
playpen. By nine months young apes are everywhere, testing the dura-

bility of the entire house. Cathy Hayes, who with her husband, a psychologist at the Yerkes Primate Laboratories in Florida, reared a baby female chimpanzee in their home, from her birth in 1947, wrote:

As the infant Viki grew, more and more of our house was exposed to her. She discovered towels, pillows, and bedding, to drag around the house and out into the yard. There was stuffed furniture for bouncing upon, chair rungs to climb over and under, mirrors to make faces at, open drawers upon which to chin herself, but especially there were doors. . . . Then Viki began climbing. This brought our pictures within her range. She entertained herself by swinging them faster and faster until they flew from the wall. She took to sailing through the air from one height to another, and we made a point of arranging our possessions as if we expected an earthquake at any minute.

One final example of how the wreckage proceeded should be sufficient to discourage anyone thinking of trying to obtain an infant ape:

In the very beginning, our windows were bordered by drapes, which hung clear to the floor in graceful folds. But, at 4 months of age, Viki began using them to pull herself erect. Thus early in our experiment, a decision had to be made. Since Viki was too young to realise that her tugging would eventually drag down the entire drapery hardware, the answer was obvious. I snipped the drapes to windowsill length, and out of Viki's reach—for two months. Then she began pulling herself up to the windowsills, using the drapes like jungle vines. Again I hacked them off, this time to mid-window. The final lopping off occurred months later, when she entered her Social Phase. Performing for visitors in the front window, she would often swing Tarzan fashion, from one short drape to the other. At that point, I reduced them to a mere valance across the top of the windows.

This hyperactivity is neither the only, nor the greatest, of the problems of keeping a baby ape. Another is the strength of its mother love. The infant ape is born with strong instincts fitting it for survival in the wild. Thus all baby apes have a strong desire to grip close to the warm stomach of their mother, and to be carried by her continuously. The gentle motion as she moves rocks them to sleep, and when she stops and sits, they wake and suckle and play beside her. Orangs and chimpanzees have an extremely strong clinging reflex on birth, which, in the wild, enables them to remain securely fastened to their mother's body, even if she hangs and swings in the trees. If they are taken from their mother and placed in a basket like a human baby, with nothing to clutch, they may grip their own hands and feet together so tightly that they are unable to undo them on their own. Gorilla infants do not develop such a strong gripping capacity until about two months old. In the wild, gorillas are slow-moving terrestrial apes, and the gorilla mother is able to support her newborn infant with an arm as she walks.

When an infant ape is removed from its mother and taken into a human household, it transfers this instinctive clinging affection to its human foster mother. Holding and carrying the ape is what fixes the new bond in the first place. Gua, a chimpanzee seven and a half months old, was taken from her mother, at the Yerkes anthropoid station, and placed in the home of Dr. and Mrs. Kellogg, who cared for her alongside their own small son for nine months about 1930 (Plate 75). The only thing that stopped Gua from crying miserably was for Dr. Kellogg to hold her in his arms, her face buried against him, and to sway gently. He wrote: "Her attachment became so strong that she had been in the human environment for fully a month before she would let go of the trouser legs of her protector [himself] for any length of time, even though he might sit quietly at a table for as long as an hour. Almost without respite she clung to him one way or another."

Dr. Ernst Lang, the director of the Basel Zoo, adopted into his home the first baby gorilla to be born in Europe, because her mother neglected her. She was named Goma, and her behavior was studied by Dr. Lang and Dr. Rudolf Schenkel. Dr. and Mrs. Lang bottle fed her every two hours day and night, changed her diapers, and carried her about. Goma gave them all her instinctive love (Plates 76 and 77). The result was that Goma could not be left alone. When the Langs went on a much-needed holiday, Goma had to go too, sitting in the back seat of the car, and every now and then hugging Dr. Lang tightly round the neck from behind, as he drove. Later, when the public at the zoo demanded to see Goma, Dr. Lang had to go into an exhibition cage along with her, for an hour in the afternoons!

All ape foster mothers have a similar story. Cathy Hayes wrote about Viki: "She sat on my lap while I ate or studied. She straddled my hips as I cooked. If she were on the floor, and I started to get away, she screamed and clung to my leg until I picked her up." Some ape foster mothers have solved the problem by hiring special keepers whose sole duty was twenty-four-hour-a-day companionship for the young ape. Barbara Harrisson, the wife of the director of the Sarawak Museum in Borneo, found that each baby orang she took into her house seemed to choose its own special foster mother. She received numerous baby orangs, illegally captured by local men in the forests after their mothers had been shot, whereupon the infants were discovered and confiscated by government officials. At one time, in the 1950's, she had five small orangs to care for all at the same time. She employed a sympathetic local youth called Bidai to help look after them, and one of the young apes, named Eve, clung to him constantly. One of the others, called Bob, chose Tom Harrisson as his guardian, and Frank preferred Barbara.

The constancy and permanent presence of the adopted mother figure are of the greatest importance for the physical health and development, as well as the happiness, of the infant ape. For example, Dr. and Mrs. Lang were obliged to go away for a few days, leaving the baby gorilla in the care of a friendly nurse, already known to Goma. However, Goma was immediately sick, developed diarrhea, and refused her food. She recovered when they returned, but wanted a lot of extra cuddling for some time. Occasionally the loss of the mother or mother substitute causes death for no apparent reason other than that the young ape loses the will to live. Barbara Harrisson had a young orang, recently arrived, who suddenly died, although the vet was unable to find any signs of illness: "I had the strong feeling that, as in the case of the male baby Tony, that had died the previous year, it was an inability to *cope* with life, and its imposed surroundings, a loss of drive for development, which followed on extreme physical neglect, and a number of psychological shocks."

Dr. Kellogg related how Gua, his adopted chimpanzee, would become "blind with fear" if he walked away faster than she could follow. She would scream and scream until she was hoarse, and run around bumping into things. "Finally she would fall prone to the sand and literally grovel in it, seeming then to be past all control, so that when she got up a moment later, her mouth, nose, and often her eyes, would be filled with sand."

If her foster parent did have to leave her for a while, Gua trailed around miserably with a piece of his clothing clutched to her. This clutching of a piece of clothing or a towel is a very common occurrence among apes raised away from their natural mothers. It no doubt results from the fact that they lack the amount of clinging and security that they normally need. Human children often develop a similar habit, perhaps for the same reasons.

Christine was an infant chimpanzee raised by Lilo Hess on a Pennsylvania farm around the year 1950. According to Mrs. Hess, Christine lugged a towel along with her wherever she went. Christine was so unhappy and so suspicious of humans, having been caged in a pet shop for some time before Lilo Hess bought her, that at first she would not relax her hold on the towel, even to be carried by her foster mother. She was eleven months old before she was willing to go to sleep without the towel, even though she had a blanket to cover her. The towel would often slip into a corner during the night, and the first thing Christine would do on waking would be to search for the towel till she found it. Viki had the same habit: "Everywhere that Viki went a towel trailed behind, clutched in one hand, a foot, or draped over her back. I had the cleanest floors and the dirtiest towels in Florida." The young gorilla, too, developed this behavior: "Goma began to drag a rag or a piece of paper behind her with her foot. . . . Often she looked behind and tittered at a long rag following her."

Another habit common to most of the baby apes whose behavior has been reported is their tendency to find their way into the beds of their foster parents. For in their natural life, their mothers do not abandon them at night as do mothers of human infants in our culture, but curl up warm and tight, their arms around their babies. Dr. Lang wrote, "As she clung to me hard, she was allowed to come into my warm bed. At this she was overjoyed, lay down against my body, and played with a button on my pyjama top, and later with my fingers: but suddenly her movements became slower and she went to sleep again, safe in my arms and in the warmth of 'the nest.'" Cathy Hayes had the same experience with Viki, and Lilo Hess reports the same tale: "She trotted up the stairs with her blanket in tow and crawled into bed with me. There she snuggled deep under the covers and went to sleep within a few seconds."

Mrs. Maria Hoyt, who in 1932 adopted an infant gorilla, employed a special keeper, who for many years slept curled up with the young Toto every night. And we humans complain that our babies cry in the night! They are instinctively protesting at being alone. Dr. Spock please note!

One of the most interesting aspects of the saga of mother love in young apes is the youngster's willingness to defend its foster parent in danger, and to show sympathy in illness or incapacity. If Dr. Kellogg, Gua's protector, threatened Mrs. Kellogg, Gua bristled and tried to bite Mrs. Kellogg, whom she normally liked very much. If Mrs. Kellogg threatened Dr. Kellogg, Gua sprang to his defense. However, if a *stranger* threatened Mrs. Kellogg, Gua defended *her*.

Mrs. Hoyt, the foster mother of Toto the gorilla, used her knowledge of this behavior in a desperate situation. Toto, now developing into an adolescent gorilla, and as strong as four men, refused one night to return to her bedroom inside her enclosure. Mrs. Hoyt and Tomas, Toto's keeper, and all the gardeners and chauffeurs, had been chasing the willful gorilla round the garden for hours, and it was already dark and pouring rain. Mrs. Hoyt, at her wits' end, tricked Toto in the following way. She herself went inside Toto's bedroom with one of the gardeners. She started to scream loudly: " 'Toto! Help me!' Almost at once I heard her feet thumping on the flagstones as she galloped towards us. Then, as she came within sight, José took my shoulders in his hands and began to shake me. When she saw that, she gave a savage threatening bark and came bounding in like an express train, charging at José with unmistakable murder in her eyes. Just in time, he managed to escape through the door and close it behind him, slamming it literally in Toto's face."

A similar story is reported by Mme. Rosalia Abreu. This remarkable woman owned a huge estate in Havana, where in 1902 she started a colony of apes and monkeys housed in big outdoor cages surrounded by thick tropical vegetation. The colony lasted for over thirty years and had numerous breeding successes with orangs and chimpanzees, a success that was unduplicated at that time in the Western world. Each animal was an individual to Mme. Abreu, and many of them were allowed to roam the grounds. Her favorites spent the nights inside her home. One day one of her chimpanzees, called Chimpita, escaped, climbed into a mango tree, and refused to come down. So, she wrote, "I went to the tree and, speaking to him, pretended that I was injured in the arm, and suffering. Immediately, on seeing that I was in trouble, he jumped from the tree, and coming to me held my arm and kissed it strongly. And so we were able to catch him."

Cathy Hayes reported that the usually boisterous Viki became quiet and concerned when Cathy was ill for a few days, and Maria Hoyt describes the gentle, affectionate way Toto, her gorilla, used to examine her carefully to see if there were any scratches. Even a broken fingernail caused her concern, and she would kiss it and blow on it, as Mrs. Hoyt had done to Toto's bruises when she was a baby.

In the wild, apes spend a long time grooming each other or themselves, parting the hairs and examining the skin for bits of dirt and other imperfections. All the foster mothers report how their young apes enjoyed their daily brushing. This mutual care of the skin and hairy surface represents another way that the infant-mother bond expresses itself in apes.

Cathy Hayes gives an amusing account of the way Viki concentrated on grooming the Hayeses: "She looked possessed, with her eyes protruding, her tongue flashing in and out, and her forefingers scratching away at our hair, our glasses, a hole in our clothes, or whatever else had seized her attention. Her system was to pick a while, then mouth the offensive spot, perhaps adding a bit of saliva, and then scratch some more." And when Cathy's husband begins to groom Viki, "She goes into a virtual trance as Keith turns back her hair, inch by inch, scratching now and then, and clacking his tongue. She sometimes places his hand on a spot which she apparently feels needs grooming. If he resists, she pushes his finger to get it started."

There are many accounts of how injured or sick apes have seemed to understand that humans are trying to help them, and have been cooperative even when unpleasant things had to be done. For example, Chimpita, the chimpanzee from the Abreu colony, escaped on another occasion, and this time broke a window by putting his arm through it. "My son thought it necessary to remove the pieces of glass and dress the arm. While he worked over it, Chimpita was quiet and patient, behaving just as a sensible person naturally would."

Various aspects of the strength of the love and trust of young apes for their foster mother and family group have been discussed so far: how during infancy in particular this love is expressed by a great need to cling to and be with the substitute mother; how this extends to defense of her person, sympathy in illness, mutual grooming, and trust in her at all times. But how does a young household ape respond to other human beings who are not part of the immediate family? All accounts agree that the infant apes, for the first year or so of life, are extremely distrustful of strangers to the house. Dr. Kellogg reported that Gua avoided all contact with strangers until she was eleven months old. She then slowly became more sociable, and by sixteen months was much more friendly. One strange fact that emerged was that both she and Donald (the Kelloggs' little boy) preferred *women* visitors to men, in spite of the fact that in Gua's case her "mother" was a man. It is just possible that this represents some basic instinct to fear adult females less than adult males. This is not reported in the other accounts, however.

The social development of Viki could be expected to be slightly ahead of the apes in the other accounts because her foster parents actively encouraged her to become habituated to large numbers of strangers. This policy was decided upon when Viki, at six months, was obviously upset by the arrival of Grandma in the house: "The little one followed me constantly, never taking her eyes off the intruder." Viki gave a "snarling display of fourteen baby teeth at her every approach," and eventually bit Grandma hard. After a phase of active social education, Viki got used to strangers, and ignored them. However, to win her personal friendship, you had to have a certain approach. When Cathy Hayes's parents-in-law arrived, Mom immediately turned to, told Viki what to do, changed her diaper with no nonsense, and was accepted. Pa was aloof and uncertain, and Viki bit him, jumped onto him, and gave him a very rough time. Later, when about two years old, she developed a very positive social phase when she would perform at the window for passersby, and enjoyed being taken to large parties.

Lilo Hess gives an account of Christine's behavior in this respect that agrees well with the foregoing accounts: "When Christine was 19 months old, her attitude toward people changed rather suddenly. She was not the shy and timid baby any longer. She liked people and was eager to please them."

Toto, too, "would simply not tolerate anyone but myself, Abdullah, my mother, Kenneth, and one of the maids." The gorilla, however, true to its more dour, less sociable nature, never went through a really positive social phase such as did the chimpanzees.

Thus it appears that the social development of the young ape follows a predictable pattern that makes sense if looked at from the point of view of survival in natural conditions. At first everyone is feared and avoided, apart from the mother. Then particular persons are accepted if they are confident and authoritative. Finally, during the second year, in the case of chimpanzees who lived in large communities, other people become attractive, and social contact is sought, although strangers are never trusted as much as members of the family. The naturally conservative, introverted gorilla remains suspicious of strangers, beyond the usual group.

But by the age of two, the young ape is discovering its own will, and becomes ready to challenge even parental authority. Lilo Hess occasionally had to use a stick to get Christine to obey. "But she still recognised authority. When someone strong and big told her to do something, she meekly obeyed." The young ape was testing out its relationship with others, discovering whom it could boss, and who bossed it. Human children, too, go through this rebellious stage, and unless authority is firm and consistent, things get out of hand.

Cathy Hayes describes the first time Viki, at fourteen months, challenged her: "One day the worst possible thing happened. She bit *me*. I have repressed the circumstances. All I remember is that it hurt and something primitive flared in my blood. Grabbing her nearest part, a furry little arm, I bit down as hard as I could." Mrs. Hayes's response settled Viki for two months. Then she became uncontrollable. "She began having temper tantrums. She refused to hand over forbidden objects, and if I was compelled to force them from her grasp, she went into a screaming fit, venting her anger on the monkey dolls by biting out hunks of their cotton insides. When I gave the command 'No! No!' she defied me. She stuck out her chest, made a sassy hooting noise, and returned to her mischief. If I slapped her, it made no impression on her. Sometimes she laughed and slapped me back."

It was clear that the ordinary human mother lacked some power of dominance that the chimpanzee mother naturally had—probably large canine teeth, strong jaws, and no inhibitions. Cathy Hayes also had to get a stick. This restored her position of dominance. She had to use it only once. After that once, Viki "abandoned her idea of mutiny without a struggle." In the case of Toto, the gorilla who got bigger and bigger, Mrs. Hoyt was eventually forced to obtain a stick with a battery and electric shock for Tomas, Toto's keeper, to use when he lost control. Later still, a snake or burning rags were the only things that worked. All this indicates that most human beings are not physically capable of exerting authority over a growing ape in the way its natural mother, backed up by fearsome adult males in the group, would be in the wild. This is partly a psychological phenomenon. Some rare people do in fact seem to compel respect and submission from an animal. And it is partly a question of being able to back up threats with physical force.

The general problem of the development of this testing of authority is well discussed in relation to Goma, the young gorilla, by Dr. Lang:

Every personal relationship is connected with a condition of social rank, or the compulsion to clarify it. At times Goma tries to bite even her most trusted friends. The more impression she makes, the sooner she repeats such attacks. Sometimes she beats unfamiliar visitors on the head, or bites them on the leg. She "assesses" the situation. She tries to establish a system of rank. . . . At 6 months she played very happily with children. She showed little shyness; she was full of initiative, and unintimidated by very robust games and petting. At times, however, she could feel the urge to bite, and the need, obviously, to force her young playmate on to the social defensive —relatively speaking—to achieve her position of superiority.

Dr. Lang's clear exposition of the function and motivation of aggressive and rebellious behavior leads us on to the subject of the *play* of the young apes in our account, with human children or with others of their kind, for one of the functions of the social play of juvenile mammals is the sorting out of dominance relationships between contemporaries. It is in the natural rough-and-tumble of play that the young individual learns methods of influencing others, how to fit into a group, how to defend his rights. And this is a very necessary learning process if the adult is to be socially at ease and confident.

Viki had few playmates, because her methods were too rough for most human children. The only ones who got on well with her were the occasional children who showed that they were not afraid. One was called Jimmy, and being seven years old he was more than Viki's equal physically, for she was only two. Gua, the Kelloggs' chimpanzee, was brought up with Donald, who was two and a half months older. Gua was always gentle and protective toward Donald, and never bit him. But with other children, especially if they giggled or pointed at her, "she would usually rush at the affected children, emitting threatening dog-like barks as she did so, and she would slap them on the shins if they had not already dashed beyond her reach." Gua also made friends with a boy, eight years old, who did not run away or giggle at her.

When Goma was nearly a year old, the Langs obtained a young male gorilla of the same age for her as a playmate. This, of course, was better than any number of human children for the normal development of the gorilla. At first Goma was plainly jealous, determined to retain her superiority, and she tried to beat him into submission, but by rather cowardly methods: "She remained haughtily at a distance, her hair still standing on end. Then she reached out quickly—as if by chance—to her fellow creature, but immediately made for safety behind me, climbed onto my knee again, and into my arms. Some time later she tried to give him a quick bite or pluck at his hair. This situation continued for a long time. Often she bit Pepe's skin quite deliberately, but he was not in the least timid, and bit back." Pepe knew how to deal with Goma, and ten days later the two young gorillas had sorted it out, and were playing in a friendly way. Goma even allowed Pepe to bite her now, in fun of course, but one feels that Pepe, even at a year old, had asserted his masculine dominance.

Toward small, helpless mammals, the young apes seem to show tenderness and sympathy. Most of the firsthand accounts on this subject concern young *female* apes. Mrs. Hoyt tells how Toto saw a litter of kittens, and gently picked up one. She held it close in her arms and gazed down at its little face. She and this kitten then became inseparable, the kitten riding on Toto's shoulders or curled in her arm, purring (Plate 78). One day, however, after the kitten had become a cat, Toto discovered that her friend was the proud mother of more kittens. Toto was very upset, and would have nothing to do with her friend from then on. Instead she chose a new kitten out of the litter to be her treasure.

Christine, the chimpanzee, also had a kitten she loved. She treated it much as she did her stuffed animals, taking it in her arms, sniffing it and kissing it, and hugging it to her the minute the box in which it came was opened. When Christine was given a treat, such as a bowl to lick from, she'd sometimes try to feed the kitten with her spoon. When the kitten fell into the pond one day, Christine was terrified, and threw herself to the ground, screaming hysterically. Apes usually are afraid of water, and Christine knew her playmate was in danger. Luckily, she was saved by Mrs. Hess. Christine also showed maternal affection toward her dolls, especially a small stuffed chimpanzee that Mrs. Hess says she treated as if it were her own child.

By no means all the play of young apes, however, is concerned with learning or practicing social relationships. Another common type of play is a matter of experimenting with, and practicing, the physical capacities of the body, and experiencing the sensations of different kinds of locomotion. All the running, jumping, leaping, climbing, acrobatic play of young apes (and humans) comes into this category. We have already quoted from Cathy Hayes's graphic account of Viki's physical development, in this respect, at the beginning of this chapter.

One day when Toto was three years old and getting very strong, she became speculatively conscious of the broad marble balustrade of the main stairway. It came down twenty feet along the stairs, with two landings and large marble posts at each. Before any of us could foresee what was on her mind, she had run to the top of the stairs, was astride the balustrade and sliding down with lightning speed. Just as I, holding my breath, thought that she was going to crash into one of the marble pillars, she turned and, seizing the post in her hands, swung her body off the balustrade, through the air around the post and onto the balustrade below, continuing her magnificent slide. Nor did her flight stop when she got to the bottom. She landed on the marble floor in a soft little ball, rolled over and over half a dozen times, then picked herself up and scampered off gleefully.

Some of the play occupations reported for the young apes can be classified as exploration by the senses. This is typical behavior with new toys of apes or humans: feeling them, turning them over, and examining, passing from hand to hand, biting them and putting them in the mouth. The Kelloggs made a detailed study of the preference in play objects of both Gua and Donald, and, broadly speaking, the two enjoyed the same range of human toys and household objects.

Gua also learned to play with sand, although she did not take to this so readily as Donald. Christine took to sand too. "She had a little shovel and pail, and after putting one or two shovelfuls into the pail, she dumped it all out, sometimes over her head, and sometimes in her mouth." Toto loved to build castles in the sand to knock them down, and in the same way built up block towers, in order, it seemed, to have the pleasure of sending them flying. Christine was the same in this respect. Mrs. Hess reports that she saw her build a tower of two or three blocks a few times on her own, but most of the time Lilo Hess had to sit with Christine and give her directions to add each block. Christine particularly liked to knock down the tower, which is probably the reason she built it in the first place.

The most striking of the ape accomplishments in this type of "sensory exploration" play is one on which all accounts agree almost to a detail. Without any teaching, all the young apes loved to look at picture books, and showed that they recognized familiar people, objects, or animals. The young gorilla Toto used to have quiet times in her playroom looking at old magazines, searching for familiar animal pictures.

Mrs. Hess writes that Christine, also, enjoyed looking at pictures in books or magazines by the time she was one year old. If Lilo Hess showed Christine photographs of apes, she would readily identify them, and if asked which figure was like herself, she would point to the photograph several times in a row. Similarly, she was able to identify pictures of cats. If she saw a picture of a cat, even a drawing of a kitten in a children's book, she would make little noises and kiss the picture.

Barbara Harrisson, the orang foster mother, used to sit over her breakfast cup of tea, reading a newspaper. The six-month-old new arrival, Ossy, was on her lap:

Soon it became apparent that Ossy not only loved the paper to play with and make a mess of it, but that he was able to recognise pictures, also. Pictures of human *faces* particularly, even if small, incited him to imprint a firm "kiss" on the face, eyes, nose, and lip area. It did not matter to him whether they were upside down or the right way up. Later I experimented with other subjects. He showed keen interest in pictures of leaves or flowers which he poked with his index finger and even tried to chew.

The Kelloggs showed Gua and Donald a film of themselves doing an experiment:

At one point in the film is shown a bit of apple which the subjects are striving to pick up from the floor. Both watch the action quietly for a while, then Gua climbs upon a writing desk immediately below the area where the pictures are projected against the wall. She reaches out and touches with her finger the image of Donald's head and face. In a later scene a moment afterward, she touches her lips to the wall in a position, which as far as we can tell, is about where the piece of apple appears in the picture. She seems indeed to be trying to pick up the apple.

Another talent the apes have, related to the previous one perhaps, is to scribble and paint. Cathy Hayes wrote of Viki at fourteen months: "As if suddenly discovering the power of the written word, Viki began to scribble on books, floors, walls, and furniture, as well as the more orthodox paper. I found her comments on assorted manuscripts, shopping lists, and on recipes I had tacked to the kitchen bulletin board." According to Maria Hoyt, Toto could draw a face: "Mother taught her how to make pictures in the air with her finger, a circle for a face, three dots inside for eyes and a nose, and a slash for a mouth. . . . Later Toto transferred this crude representation of a face to the sidewalk with soft white limestone."

The biggest contribution on this subject has been made by Desmond Morris, the Curator of Mammals at the London Zoo, who encouraged a young male chimpanzee called Congo to draw on paper with a pencil, and to paint with a brush. Congo's paintings were on exhibition in 1957, and many of his originals are now owned by famous people.

His characteristic creation is of a fan pattern of lines, drawn inward toward Congo from the edges of the paper. Dr. Morris did not attempt to influence Congo in his painting. His only intervention was to hand him a new brush with a different color on it, when his interest began to flag. The results are colorful, exciting, and structured. Dr. Morris also experimented with Congo to find out what determined the position of the lines he drew. On a blank card, there was a tendency to mark the center and the corners, and to draw the fan pattern. If there was a blot on the card, Congo's lines were drawn to this. If a square was drawn in the center of the card, Congo would draw inside it. But if the square was to one side, he would balance it with marks on the other side. Thus Dr. Morris argued, on the basis of these and many more tests, that chimpanzees do show the basic elements of composition and patterning, which are the structure of human art.

Another entertaining form of the play of juvenile apes can also be classified as play involving exploration by the senses. This involved a propensity to ornament their own bodies in various ways, an odd characteristic indeed, but one that also shows itself in young chimpanzees and gorillas in the wild. Toto was so fascinated by Maria Hoyt's jewelry that she had to give her a bracelet and necklace of her own. Thereafter Mrs. Hoyt had to remember to remove all items of jewelry before going to visit Toto. Toto also loved to raid the laundry room, sending the servants scattering. She would tear the sheets to shreds, then race around the garden covered in a blanket.

Cathy Hayes records:

Not only towels, but rags, magazines, sprays of foliage, even the mops are used by Viki to decorate herself. And during these sweltering July days when I tried to keep Viki cool by letting her go native, she repaid my concern by struggling back into the clothes I had just peeled from her. And one day, as the mercury climbed past 100 degrees in the shade, she draped a 10-pound woollen blanket over her back and ran up and down the dirt road in the hot sun.

Gua showed the same characteristic behavior:

Thus she would sometimes place a blanket or a piece of clothing over her shoulders and drag it around with her; she would put small branches containing foliage upon her back and similarly carry or trail them; or she would wrap herself in hanging tree moss or in rags by putting them behind her back and holding them with both hands in front. She would thereupon walk upright with a train following in her wake, towards which she would gaze with a play smile, moving usually in a wide circle as she did so.

The Kelloggs record that "nothing of an exactly similar nature was ever observed in the behavior of the child," which was, of course, a boy. The "dressing up" of little girls, however, presents a striking comparison with the above quotation.

Christine's behavior was even more typically feminine. She would often adorn herself with strange items: a saucepan or a paper bag on her head, carrots or a piece of cloth around her neck. Then she would pose in front of a mirror, admiring herself, smiling and patting the mirror. In the Rosalia Abreu colony of apes in Havana, Yerkes reports on two adolescent female chimpanzees, Sita and Malapelga, who used to take fruits such as oranges and mangoes, crush and split them, and place them on their shoulders. It is remarkable that every single instance quoted here of this behavior concerns a *female* chimpanzee or gorilla. As most of the pet apes have been female, this may only reflect that fact. But even zoo reports of this habit seem to be of females.

In our discussion of the play of young apes reared as individuals, we have so far ranged over social play and its functions, locomotor play, and play involving exploration of the senses such as response to toys, and love of picture books, painting, and self-ornamentation. But play is a vast subject; in fact most of the waking activity of all juvenile mammals, not only young apes, is spent on play of one kind or another. Play, looked at another way, is really the "work" of juveniles, for indeed it is often accompanied by immense concentration, and a motivation to work at something till it is mastered.

Nowhere is this more apparent than in the astonishing talents of young apes to master mechanical devices within and outside the house. Goma had to be restrained from handling the gear lever on a car journey with her foster parents. She also easily mastered doorlatches and light switches by the time she was a year old. At one year of age, Christine the chimpanzee turned on all the taps by herself and could get herself a drink. She could also open doors, and used to slam them shut behind her if she wanted peace and quiet to do something she knew was naughty. Gua was about a year ahead of Donald in her capacity to deal with mechanical principles:

By the time the ape had attained the age of 13½ months, she was observed to unlatch the front door of the house in a manner which appeared anything but accidental. This she accomplished by climbing upon a small piece of furniture beside it, reaching from the furniture to the knob with her right hand, and turning the knob successively to the right and to the left by extending and flexing her arm. As soon as the latch was released she pulled the door open at once.

The Hayes, unwisely, in a series of tests of imitation, showed Viki how to turn a key in a lock. A short while later, Cathy Hayes was washing the car with Viki playing inside the car, out of the wet. Suddenly the car engine started, and the car jumped backward in reverse gear. Luckily, it stalled.

Of all the apes, however, it is the orang that, from all reports, shows the greatest persistence and natural interest in mechanical principles. Two examples illustrate this. One of Barbara Harrisson's young orangs, named Bob, was eventually sent off to the San Diego Zoo, when he was about three years old. A little while after his arrival, the Harrissons received the following letter from the zoo:

The day Bob arrived at the Zoo he was placed in our hospital for routine check-up and quarantine. During the same evening I received a phone call from Barbara Kadas, our nursery attendant, saying that our new arrival was taking his cage apart. When I reached the hospital, he was just pushing his head through an opening that he had made by untwisting a strand of the heavy link. He had already shoved out his blanket and several toys that were in the cage—evidently with no intention of returning. When he saw me he evidenced no sign of anger or frustration, but simply held out his arms to be picked up. The cage was repaired and strengthened and he was returned. The next day we discovered him diligently working away at another opening he had made in the top.

Bob was next confined in a larger, more sturdy enclosure in the hospital yard, where he promptly went to work again, coming out during the night and forcing an opening in another cage housing penguins. Here he was found by his keeper in the morning. No attempt had been made to harm the penguins. We then decided to place Bob temporarily in a heavily barred cage that had been recently used to house a big grizzly bear, and had also, in the past, held lions, pumas, and other large animals. Next morning he was found in the hospital feeding-room where he had spent the night dining sumptuously on bananas, apples, grapes and other goodies. He had patiently worked one of the bars loose, more a case of skill than strength.

The other example of orang persistence in this respect is also from the San Diego Zoo, a generation earlier, in Mrs. Belle Benchley's account of her personal friendships with some of the apes there, in the thirties and forties when she was in charge of the zoo. There was one old female orang called Jiggs:

I still believe that she was the smartest ape I ever knew, regardless of species. Her use of the principle of the lever was not aimless poking and prying for the fun of doing. It was a sure process applied to the most vulnerable part of the cage always. There was never a lost motion with Jiggs. If by chance or a trick, she secured a stout bar, she would walk to the side of her cage and put the end of her lever under the largest loop in the chain link she had noted and remembered, pending the time she could go to work on it. Right there where the wires or bolts would be farthest apart, she would insert the bar until she had achieved real leverage; then she would put her entire weight, as well as her great strength on it. She nearly escaped several times.

The final category of play activities observed in young apes is, perhaps, the most interesting of all. I am referring to the type of behavior that is typical of the species in its natural environment and that appears spontaneously, at a certain point in the development of the young animal, without training or even the opportunity to imitate. This instinctive behavior includes grooming, which has already been mentioned in our discussion of the expression of familial affection in apes, and *nest building*. In the wild, all three of the large apes build strong nests of woven branches and plants to sleep and rest in. In captivity, even when the infant apes have been removed from their mothers at birth, they start to construct nests of any materials to hand. For example, Dr. Lang who cared for Goma from the time she was thirty-six hours old, after her birth in the zoo, reports:

One evening I was sitting alone with Goma in front of the house. She was playing with the lowest branches of a shrub, pulling them down, breaking them off, putting her foot on them, tearing the fibres out one by one and happily beating the leaves. Suddenly she began to arrange the branches near her, in the way chimpanzees do when they want to build a nest on the ground. As darkness began falling she came over to me on the garden seat, but turned back to the shrub to arrange the branches. . . . We got the impression from Goma that nest-building was a necessity with the onset of darkness and that perhaps the essentials of this technique were innate.

Goma was about one year old at the time of this observation.

Toto, who was cared for by Mrs. Hoyt from a few months of age, at which time she still had to be carried everywhere, used to make simple nests of palm leaves on the ground for a daytime nap in her shady enclosure.

Home-raised female chimpanzees have also attempted to make nests out of different materials. Dr. Kellogg considered this topic very seriously:

A question of evident significance at this point is whether Gua ever displayed anything in the nature of *chimpanzee nest-building*. . . . Gua certainly had no experience in this behaviour nor had she in all probability ever observed older apes engaged in such activities. Nevertheless, after she had been sleeping on a soft mattress for a few weeks, she began nightly to disarrange and disturb the bed clothing to so great an extent before she finally fell asleep that serious preventive measures were taken. Such behaviour persisted, except for occasional intermissions, until the end of the research.

And it persisted in spite of punishment. Gua was determined to structure her sleeping area. The boy Donald did *not* do this, needless to say. Lilo Hess wrote that Christine, at age one, "made a sort of nest out of a blanket and towels when she went to sleep in her playpen."

This behavior appeared spontaneously in these young, inexperienced apes. If, however, circumstances had been unfavorable—if, for example, they had been denied access to nesting materials of any kind—typical nest-building behavior could never have developed. For it is known that there is a "critical period" for many instinctive responses in the growth of the young animal, when the performance of a particular instinctive sequence of actions is facilitated in the correct environment. If this critical period passes without the performance of the actions, the behavior pattern may never develop. However, it can still be learned. Some observations by Barbara Harrisson on nest building in her baby orangs show this clearly. One of her orangs, called Nigel, was about two years old when he arrived. He was upset by having been chained up for some months, and at first he seemed frightened of the trees in the Harrisson's garden. However, on the third day he started climbing, and did not come down with the others at dusk for his supper. At 6:00 P.M. he made a nest and slept in it. He did this often after that. The two other young orangs who played with him, about the same age, had been captured at an early age, and had had no opportunity to build nests while in captivity in local villages. This had inhibited the normal development of nest building in them. However, on the example of Nigel, they at once started to do so readily, progressing quickly from scrappy ones to proper nests.

Another interesting item of behavior that is frequently reported in the play of young apes and that again develops without teaching or example if materials are available, is the use of sticks or other objects as tools or weapons. Viki, for example, poked twigs into ant holes. In the wild this is a meaningful activity, obtaining a great chimpanzee delicacy, termites. Orangs, too, do this, quite spontaneously. "He [Bob] would poke for ants and other insects." Christine used a stick against the frogs in her garden. She would pick up a stick and start to work getting rid of the frogs by beating the bank of the pond. Whenever she spotted a frog, she'd touch him with the stick and laugh as he jumped away.

Reports of gorillas spontaneously using an object as a tool are rare, but Toto certainly did use objects as *weapons*. "The gardener had to be scrupulously careful not to leave any tool lying unattended even for a moment, because no-one knew when Toto, passing by, might decide to use a rake, or shovel, or pruning shears as a weapon of attack." If the gorilla's meals were two minutes late she would tear into the kitchen, scattering the servants, and fling plates, cutlery, whole drawers containing silverware against the door through which they had all disappeared. She threw tables and chairs at her keeper Tomas when he annoyed her. And one day, after she was locked in her enclosure because the Pomeranian dog she detested was being taken for a walk in the grounds, Tomas noticed her sitting in an unusual attitude, close to the wire, one hand behind her back. He was able quickly to remove from her grasp a heavy rock, just as the pom approached.

All the above examples occurred spontaneously, on the ape's own initiative, showing how natural a behavior pattern—using objects as implements—is to apes. Through experience, chimpanzees can become almost as efficient tool users as humans. Viki at six years old lit cigarettes with a lighter, pulled out her own loose tooth with a pair of pliers in front of the mirror, dug in the garden, and threw objects to knock down bananas.

A final example of innate behavior patterns that occur in the play of apes is their drumming, dancing and singing. Apes, in maturity, have tendencies to one or more of these forms of primitive rhythmic expression, from the roots of which stem our human music and dance. In zoos, chimpanzees can be stimulated by the audience to start clapping and stamping, getting faster, and usually finishing up with a tremendous display of banging or drumming on a resonant partition door of some kind. Loud whooping noises are made at the same time.

Gorillas in zoos beat their enormous chests with cupped hands, as a form of display. In the wild, the chest beating occurs in the context of a predictable series of actions, beginning with hooting noises; then the gorilla tears at the vegetation, rises on his legs, beats his chest, then kicks his legs, and starts to run, tearing at the plants, uprooting them, throwing them, and thumping on the ground. This, too, is a social behavior pattern.

One story of Mrs. Hoyt's about Toto is relevant here. A neighbor's balcony overlooked part of the Hoyt's garden, and on fine days, when Toto was out, Mrs. Hoyt's neighbor used to bring a gramophone out onto the balcony and dance to the music. Toto "would stand and begin to dance too, lifting one foot and then the other, stamping in perfect rhythm with the music or pirouetting with one foot constantly on the ground and making a perfect circle on the grass. . . . Her happiness in the dance would gradually work itself up to such a pitch of pure ecstatic excitement that if I stayed close to her she would, by the time the climax of her joy had been reached, tear my dress to tatters." This is reminiscent of wild gorilla displays.

Goma, too, got uncontrollably excited at her first birthday party. "The urge to perform overtook Goma; she ran wildly among the chairs, and threw some of them about. She pulled the children's dresses and even one little girl's long hair, and bit a little boy on the leg and made him cry." Goma was also reported to drum on the floor with the flat of her hands in excited play. Both Viki and Gua were reported to "whirl" from time to time, whereas Donald did not, and seemed to dislike being whirled by others.

One of Barbara Harrisson's orangs, Bob, "would race away madly, turning head over heels across the lawn. Sometimes he would dance about, standing upright for a second or two with his feet well apart; then waving his arms like a windmill to keep his balance, he would stagger a few paces or walk in a semicircle giving the impression of a drunken bear-like dance."

How far have these self-appointed foster parents succeeded in educating the ape to the customs of civilized living? To what extent can an ape adapt to the life of a human household?

All the infant apes learned at about the same time as a human infant how to use a spoon and feed themselves with it, how to drink from a cup, and how to sit on a chair at table for meals (see Plate 79). Many of the problems of infant ape and foster parent were identical to those met with in human babies. Lilo Hess wrote of Christine: "She liked to feed herself, but by now I was not so eager for her to do it, since she started to play with her food. She piled up little mounds on the side of her dish and hit them with the spoon, laughing as it splashed. Or she fed her teddy bear or another toy some of the food."

All the foster parents found that the young apes, in spite of the predominant vegetarianism of these species in the wild, took quite readily to a mixed diet similar to that of a human child, with a little more emphasis on raw salad and fruits. Gua, however, expressed definite dislikes in the food line, which the Kelloggs tried to overcome. "Thus if we disguised the mashed green beans by straining their pulp into Gua's milk she might eat them. The alternating of spoonfuls of beans or spinach with spoonfuls of milk was another device which worked well enough during the early months. Strong-arm procedures of forcing food upon her, as for example by holding the lips closed, or of starving her into eating the rejected dishes, or of shutting her off in a room by herself or in her bed when she would not eat, were also attempted once or twice but never with enough success to warrant their continuation. In one such instance, to our great surprise, Gua went without eating for as long as 43 hours because she refused some specially prepared infants' soup."

Viki, the Hayes chimpanzee, like many human children, "prefers to eat on the run," and had sudden whims. "Some days she dines exclusively on pork and beans, for example, or watermelon, or marshmallows, or laundry starch, or green onions and radishes." Would the Kelloggs ever have allowed this?

Toto took to a rich diet of luxury foods in the grand manner. She had two great likes, rare meat and black bean soup, neither of which seems remotely like the natural diet of her forest relations—stalks, leaves and pith. Her daily menu was formidable in her adolescent years:

> Breakfast: A quart of milk with cereal and raisins
> Midmorning: Orange juice
> Lunch: Black bean soup, 5 eggs, chicken or rare steak
> Afternoon: Dish of baked apples
> Before bed: Plate of fruit, lettuce, nuts, and milk.

All this Toto ate properly, sitting up at a table in her own dining room, with her keeper Tomas. She always examined Tomas's tray carefully to make sure he had been given nothing that she had not got.

Although the young apes seemed readily to take to the normal diet eaten by human beings, they are all reported to supplement it with other items they take themselves. They all seemed to have a tendency to catch and eat insects:

Toto loved ants. Although it is impossible that she can remember anything about African bush life, her behaviour in many respects was, in this as in many other things, exactly what it would have been if she had been brought up by her mother. When she saw a column of ants going up a tree she would brush her arm against it, with the fur in the direction opposite that which the ants were going, and then licked the whole off with one swipe of her tongue.

Nigel and Frank, the young orangs, were on board ship on their way to a European zoo, when suddenly a large pink locust landed in their cage. "Frank moved up to the high shelf and got into 'attack position' standing on all fours. He bashed at it with one fist, squashing it down." He then chewed it up.

Viki liked grasshoppers. "At dusk we watched the lily leaves become lined with grasshoppers, who are said to dislike sleeping on the damp ground. Viki with budding gourmet tendencies, plucked a few of these each afternoon, and chewed them solemnly, spitting out the tough exoskeletons."

Gua, as usual, got into trouble. "She was at first observed to pick up insects which came within her reach and immediately to place them in her mouth. They were then apparently chewed for their juices, the crushed shell being later ejected. Small insects she would often seize with her lips directly, in spite of our persistent admonition against this."

Goma's weakness was flowers, especially roses, and she used to try to supplement her diet this way. On her first birthday the Langs arranged a special treat. "At the beginning of the party Pepe presented his little hostess with a bouquet of roses which Goma enthusiastically put into her mouth and consumed."

Most apes are easily taught to undress and dress themselves. Viki could do so, and seemed to prefer wearing clothes to being naked. However, if she felt angry about something, she would tear her clothes in fury. Toto used to pull on a sweater and socks when the weather turned cool. Gua was put into child's shoes straight away, and later the Kelloggs found that she had, as a result, lost the ability to use her feet to grasp things. Apes readily learn other aspects of body care too. For example, Christine brushed her hair, cleaned her teeth, and washed her own clothes.

Perhaps the most interesting and controversial item on the social training routine of at least some of the ape foster parents has been an attempt to toilet-train their apes. In the wild, an ape has no need of a routine of elimination in a particular place. All the large apes are nomadic, and live in tropical vegetation. It is only home-based or territorial animals, such as man, that have to develop toilet routines so as not to foul the home. As Barbara Harrisson put it: "It is probably impossible to teach an orang that certain spaces should be used for certain purposes, because the animal's instincts are adapted to living in trees where everything drops down out of sight and smell. But they have a distinct tendency to keep their bodies and nests clean." If the little Ossy "felt a need while clinging to my body, he lifted his bottom away from me." This was without training from Barbara. So much appears instinctive, for the Kelloggs reported the same with Gua when she first arrived. Or it may be due to very early training by ape mothers, who had been seen to hold infants at arms' length during elimination.

Viki's foster parents started off with high hopes for Viki's potty training, but soon realized they were fighting nature, and admitted that this was "the one area of her education in which we have been most eminently unsuccessful."

The Kelloggs, however, put a truly Herculean effort into training Gua, at the age of seven and a half months, and Donald, who was ten months, to use a "nursery chair" for all elimination. It may seem amazing that they attempted so early with the child, let alone the ape; but in the thirties this was a widespread practice. The mind boggles at the patience and persistence involved. Both Donald and Gua were placed on their nursery chairs upon awakening, after each meal, and at approximately half-hour intervals throughout the day, and in addition on all occasions when one of them managed to indicate a need.

Gua was at an enormous disadvantage. She drank vast quantities of water, and as she also had relatively fewer sweat glands, the result was that she had to urinate 17 to 31 times a day, in comparison to the child's 13 to 23. She also defecated 4 to 7 times a day, while the child had only one motion. So even stricter measures were introduced for Gua, to increase her motivation for good toilet training—she was slapped or whipped following an error.

After a month's training the Kelloggs succeeded in getting Gua to defecate in the nursery chair, but two months after this she was still making an average of four bladder errors each day. The child during the daytime was completely trained, his only errors being in sleep or upon awakening.

The next step of the program was to get the young ape and child to indicate when an elimination was imminent. Gua's first attempts in this direction were to cry "oo-oo" as she was in the act of making a puddle. Later, however, she learned to indicate on about half the occasions what was about to happen, by hopping about with both hands or one foot pressed hard against her bottom.

Gua, of course, like Viki, was very young at the time of attempted training. It may be easier with an older ape, for Mrs. Hoyt records in her account of Toto the gorilla how at the age of three years Toto was toilet trained. They had constructed for her a special bed. "It had a spring and a mattress like a proper bed, but in one corner the mattress and spring were cut out and under it was placed a vessel. As a result, Toto immediately achieved superiority over human children in one respect at least. Her bed was always clean and dry. She supplemented the use of her own private equipment at night by use of the toilet during the daytime." No details are given by Mrs. Hoyt of how Toto was trained to use a daytime toilet.

In spite of their avoidance of bodies of water in the wild, young apes can be trained to have and enjoy a daily bath. Their fear does exist, however, innately, if they are not habituated against it. For example, we have previously mentioned how Christine screamed hysterically when her cat fell in the pond. In the same way, when Mrs. Hoyt one day went for a swim, Toto had a fit of terror by the pool, screaming until Mrs. Hoyt got out. Christine would play happily at the edge of the pond, patting the water or stirring it with sticks, but would not go in.

However, Viki learned to put up with the soaping, and enjoyed rinsing herself with the shower. In fact, Viki became an addict (Plate 80):

Now during her bath, Viki began paddling her hands in the water. Then she hung onto the edge of the tub and kicked with her feet. When I held her under the tummy, as children are held for swimming lessons, she made the proper motions. I then took my hands away, and to my amazement, she remained completely suspended for five seconds before her feet sought bottom. She seemed delighted. Although she coughed and sputtered from the water in her nose, she always laughed and went back for more. Once again, we almost had cause to regret her latest achievement. She became so fond of water that one wintry day, she ran away to Mrs. Clarke's and jumped into the ice-cold fish pond.

There was more resistance with Gua, because she was already seven and a half months, and old enough to be frightened of new experiences in themselves. "In the beginning, it is true, she showed but little liking for her bath, and if her head went under the stream of the faucet or if she was momentarily submerged, she appeared terrified. But her adaptation to the new medium was nearly as rapid as it was to other features of her environment, so that before long she would enter the heavy torrent of a shower bath if simply called by the experimenter." At ten months the Kelloggs reported that she would play at the edge of a small pool, but not with the enthusiasm of the child. "On one or two occasions she was induced, after some wailing, to enter the pool herself and move through it to the opposite side where the experimenter was calling her."

A rather different adaptation to the human way of living, which most foster parents of apes have encouraged, is erect bipedal walking. The Kelloggs actively trained Gua, from her arrival at seven and a half months, to walk upright, by giving her a "baby-walker," and by taking her for walks, holding one or both her hands, a thing she accepted readily from the start.

Her progress record showed that at eight months she was able to stand alone for short periods; at nine months she could walk three meters unaided; and "at the age of 9½ months she stood or walked upright fully half the time when she was out-of-doors, but not to such a great extent in the house." By twelve and a half months she was running erect out of doors (Plate 81).

However, it seems unlikely that Gua's erect walking was very much influenced by the Kellogg's training. For Christine, without any training or encouragement from Lilo Hess, started to *try* to walk upright at ten months, and by eleven months old she was on her feet a good part of the time. Her walking seems to have been stimulated by the carrying of objects, for when she was upright she was usually carrying a towel or a toy. Lilo Hess confirms, too, that being *outside* appears to increase the amount of upright locomotion. When Christine played outdoors she often stood upright when playing in the sand or while splashing about in a shallow lid filled with water. To begin with, she would take short runs erect, running fast to keep her balance, but after a while she was able to trot along in leisurely fashion, swaying from side to side only slightly.

Goma was occasionally encouraged to walk this way by holding her hand, but when erect walking did become common, at nearly a year old, it appeared to be spontaneously motivated. "It was at this time that we first noticed Goma trying to walk upright. She had drawn herself up against a chair and now walked five steps in a standing position. Soon she could walk halfway across the room. At play too we saw her pick up a toy and run away with it upright." It seems probable on the basis of these reports, that walking and running erect develop naturally in young apes but that in human surroundings it is encouraged to be more frequent than is normal in apes.

For all young human children, the basic values and skills and traditional ways of doing things, in any particular culture, are picked up by imitation, beginning in, and of most importance in, the toddler stage. Human infants are possessed with an enormous motivation to imitate everything their parents do; imitation is an end in itself, for there are no other rewards, nor does the child understand the reason for, say, washing the floor, yet it washes vigorously alongside the mother.

It is therefore interesting to inquire whether young apes, too, show this insatiable desire to do what their foster parents do, and if they do, whether they acquire skills adequately in this manner, with no other reward.

Viki certainly did imitate Cathy Hayes:

Viki showed her first evidence of imitation at 16 months of age, when she began crudely copying my household routine—dusting, washing dishes, pushing the vacuum cleaner about. . . . As Viki grew, such imitative play became more frequent until every tool we used, every little action, was apt to result in her attempts at duplication—hair brushing, fingernail filing, eyebrow tweezing, the use of a saw, a drill, a bottle opener, a pencil sharpener.

She became an actual help at one stage of the process of washing clothes since "her strong hands can wring the laundry drier than mine are able to do." Lilo Hess had a similar story. When Christine was around twenty months old, she began to copy some of Mrs. Hess's actions. She would imitate Mrs. Hess's movements in doing such household chores as sweeping with a broom or scrubbing the floor with a scrub brush.

Viki started spontaneous imitative behavior at sixteen months and Christine at twenty months. The Kelloggs studied Gua from seven and a half months until she was sixteen and a half months old, and reported that they found little evidence of imitation in her activities. In view of the others' finding, this is understandable, but the Kelloggs also reported that Donald started imitative behavior at under one year of age, when he would attempt to brush his hair, close drawers, push a broom back and forth on the floor, and shake hands. A few months later, he joined in activities of his mother's, such as helping her sort oranges into two baskets. Donald also imitated *Gua,* and even managed to produce some chimp-like sounds before he learned human words. So it appears that although the ape has a faster rate of maturation than the human child, it starts imitative behavior at a *later* age. This indicates that imitation may have a lesser function in the development of apes than it does in man, and that man may have a greater capacity to learn in this way.

As the final subject in this discussion of the ability of young apes to adapt to a civilized human way of life, mention might be made of the extent to which they can be taught obedience. Certainly they never learn the blind obedience of a dog. This may be partly due to the fact, already mentioned in our discussion of the growing ape, that it is difficult indeed to get an ape to accept you as master, such is its drive for dominance at a certain stage of development. The author recently saw a remarkable film made in 1966 at the Ngoya Zoo in Japan. In 1959 three newly captured baby gorillas of approximately one year of age were placed in the total care of one keeper, Rikizo Asai. The gorillas lived in their cage, but the keeper seemed to spend most of his time in there with them, and even ate his own meals in their view just outside the cage. While caring for the gorillas with extraordinary devotion, he believed that it was essential that they accept him as absolute master. To this end, he initiated a remarkable training procedure: while the gorillas were eating their meals, he subjected them to cuffs on the mouth, head and body and constantly teased them by waving bits of food beyond their reach; he kept up a barrage of bangs and rattles, forcing the gorillas to attend to him all the time. This unusual form of conditioning appears to have had the required results and the gorillas and the man now have a very close, intimate relationship, with the gorillas accepting him completely as their master. They appear to love him rather than fear him, and willingly perform with him before audiences in a way that is usual only in young chimpanzees. They wear clothes, have tea parties and even play in a percussion band while dancing in an upright posture. These gorillas are already bigger and heavier than their keeper and are entering adolescence. Whether Rikizo Asai's method of dominating them will succeed into their massive introverted maturity will be interesting to discover.

Apes are intelligent, and won't do something if they do not understand the issues involved. An experiment or two done with Gua illus-trate this. To test her obedience, the Kelloggs sat her on a chair in a room, and said, "Stay there, Gua," which she understood. She remained on the chair as long as the Kelloggs remained in the room. They then left but were able to watch her without her knowing it. Gua got off the chair when they left, but hastily got back on when she heard some-one approaching the door. Her desire was to please her foster parents, but she had no sense of *duty* to remain at her post if they were not there. On another occasion she was also told to sit still on her stool, which was at the other side of the room. She desperately wanted to get close to her "mother," Dr. Kellogg, but feared to incur his displeasure by not sitting on her stool. After some minutes of restlessness she solved the problem to her own satisfaction. She suddenly got off the stool, quickly pushed it over to be next to Dr. Kellogg, then rapidly remounted and sat on it.

The most important question of all that is raised by the examination of the accounts of these apes that have been reared with every oppor-tunity given to a human child, is: What becomes of them? They are reared with humans, as humans, pampered with civilized living, taught human skills. They are loved as children, and there can be no doubt that they love in return. As juveniles, their development and behavior bear a striking resemblance to that of a human child; and this is because we and the large apes once had a common ancestor. But when the adult animal is considered, the differences due to specializa-tion for varying habitat, diet, manner of life become clear. For when the ape matures he is found to have physical and physiological capacities and powerful instincts to go with them, that fit him for survival in the forest—quite a different set of circumstances than those his human foster parents are adapted to. The juvenile ape appears adaptable and plastic and full of learning power. But it does not learn to be human or have human motives. It develops, instead, in ac-cordance with the program of its genes, selected in millions of years of forest living.

So the answer to our earlier question, How far can an ape adapt to the life of a human household? seems to be that while a lot of civilized customs can be trained *in*, a lot of uncivilized instincts cannot be trained *out*. And the latter increase with the growing maturity of the ape, as the story of Toto's adolescence and maturity, which I am about to relate, shows beyond any doubt.

Usually pet apes are handed over to zoos before adolescence, because it is well known that at this time they become moody and un-predictable. One person who broke this rule was Mrs. Hoyt, who kept Toto until she was almost adult, and even then remained in touch with her. It is with the beautiful story of Toto, and with its tragic moments, that I wish to end this chapter. We have already met Toto often; here is the rest of her story.

Mrs. Hoyt always felt she owed Toto something for the manner of the animal's mother's death, for it was when she and her husband were on a collecting trip in Africa in 1932, that all Toto's group, in-cluding her mother, were killed. Mr. Hoyt shot only the large male, which he wanted as a specimen for the New York Museum of Natural History, but the natives, hungry for meat, rebelled, and killed the entire group. Only Toto was left, a baby of a few months, incapable of locomotion, crying and clinging to its dead mother. It saw Mrs. Hoyt and, we are told, leaped into her arms. And so began an incredible and moving relationship. The Hoyts settled in Havana, in a large house with extensive grounds. The early years were quite obviously de-lightful, although already, at three years of age, Toto "had the strength of 2 men, and the ingenuity of a dozen boys." With her growing strength, Toto was able to wreck the house. If she failed to open a door by the latch, she simply pushed, and crashed through it. Lady guests were usually terrified. So the Hoyts built Toto a special apartment in the garden, consisting of two rooms, and an outdoor enclosure covered with tropical vines for shade, as Toto disliked being in the sunshine. A large iron bedstead, with a barred roof which could be locked on at night, was fastened to the floor, because Toto had once used the bed-stead as a weapon against her keeper, Tomas, who shared her apart-ment with her.

But Toto grew out of childhood, and could not control her gigantic strength. She could not understand why, when she pushed Mrs. Hoyt in play, her beloved foster mother fell backward onto the flagstones, breaking both her wrists. Toto was ashamed, and for long after the wrists were healed, she took them from time to time in her hands, and examined them and kissed them gently.

Powerful instincts took hold of Toto now and then, instincts to dis-play wildly, when excited; but in her human environment this was dangerous for property and persons. Toto developed hatreds of certain members of the large staff of servants and gardeners, and some of the dogs. Drastic incidents happened, and were tolerated by Mrs. Hoyt's household because of the love the Hoyts bore for Toto, and she for them. For example, the gorilla, who by now was gigantic, pursued a terrified gardener up his ladder, so that he had to leap off. She picked up a small Japanese servant in her great arms, carried the terrified man to the top of her enclosure, and dropped him.

Toto now had estrous cycles, and for a few days each month, became surly, and more uncontrollable than usual. She fell in love each time, with one or other of the male staff, and followed him around, trying to touch the frightened individual. All this time, Toto was allowed the freedom of the grounds during the day, because Mrs. Hoyt could not bear to have the animal locked in her enclosure, for she went into rages at being restricted (Plate 82).

Tomas now had to be equipped with an electric prod, leather sheaths to protect his arms from bites, and a snake curled up in a bag around his waist, as this was the only thing that terrified Toto into submission if she was feeling rebellious. He had a wooden shield put up in Toto's room so that he could escape behind it, like a bullfighter, when Toto started throwing furniture. Tomas also had a whistle to blow when Toto went on a "spree," meaning on a destructive rampage. When he blew it, all the servants fled into the house, the doors were bolted, and the windows were fastened.

Tomas even had to surround Toto's bed with a hedge of thorn branches, with a small gap through which he could drive her, sometimes with blazing rags, into her bed, while he got the roof fastened down on her. These are the facts, related quite simply by Mrs. Hoyt. They are astonishing, and could have happened without the law being concerned only in a place like prerevolutionary Havana. However, throughout the story runs the thread of the great affection between Toto and Mrs. Hoyt. For Toto was not always being wild and rebellious. While Mr. and Mrs. Hoyt were on a holiday trip to New York, Mr. Hoyt died, and his wife, numb with grief, returned to Havana alone. When she went to see Toto, the gorilla greeted her and looked beyond her to find Mr. Hoyt. She looked puzzled. Then she took Mrs. Hoyt's hand, and gently led her into the house and through all the rooms, looking for Mr. Hoyt. Not finding him, she led Maria out again, round the chicken houses and garden sheds, and finally into all the cars in the garage. At this point Mrs. Hoyt began to weep uncontrollably. Toto gently wiped her eyes, kissed her, and embraced her.

Because of this affection between them, and the near-human sympathy and understanding that Toto was capable of, Mrs. Hoyt could not bring herself to hand Toto over to a zoo. But matters got worse.

Plate 57.   "Hunter killed by a gorilla" (from P. Du Chaillu).

Plate 58.   "My first gorilla" (from P. Du Chaillu).

Plate 59. Chimpanzees under their rain shelters, as imagined by Du Chaillu.

Plate 60. Gorilla family, from an edition of Brehm's *Tierleben*.

Plates 61 and 62. *Above:* Adult male mountain gorilla in the wild. *Below:* Wild juvenile mountain gorilla.

Plate 64. Locomotor patterns of wild gibbons, sketched by W. T. Hornaday. 1–4. Swinging through the treetops. 5. Walking on level ground. 6. Climbing through the treetops.

Plate 63. Gorilla nest.

Plate 65.   Adult female gibbon *(Hylobates lar)* in the wild.

Plate 66.   Wild adult male gibbon *(Hylobates lar)* feeding on new leaves.

Plate 67. Female orangutan, her baby and nest, sketched by W. T. Hornaday.

Plate 68.   Orang habitat — the swamp forest bordering the South China Sea in Sarawak.

Plate 69.   Nest of an orangutan in Sarawak.

Plates 70 and 71. Wild orang in Sabah.

Plate 72. Arthur, a male orangutan, aged five years, near a cave in Bako National Park, Sarawak.

Plate 73. Cynthia, a three-year-old female orang, nesting on the ground at Bako.

Plate 74. George, a 2½-year-old male, preparing to sleep at Bako.

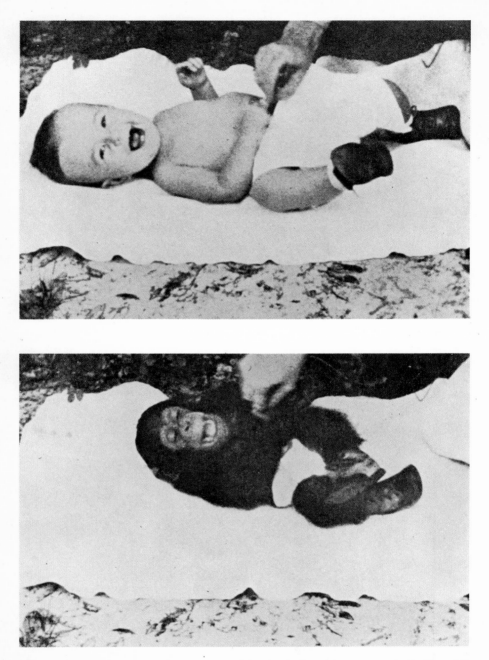

Plate 75. Donald, the baby boy, and Gua, the baby chimpanzee, both "laugh" when tickled.

Plates 76 and 77. *Left:* Goma, as a baby, would clutch her feet together tightly in her crib. *Below:* Later, Goma had the run of the Langs' garden.

Plates 78 and 79. *Left:* Toto, the adult female gorilla belonging to Mrs. Hoyt, with a feline friend. *Right:* Gua drinking.

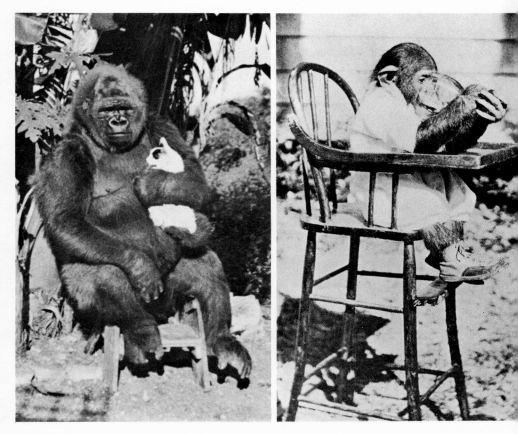

Plate 80.   Viki, the Hayes' chimpanzee, in her bath.

Plate 81. Gua walking upright.

Plate 82. Mrs. Hoyt and
Toto in the garden
at Havana.

Grocery boys threw their deliveries over the wall because they were too scared to enter. Even Maria had to be prepared at all times for Toto's mood to undergo a sudden change, for, without warning, the gorilla "would stand to full height and charge like an angry bull, with such speed that the only way to avoid being hit, was to fall to the ground and roll away." Sometimes she would seize Maria by the arms or part of her dress, and drag her for yards over the lawn or walk, or through a sandpile. Mrs. Hoyt and Tomas developed a technique of falling limply or of wrapping themselves around trees when out for a walk in the grounds with Toto.

In 1941, when Toto was nine years old, Mrs. Hoyt agreed that the animal would have to live elsewhere. She arranged to sell her to Ringling Brothers circus, as a mate for Gargantua, the famous male gorilla. Tomas went along too, as permanent companion to Toto, sharing her wagon, and cooking the food she was accustomed to (Plate 83). For most of the first year, Mrs. Hoyt also followed the circus over the States, living with Toto at every stop. Toto had her own wagon with two compartments, but none of the freedom to roam that she had in Havana. Mrs. Hoyt's book, published in 1941, ends on a self-questioning, unfinished note, as if she were uncertain that there was not some better solution to the problem of caring for the gorilla. And indeed, in 1956, Mrs. Hoyt bought back her friend Toto and took her to live in New York with her. Both were still healthy in 1962.

But Toto is the exception, and the sad moral is, I fear, that almost the only possible end for a captive baby ape, however promising and affectionate, is to spend its adult life behind bars.

CHAPTER 9

The Abilities of Apes

HUMAN BEINGS, NOT animals, devise tests of animal intelligence, and in doing so we tend to test for the existence of capabilities upon which *we*, as a species, put high value; capabilities that have been responsible for our own survival and success as a species. Thus, looked at one way, human intelligence tests applied to apes have little meaning. For if the ape succeeds, this merely indicates that the capacity to respond adaptively in such a situation is one that has been important to both man and ape in their common evolution; if the ape fails, this does not necessarily indicate that it is stupid, but simply that such a way of responding has not been selected in the ape's forest life. Many examples of this type of failure will be mentioned in the following pages.

Nevertheless, some apes are cleverer than others; and, in my opinion, the chief value in giving intelligence tests to apes lies in the opportunity they give of studying the operation of humanoid thought processes at relatively simple levels.

Most of the really thorough contributions to our knowledge of ape abilities and mental processes were made during the early decades of this century, when collections of captive apes were much rarer than they are today. In 1914, Wolfgang Köhler found himself in charge of an anthropoid station situated at Tenerife in the Canary Islands. There were eight young chimpanzees there, and one adult female. Most of the young ones were between four and seven years of age at the time of Köhler's experiments. He investigated the problem-solving abilities of these chimpanzees by means of a series of tests. He also tested some other animals and some children on a few of the tests, for purposes of comparison.

The simplest test was the Roundabout Methods Test. An incentive, such as a banana or orange, was placed on the far side of a fence. For all the chimpanzees it was a simple and immediate matter to make a detour around the fence to pick up the prize. A dog tested on the same problem also made an immediate detour. But when, on the next test, the meat was placed directly in front of the dog, on the other side of the fence but very close to it, the dog failed. She "pushed again and again with her nose at the wire fence, but did not budge from the spot." Chimpanzees continued to make the detour. Hens found the problem impossible: "They keep rushing up against the obstruction when they see their objective in front of them through the wire fence, rush from one side to another all a-fluster." They never learned the detour. A baby girl, however, although only one and a quarter years old and barely walking, was already able to solve the detour problem. "First she pushed towards the object, i.e. against the partition, then looked round slowly, let her eyes run along the blind alley, suddenly laughed joyfully, and in one movement was off at a trot round the corner to the objective."

On the next test, the Use of Implements, the chimpanzee again succeeded where the dog failed. The incentive lay three yards beyond the cage bars, attached to a piece of string, of which the near end was within reach of the bars. "One glance at the objective, and the animal began to pull on the rope, gazing not at the rope, but at the distant objective." A dog has the physical means of pulling in the string, by teeth or forepaws, and no doubt would readily do so after training. But the dog tested by Köhler showed no understanding of the solution: she "paid no attention to the string which was lying just under her nose—whilst at the same time she showed the liveliest interest in the distant objective."

Further string experiments suggested that the chimpanzee had a primitive concept of "connexion" but that this involved merely visual contact. For if a string lay close to the incentive but not touching, the chimpanzee Sultan pulled it in; if the string was clearly separated from the object, he did not attempt to pull. If several strings ran from the direction of the banana, crisscrossing over, but only one was attached, Sultan paid little attention, and pulled quickly at the string that appeared to cover the distance by the shortest route.

The most interesting series of experiments involved the chimpanzee's manipulation of a stick in the solution. The incentive was placed outside the cage bars, beyond arm's reach. A stick was placed close by, within the cage. The account of the behavior of Nueva, a four-year-old female, gives a typical sequence of events in the solution of this problem by the chimpanzees: "Thus between lamentations and entreaties, some time passes, until—about 7 minutes after the fruit has been exhibited to her—she suddenly casts a look at the stick, ceases her moaning, seizes the stick, stretches it out of the cage, and succeeds, though somewhat clumsily, in drawing the bananas within arm's length. Moreover, Nueva at once puts the end of her stick behind and beyond the objective." Two days later the bananas were again placed beyond the bars, but no stick was given to Nueva. "She at once tried to pull it towards her with rags lying in her cage, with straws, and finally with her tin drinking-bowl which stood in front of the bars, or to beat it towards her—using the rags—and sometimes successfully."

In further experiments on the use of implements, six young apes of the colony were enclosed together in a room where a bunch of bananas was suspended from the ceiling.

All six apes vainly endeavoured to reach the fruit by leaping up from the ground. Sultan soon relinquished this attempt, paced restlessly up and down, suddenly stood still in front of the box, seized it, tipped it hastily towards the objective, but began to climb upon it at a (horizontal) distance of ½ metre, and springing upwards with all his force, tore down the bananas. About five minutes had elapsed since the fastening of the fruit; from the momentary pause before the box, to the first bite into the banana, only a few seconds elapsed, a perfectly continuous action after the first hesitation.

On the basis of his observations of the chimpanzee in such tests as those described above, Köhler maintained that the typical solution was achieved by what he termed "insight" and that this involved a sudden perception of the relationship between, say, the stick and the banana. Other workers on ape or on human problem-solving have used other terms, but most have agreed that, in certain circumstances, there can be a process of sudden solution, which must involve an image, an idea, or a hypothesis that anticipates the results of the subject's consequent actions. From this point on, the subject acts *purposively*. In humans, the same process normally involves verbal consideration of the problem, and is then called "reasoning."

Many factors affect the probability of the chimpanzee achieving an insightful solution of the problem. Köhler deduced that the chimpanzees depended greatly on the *visual* arrangement of the problem situation. For example, in the stick-and-banana test, after vainly reaching, the frustrated animal often sat for a few minutes staring at the incentive. If the stick lay in his field of vision at this time, it was probable that he would leap up and grab it to get the bananas. But if the stick lay behind the ape, and even if he turned around and saw it there, insight would not occur, because in doing so he lost sight of the objective. This was typical only of the first time of encountering the situation. Later, of course, the sophisticated chimpanzees went searching for tools. Another aspect of visual importance was whether the potential implement stood out from the background. One day, for example, the apes failed in the box problem because Tercera, one of the females, had sat comfortably on the box to watch the proceedings.

Another important factor influencing the probability of insightful solution of a problem was the previous experience of the ape. Köhler took it for granted that the chimpanzees used in his experiments were familiar with the use of sticks and branches from their early years, when they were living wild in the Cameroons. He accepted this as the natural state of affairs. H. G. Birch, a research worker at the Yerkes Primate Laboratories, showed in 1945 that opportunity to play with sticks does contribute to problem solution. His subjects were six chimpanzees, four to five years old, reared from birth in the Yerkes chimpanzee nursery. Only one, named Jojo, had been observed to play with a stick, using it to flick a switch off and on. These chimpanzees were tested with the bananas beyond the bars, and a stick to hand within the cage. Only one, Jojo, solved the problem properly. All six then spent the next three days with all kinds of sticks available to play and experiment with. They were then tested on the banana problem once more, and all six solved it immediately. None of their three days' play had given them an opportunity to practice drawing in food in the way required in the test. What they had learned, according to Birch, was an "arm-stick extension pattern," and this was essential to the insightful solution of the problem.

However, in other of Köhler's experiments, such as the box problems, the apes can have had little practice in their wild life. "How often, in any case," he wrote, "could a chimpanzee, under his normal conditions of life, be in a position to need, for example, a footstool, to reach a high object—presumably the fruit on a tree?" It appears from later experiments, reported in 1952 by P. H. Schiller, also a scientist at the Yerkes Laboratories, that chimpanzees reared in captivity from birth, do not show such intelligent behavior when confronted with the box or stick problems, as did Köhler's chimpanzees. This indicates that the wild experience of Köhler's subjects, and their relatively natural conditions even in captivity, allowed them to acquire manipulative skills and concepts of spatial dynamics lacking in Schiller's animals.

Schiller's chimpanzees, when given the opportunity, played with sticks and dragged boxes around, even stacked them, but did not use these implements in the test situation, to obtain the fruit, until they had had a number of trials. Schiller found that the older the chimpanzee, the fewer trials it needed to obtain the solution. Schiller's results, in the light of Birch's and Köhler's findings, suggest two more factors that influence the development of intelligent behavior in a problem situation—the age of the subject and the richness of the early environment.

Another experiment done by Birch investigated the effects of different degrees of hunger on the ability of his chimpanzee to solve the problems. He tested his subjects on the confusing-strings problem and on the stick-using problem, after they had been 2, 6, 12, 24, 36, or 48 hours without food. He found that at a low degree of hunger the chimpanzees showed lack of interest in the problems, and were easily distracted onto something else. However, Birch's incentive lying beyond the bars of the cage consisted of only 1/30th of a medium-sized orange! Whereas Köhler's chimpanzees, without any food deprivation, worked quite well for whole bunches of bananas, Birch found that at 36 and 48 hours of hunger, the subjects were so desperate to get at the tiny slice of fruit that they tended not to notice the other relevant features in the environment, such as the stick. For example, the very hungry groups made between them 117 futile reaches toward the food with their hands in 3½ minutes, whereas the low-hunger groups made only 25 such wasted efforts in 6 minutes. The best and quickest solutions were made by chimpanzees who were between 6 and 24 hours hungry, because they were hungry enough to persist with the problem, but not so desperate that they could respond only to the sight of the fruit. Birch's very careful and comprehensive work fully corroborated Köhler's conclusions that the typical solution by the chimpanzees was a sudden purposeful insightful one, though occasional accidental solutions did occur. His results however showed that 78 percent of the solutions, irrespective of degree of hunger, were insightful.

A final factor that affects the likelihood of a given chimpanzee achieving an intelligent solution to a problem is the obvious one of its own particular brain capacity; for as in humans, some chimpanzees possess a higher potential of intelligence than others. H. W. Nissen was at the Yerkes Primate Laboratories for more than twenty years, and watched scores of chimpanzees grow up, breed, and produce young. Most of these he got to know as individuals on a friendly basis owing to the frequent behavioral experiments they were doing for him. The environment was controlled and to a large extent constant for each animal. Most had been reared from birth in the Yerkes nursery. Nissen wrote, "In every learning experiment we have ever done, and these must be numbered in the hundreds—individuals have varied widely in speed and accuracy of performance." He went on to describe the case of Jenny and Jojo who were half-sisters, born about the same time, and reared together in the nursery. As juveniles they were housed with other young chimpanzees in an enclosure containing an oak tree. "It is here that Jojo's exceptional tool-using talents became manifest. Twigs and branches were freely available and Jojo was soon using these far more than her companions. Selecting a stick of proper length, thickness and strength, she pushed it through the meshes of the hardware cloth door to flip the light switch up and down, on and off until the switch wore out." Though the others had the same opportunities and could have imitated Jojo, none performed any of her antics. "Give Jenny a stick and she may chew it, or at the most use it to clean her ears."

We have discussed certain factors that affect the probability of an insightful solution: the layout of the problem situation, previous experience with the implements to be used, the more general perceptual and manipulative experience afforded by a rich environment, the degree of maturation of the subject, the amount of motivation, and the brain potentiality. None of these factors detracts from the fact that chimpanzees as a species are able to perceive relationships, anticipate the results of their actions, and act purposively in some situations. In this respect they show a higher degree of intelligence than monkeys, as experiments have shown.

Both Yerkes and, later, Schiller tested monkeys on the stick-and-box problems, in comparison with apes. Yerkes used two monkeys as subjects, one rhesus macaque and one crab-eating macaque. The latter was already a tool user, in that it could hammer nails in accurately, and draw a nail over the teeth of a saw to make a noise. Neither of these monkeys, however, saw the relationship between the stick in their cage and the fruit beyond their reach. Neither monkey, in the box test, made any attempts to move the boxes, or even attended to them at all. Yerkes states that his results "indicate a vast gulf, psychologically, between monkey and ape." In Schiller's experiments, rhesus and spider monkeys required four hundred to five hundred trials before achieving success on the stick problem, when the food lay on the near side of the stick, ready to be drawn in with one pull. No monkey learned to get the fruit if it lay behind the stick. Only very occasionally have exceptional monkeys, usually capuchins, approached in problem-solving experiments the performances of apes. Such a rare subject was P. Y., studied by Heinrich Klüver. This monkey after death was found to have possessed an unusually large development of the forebrain.

Experiments in general, however, demonstrate superior mental ability in the chimpanzee. Humans, on the other hand, as is to be expected, succeed more speedily and at a lower age than chimpanzees. Köhler tested a boy of two on the stick problem:

He is put into a railed-off space, such as is often used for little children. The walls are so low that they reach only to his breast. Inside lies a light stick; outside, out of his reach, the objective. In a little while the stick is picked up as a matter of course, and the objective pulled to him with it. The skill with which this is done is distinctly less than that of Sultan, who is twice as old as the child, but greater than that of Rana and Tercera, [two other chimpanzees] who are about the same age as Sultan. In whatever way the use of the implement may have developed, it certainly takes place.

In later experiments on his chimpanzees, Köhler showed how they were able to solve problems of much greater complexity than the simple stick and box tests. The following example illustrates the coordinated and purposeful method by which Sultan finally solved a problem. The incentive lay some distance beyond the bars. The long stick he needed to obtain the fruit also lay outside the bars, just out of his reach. Inside the cage was a shorter stick.

Sultan tries to reach the fruit with the smaller of the two sticks. Not succeeding, he tears at a piece of wire that projects from the netting of his cage, but that too is in vain. Then he gazes about him (there are always in the course of these tests some long pauses, during which the animals scrutinise the whole visible area). He suddenly picks up the little stick once more, goes up to the bars directly opposite to the long stick, scratches it towards him with the auxiliary, seizes it, and goes with it to the point opposite the objective, which he secures. From the moment his eyes fall upon the long stick, his procedure forms one consecutive whole.

In one much-quoted experiment, Sultan managed to fit two sticks together, to make a long stick to get the bananas.

Many of Köhler's more complex tests of problem-solving ability demonstrate the limitations of chimpanzee intelligence. Sultan usually hit on the best solution, but the others, among which there were big differences in ability, often failed utterly. In some tests a stick had to be used to push the fruit *away* from the chimpanzee, which stood outside a large box in which the fruit was contained. The ape could then run round and collect it from a point of access at the far side. Sultan solved this by accident in the first instance, but thereafter understood the principle, and succeeded on his own. Some of the other chimpanzees were unable to do anything other than pull the fruit toward them, although they could not get their hands to it on the near side.

What to us is a simple, obvious device—a ring hooked over a nail —was incomprehensible to the chimpanzees. In this problem, the fruit lay beyond the bars as usual, but the stick was tied to a rope, on one end of which was the ring, hooped over the nail. To obtain free use of the stick, the subject had merely to lift the ring off the nail in one simple movement. "Sultan pulls at the stick in the direction of the bars (and of the objective), chews and gnaws at the rope where it is tied to the stick, notices the connexion ring-nail only after considerable time, and then does not lift the wide open ring up a few centimetres, but tries to pull out or break off the nail! The final solution is that the stick itself is broken above the middle with a great effort, and the objective reached with the free part." On the next test, Sultan noticed the ring on the nail, and lifted it off, but the other chimpanzees never solved this puzzle at all.

The problems requiring the stacking of boxes for their solution are particularly interesting (see Plates 84 and 85). As we saw before, a chimpanzee is capable of solving the simpler problem of dragging *one* box across the floor to a position beneath a hanging bunch of bananas. It does this in a purposeful way, even though, as Köhler pointed out, it can have had no opportunity to practice this in the wild. However, the problem of putting one box on top of another in order to gain the prize produces all sorts of difficulties that surprise the human onlooker. From Köhler's descriptions of his subjects' behavior in these tests, it appears that they arrived at the *idea* that the second box must be used to make the first box higher, without having the necessary experience of how to achieve it:

At first everything goes well; as soon as the animals are quite familiar with the situation, and are convinced that they cannot obtain the objective with *one* box, a moment arrives when the second box is suddenly drawn into the task. They then drag it up (Tshego) or carry it just to the first box and all of a sudden stop and hesitate. With uncertain movements they wave the second one to and fro over the first (unless they drop it to the ground immediately, not knowing what to do with it as Sultan once did) and if you did not know that the animals see perfectly well in the ordinary sense of the word, you might believe that you were watching extremely weak-sighted creatures, that cannot clearly see where the first box is standing.

It is clear that to the chimpanzees, the concepts of gravity and statics do not occur naturally, and even when, according to Köhler, they are given plenty of opportunity to practice, they get no better. "Almost everything arising as 'questions of statics' during the building operations, he solves not with insight, but by trying around blindly. . . . This is where the chimpanzee seems to reach the limit of his capacity."

The operation of innate or previously acquired balancing mechanisms is evident here. For the chimpanzees judge the safety of a structure by the methods that might serve them best when testing branches in the trees:

If the upper box is brought into a position in which it stands quite satisfactorily from a static point of view, but in which it may still wobble a little (this motion having no significance) it is often taken, or turned, out of this good position, if either hand or foot discovers the oscillation; for the optics of the position has here no further noticeable significance for the chimpanzee's control over the situation. If by chance, or in any other way, the upper box comes into any position where it does not for the moment wobble, the chimpanzee will certainly climb up, even though a mere touch or friction at some point has for the moment steadied the box; really it may be quite unsteady and may fall over at once if weight is put on it. Thus Sultan, quite as a matter of course, once tried to climb up on the second box when it was precariously balanced on one corner only of the other one.

We have so far discussed at some length the problem-solving abilities of chimpanzees, as demonstrated in the work of Köhler, and more recent workers at the Yerkes Primate Laboratories. But what of the other apes? Do they show comparable "insight" too, or are chimpanzees unique?

One of Professor Yerkes's first major pieces of research was an investigation into what he termed "Ideational Behaviour" in an orangutan named Julius. Julius solved the problem of the bananas beyond the bars by the use of a stick, immediately. Yerkes also tested him on the box problem, but rather unfairly, for the first experiment required Julius to stack *two* boxes, which as we have seen with the chimpanzees represents a more difficult problem than the human observer tends to think. Not surprisingly, Julius did not reach the bananas, but in a ten-minute test period he attempted several different methods of a sensible nature. He climbed up the wall in different places to see if he could reach out; he actually placed the *larger* of the two boxes under the bananas, stood on it and reached upward; he approached Yerkes, who was standing in one corner of the cage, led him beneath the bananas, raised Yerkes's arm, and tried to climb upon it, but was prevented from doing so! Yerkes wrote: "I was amazed by Julius' behaviour this morning, for it was far more deliberate and apparently reflective as well as more persistently directed towards the goal than I had anticipated." After a few days' practice with the boxes, during which he had the solution of stacking the two boxes demonstrated to him by Yerkes, Julius was able to solve the problem. In all the tests of a practical nature given to him, Julius performed with the interest and adaptivity of a chimpanzee.

The only work on a gibbon using tests comparable to those described above was reported in 1927 by K. Drescher and W. Trendelenburg, and gave results on a rake problem comparable to those on monkeys. "It drew in the fruit when it lay in front of the rake, but made no movements to place the rake behind the fruit when it lay farther away." P. Guillaume and I. Meyerson also found that gibbons had no aptitude in this direction.

In the 1920's Yerkes worked intensively for three winters with a female mountain gorilla named Congo, who was aged five years at the start of the tests. Gorillas have conventionally been thought to be phylogenetically much more closely related to chimpanzees than is the orang (see Chapter 4), yet it is remarkable that, in problem-solving experiments, the gorilla is the odd one out of the large apes, while chimpanzee and orang show similar abilities. For example, contrast Congo's behavior in the usual stick-and-banana problem: "It became increasingly clear that she had neither natural nor acquired ability to use sticks, straws, or functionally similar objects in her cage to aid her in reaching desired food. She used but two methods: the attempt to squeeze her head and body through the feeding aperture, and reaching with extended arm." Her temper and bearing throughout were also totally different from the agitation and complaining of frustrated chimpanzees or orangs. "She was hungry, evidently wanted the food, and yet acted calmly. Surprising also to the observer were Congo's poise in the experiment, her deliberateness of movement and adaptive effort, and her self-control and emotional stability."

From her behavior it is plain that although Congo could not solve the problem, she was in a different class from the monkeys who also failed, because the cause of their failure was an inability to attend for more than a minute or two, and a total lack of calm, deliberate behavior in the test situation. Congo's dullness in the use of a stick is, however, very surprising, considering that, like the other apes, gorilla ancestors have an arboreal history. Yerkes next demonstrated the solution of the problem to her, but Congo did not imitate. When he then placed the stick touching the apple, Congo grasped it and the apple rolled toward her. But even then, although she had achieved success, Congo had not understood the method of solution. "Whenever the stick happened to come into contact with the apple, or be left by me in that position, she eagerly seized it and swept the apple towards her left. If, however, the stick was placed on the left side of the apple, instead of the right side, she would make precisely the same motion, sweeping it futilely toward her left and there abandoning it." Eventually Congo learned to use the stick, but even after practice her skill "continued to be very crude, consisting chiefly of pushing, throwing, jabbing, instead of well coordinated, steady directed movements." When the stick was placed inside Congo's cage instead of in position near the incentive, "Congo gave no indication of association of the stick with the problematic situation, and after a few trials we recorded failure of solution."

One might be tempted to assume, from these unexpected results, that Yerkes was dealing here with a particularly stupid gorilla, but two facts indicate that his observations may be typical. First, there are no authentic reports from the wild of gorillas using any form of implement, though such reports exist for wild orangs (page 161) and wild chimpanzees (page 123); also, throwing of objects is reported less frequently from zoos for gorillas than for chimpanzees or orangs. Second, the gorilla Congo when given other types of test, involving memory, for example, performed as well as, or better than, a chimpanzee. In one test, where the subject had to remember which can contained food, the cans being differentiated only by color, Congo made more correct choices than a chimpanzee. But in using sticks, piling boxes, undoing any mechanical devices—problems all quickly mastered by the other large apes—Congo was a failure. However, although Congo was inept and not quick to pick things up, when she did learn something, she learned it completely and forever. Experiments in succeeding years, after time gaps of several months, showed that Congo forgot none of her training, and even tended to show *improvement*, although she had had no practice in the interim. As her success increased, so did her motivation toward the tests. And throughout, Congo remained calm and deliberate, never wasting energy on useless attempts or emotional outbursts.

Comparisons such as these, between the behavior of the three large apes in captivity, show how impossible it is to devise test situations that can measure "intelligent" behavior without becoming involved in innate behavior tendencies, which occur naturally in all species, in adaptation to their way of life in the wild. Consider for a moment the demands of life in the wild for chimpanzees and orangs. Both species find most of their food in trees, and have adapted, as species, to branch manipulation. In contrast, the wild gorilla feeds mainly on pith and roots, and is not such a natural manipulator of branches. The gorilla's food is all around it, whereas it is a natural situation for a chimpanzee or orang to have to devise roundabout methods to obtain inaccessible clumps of hanging fruit. Second, both chimpanzees and orangs depend on seasonal location of fruits, and this enters into both their superior capacity to appreciate spatial relationships, and the greater energy they put into the test situations. Searching about in the undergrowth, as gorillas do, requires on the other hand dogged persistence and patience, which they show in tests.

Nevertheless, such comparative experiments are immensely valuable, even if inconclusive in absolute terms. Since Yerkes's and Köhler's pioneer work, there have been relatively few other important contributions to our understanding of problem solving in the apes. Some experiments, however, were done at the San Diego Zoo, which has long been famous for its apes. In the thirties, H. C. Bingham, of the Yerkes Primate Laboratories, did some tests, which were reported by Mrs. B. J. Benchley, in her own terms, in 1942.

Mrs. Benchley's account is interesting because it describes some experiments in which the gorillas come out best by virtue of their sterling virtues of patience, persistence, and nonexcitement, mentioned above. These tests used what were called slot boxes. These boxes were 5 feet long and 6 inches square, fastened horizontally to the cage bars inside the cage. In the middle on the top surface was a 2-foot-long slot, wide enough to admit the fingers of an ape, but not wide enough to allow it to hold or remove an object inside the box. Two more similar slots, on the frontal surface, were situated toward either end of the box. The box was closed at one end, and fruit was placed near the closed end. The solution to the problem was to slide the fruit along by working the slots with both hands until it was pushed out at the open end. There were two gorillas sharing the cage, wild-born and captured together, Mbongo and Ngagi. First one gorilla, then the other, attempted the problem, each patiently waiting until the other had finished:

He [Mbongo] moved this time with greater caution, slowly shoving the fruit along to a spot where he could see it through the top slot. At this point he held the fruit between the fingers of his right hand in the upper slot, and his left hand in the side slot. He tried several times to manipulate it in some way to get it through the slots. I thought once he had quit, and again that he had lost the fruit, but suddenly poking the big fingers of his left hand down into the top slot, he slid it along easily. His right hand was ready at the third slot, and the fruit moved out in the matter of a surprisingly few minutes.

Ngagi had been observing carefully the progress of Mbongo, and when the fruit rolled out, he took it. Mbongo was already trying to get at a second piece. "This time Ngagi held out his great palm and the apple rolled into it." This altruistic behavior of Mbongo's, doing all the hard work while Ngagi collected the prize, is certainly unusual in accounts of behavior of the other great apes. Mbongo got better and better in succeeding days, with Ngagi watching and eating the fruit. Then one day Ngagi grunted, and Mbongo moved away. Ngagi then performed as rapidly as Mbongo had been doing, proving his own careful observation and capacity to imitate. The regular tests had a great influence on the well-being of the two gorillas, who looked forward immensely to their test sessions, and also became more lively in other ways.

The behavior of the other apes in the zoo on the same slot-box problem was strikingly different. The chimpanzees were interested only in the fruit and not in the way the box worked, as Mbongo had seemed to be. They solved the problem impatiently by breaking the fruit up into little mashed pieces with their fingers and fishing these out through the slots. Also, they kept approaching the experimenters, asking for help, which the gorillas never did. The orangs also had no time for the slot box. "They used their technical skill to remove the box; their strength to destroy it; but at no time did they solve the problem of removing the fruit either whole or piecemeal."

Some experiments rather similar in type were done on a young female gibbon, obtained by Louis Boutan in about 1908. Much less work has been done in this field on the gibbon than on the large apes. Pepée, the gibbon, was presented on each test with a box, one side of which was made of wire. Fruit inside the box could be seen through the wire. A hinged door was in the top of the box, which, when one or more sliding bars had been removed, could be raised by a knob to obtain the prize. After trial-and-error experience with these boxes, the gibbon appeared to learn the function of the sliding bars and the knob, for different combinations were later dealt with efficiently, without mistakes. Pepée also retained perfectly her level of performance after a three-month holiday in the country. Boutan noted that once the gibbon arrived at the solution, her performance immediately became perfect and she showed evidence of understanding the method of solution. Yerkes commented on this: "It seems then that Boutan discovered from his observation of the gibbon what was revealed to Köhler in his experimental study of the chimpanzee and to Yerkes in his work with the orang-utan; namely sudden or immediate adaptation."

Another study of problem solving in a gibbon was done by Fae Hall at the London Zoo in 1960. The tests given were not for the most part the standard ones used in experiments with the larger apes, but are nevertheless of great interest. The gibbon was never made hungry for the tests, but worked at all times for the incentive of an extra grape. The first problem consisted of three plastic boxes inside each other, with a grape visible in the center one. Each box was fastened by an elastic band. Honey, the gibbon, was a female, four and a half years old, not fully mature. She attacked the boxes in trial-and-error fashion, tossing and pulling them from foot to hand for several minutes of intense concentration. It was the concentration that chiefly impressed Hall. Finally, Honey obtained the grape. There is evidence that, as in the other apes, older age, even without direct experience of similar problems, is an asset in intelligence tests, for as a comparison, an adult female gibbon called Cleo was also given the plastic-box test, and showed more comprehension of the nature of the problem by actually pulling at the elastic bands to get them off the boxes.

Another problem given to Honey was a stylus maze, where in order to release a grape she had to guide a stylus along a T-maze which could be angled in different positions. She learned to obtain the grape in one position of the maze. When it was reversed, Honey showed flexibility of response by calmly walking around the apparatus to the other side, where the problem immediately became the one that she was used to solving. From these and other tests given to Honey, it appears that the curiosity and adaptability characteristic of the apes is also present in gibbons and that their persistence and application to tasks may be greater than that of monkeys.

Thus, to summarize briefly the results of problem-solving tests on the apes, it appears that all of them can show, in certain situations, evidence of a mental process in which the solution to a problem is perceived in the form of an idea of the consequences of the subject's anticipated actions and that this leads to purposive behavior when the animal encounters the same or essentially similar situations. This "idea" results from prior experience and innate properties of brain organization. In addition, each of the apes seems to have especially well-developed talents in particular directions. The chimpanzee appears to excel in the use of implements, and in general plasticity of behavior. Orangs have similar abilities but show a particular flair for mechanical contraptions. Gorillas seem to be rather less implement-minded, but show great funds of calm persistence and dogged determination that sometimes allow them to succeed where the others fail. The gibbon may be more like the monkeys in its capacities; nevertheless, it impressed Hall with its application to the task and its flexibility of response.

It is in these tests of problem solving discussed so far that the mental abilities of the apes are best studied. For in the constructive manipulation of the environment in the search for a solution, stages in the process by which the subject attempts and finally suceeds can be described and analyzed.

Very many other kinds of tests have been given to captive apes, some of which will be mentioned shortly. Whole types of tests, however, will have to be left out of the discussion. These include all those investigating chiefly the perceptual and discriminatory processes of the apes, which show that an ape tends to make judgments, see patterns, perceive relative size, or brightness, generalize shape and color, in much the same way that humans do. Other tests involve memory, or delayed response to a situation, and here again apes come nearest to humans in performance. Each study, however, shows very great differences in performance between one individual ape and another.

We shall now look at a few other ways in which faculties that we would term intelligence in a human being are tested in apes.

One series of experiments made by Yerkes on an orang, two monkeys, and some other animals is of especial interest. He set up a row of nine boxes, each big enough to contain an animal. Each box had an entrance door in front of the subject, and an exit door from the far side of the box. On each test a selection of these boxes had open doors. One of them contained a food reward, hidden under a receptacle. Yerkes wanted to find out if his subjects could learn to choose the correct box by obeying certain principles. The first principle he tried was that the last open box on the left was the correct one. At first sight the results are surprising. Crows learned this in 50 to 100 trials. Rats learned in 170 to 350 trials, and pigs in 50. One monkey learned in 70 trials, the other in 132. And Julius, the orang? It took Julius 290 trials to learn this simple concept, putting him behind all the animals tested except the slowest of the rats!

Why was Julius's score so low? It seems that he worked with *methods* different from those of the other experimental subjects. They all started with high errors, and by trial and error gradually eliminated wrong choices, until they were making a high percentage of correct ones. But right from the start Julius appeared to think he could beat the system, and chose on the basis of a *hypothesis* decided upon by himself. This was that the open door nearest to the starting position was the correct one. In fact his hypothesis yielded him consistently 60 percent correct choices from the beginning. Thus, for the first 200 trials Julius chose this way, and was satisfied with the results. But Yerkes was not. After 230 trials he arranged the selection of boxes to choose from in such a way that the nearest one was *never* correct. For the next 60 trials Julius made all mistakes, and rapidly became discouraged. On trial 289 Julius made 7/10 incorrect choices. On trial 290 he made 10/10 *correct*, and made no further mistakes on subsequent trials. This is a remarkable result, and the learning curve of Julius's responses plotted on a graph is unique (Figure 15). Yerkes wrote that he was "justified in concluding from the evidence at hand that the orangutan solved this simple problem ideationally." A human, too, would solve such a problem by trying one hypothesis after another, until he hit upon the correct one.

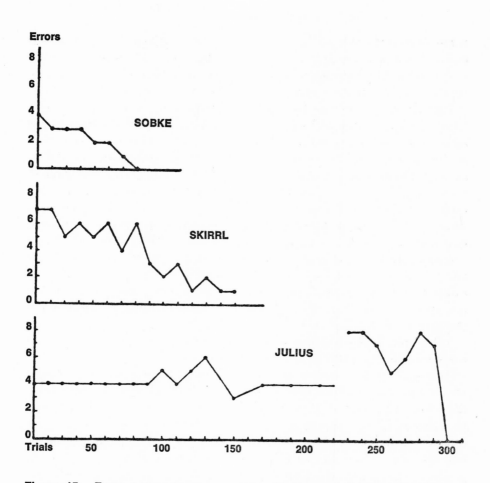

Figure 15. Error curves for two monkeys, Sobke and Skirrl, and Julius the orangutan.

On the next problem, the principle governing the choice of box was more complex. The animals were required to learn that the reward was in the *second* of the open boxes from the right. Julius failed entirely on this, but used the same method as before, acting on the basis of one hypothesis after another so consistently that on any day Yerkes was able to predict with 90 to 100 percent accuracy which box he would choose. But Julius soon got discouraged, and stopped trying. There are, it seems, dangers in being too bright, for the monkeys tested succeeded finally on the basis of large numbers of trial-and-error choices, the correct responses gradually becoming reinforced. One monkey required 400 trials, the other, 1,070. Pigs learned to choose correctly after 340 to 600 trials, but rats and crows had not learned after 800, at which point their tests were discontinued.

One of Köhler's original tests—the one where Sultan had to choose between two or more crossed strings, only one of which was attached to the banana—was frequently used in later years, especially by workers at the Yerkes Primate Laboratories, as a test for comparing the abilities of various types of monkeys and apes. The "patterned string tests," as they became known, could be graded in order of difficulty to form a sort of IQ test.

G. Finch gave a series of eleven string tests, starting from two simple parallel strings, and increasing in difficulty to visually confusing combinations of strings crisscrossing over and back again. A few years earlier, identical tests had been given by Harry Harlow to a number of species of monkeys. The chimpanzees solved all eleven problems, whereas even the cleverest of the monkeys, the spider, could not get beyond grade nine. Gorillas, tested by A. H. Riesen and others, were as good as chimpanzees. Honey, the London Zoo gibbon, was also given some of the simpler patterned string tests, and was able to learn the correct one to pull after a number of repetitions of each pattern. The wily adult female Cleo, however, was able to solve the complicated pattern of the two strings crossed over twice by following along the string with her eye as a human would.

And of course it is the *behavior* of the apes when confronted with this kind of test that is the interesting thing if one is attempting to understand the types of thought processes of which they are capable. Often, however, the behavior is not reported in publications. H. G. Birch did give accounts of his chimpanzees in the patterned-string situation. He confirmed the findings of Yerkes and Köhler that the apes typically have a systematic approach to a problem. For example Art, faced with the crossed-string situation, worked on the hypothesis that the linearly most direct string toward the fruit was the right one. As it happened in the alternated presentation of the tests, this worked out to be right 50 percent of the time. Jojo, the most intelligent of his subjects, referred to by H. W. Nissen above, developed a clever way of working it out. "Before making a selection she would crouch down until her eye was level with the table and sight along the string to the food, then select the string making a direct line with the food." It is observations of this sort that tell us that the individual chimpanzee, at any rate, has the capacity to understand the nature of the problem facing it, and to proceed rationally.

To *learn* new skills and to respond to new situations are perhaps the most important factors in human intelligence. Of especial value is cumulative learning, or learning sets, whereby having learned an efficient way of dealing with a situation, one is able to adapt the response to another situation, which is similar but not the same, by a process of generalization. In recent decades much work has been done on the abilities of monkeys and apes to learn cumulatively in this way, using consecutive series of choice tests. The subject is required to choose one of two or more stimulus objects, for example, the odd one out of an array of circles and a triangle, a card with three objects on it, a particular color, an object similar to a show object, or simply one particular stimulus object out of two. The equipment used in testing choice discrimination and concept formation in learning experiments of the kind described has been developed and refined to the extent that in some cases the experimenter's only work is to arrange for the programing of a number of tests in a computer unit. The subjects enter a special test cubicle, where they are faced with an automatic display panel, usually electronically controlled, which flashes on the choice of stimulus (see Plates 86 and 87). The subject responds by pressing a button below the stimulus of his choice. If this is correct, a tidbit is delivered. If it is incorrect he gets nothing; alternatively he may get punished by means of a mild electric shock or by being plunged into darkness. The results of thousands of discrimination tests, automatically presented, are processed by the computer for perusal by the experimenter. Some experiments of this type, which have potential interest for the subject of this chapter, were done by D. M. Rumbaugh on learning sets in gorillas, chimpanzees, and orangs, with a view to comparing the capacities of the three species.

He familiarized a young gorilla, chimpanzee, and orang with the apparatus, requiring them to learn a discrimination between a circle and a square, the correct choice being rewarded. The gorilla learned this initial problem in 139 trials, the chimpanzee in 273, the orang in 280. Next came the learning-set series of 600 different problems, each of which required the choice between two household objects, for 6 trials, after which two more objects were presented for the next problem. After 400 different problems had been presented, the efficiency of the learning sets established was measured by taking the percentage of correct choices on trial 2 of the last 200 problems, that is, how efficiently did each subject learn to adapt to the new problems and how quickly did he fix on the correct choice each time? The gorilla did best again with a trial-2 efficiency of 70 percent correct choices. The chimpanzee had 60 percent, the orang 58 percent. These results could be taken to support the Belle Benchley account of the patient, persistent ability of her gorillas to solve problems of some kinds that chimpanzees and orangs failed in. It would be interesting to know whether the superior performance of the gorilla was due to superior ability or simply greater interest, patience, motivation, or some other psychological factor. Three thousand trials is a long time for an ape.

In some other experiments, Rumbaugh tested other apes of older age groups, and his results indicated that gorillas got better at learning-set experiments the older they were, while chimpanzees were more variable, reaching a peak of achievement earlier than the gorillas. Orangs appeared to start at a high level of achievement, but the older orangs did less well than the younger. Only one subject was tested for most age groups, and until more behavioral data are accumulated the exact significance of these results remains uncertain. However, it seems that in learning experiments, gorillas are at least as good as the other large apes. The capacity for persistence and determination already discussed perhaps enables them to do even better in some experiments.

Finally, Rumbaugh put together the results on learning-set experiments in a group of squirrel monkeys and in his apes. It was apparent that while some squirrel monkeys were capable of learning how to do discrimination problems as efficiently as apes, they were not able to adjust to the changes and reversals of the problems as efficiently as could the apes. Rumbaugh thinks that this ability to respond rapidly to a new problem in the correct way is a good measure of species difference in intelligence.

There remain, however, many other measures of intelligence in the human sense of the word. One is a social value without which the human species could not have survived—the capacity to cooperate with others on a task for the common good. Cooperation of different individuals in teamwork for the mutual benefit of all is a typically human behavior, and appears to involve the intelligent ability to postpone immediate and selfish motives for the later good of all. From what we know of the humanoid thought processes of the apes, especially chimpanzees, we might expect that they would spontaneously learn to cooperate if the situation demanded it, and if the circumstances were fully obvious to the animals. However, such is not the case, as M. P. Crawford showed in his experiments on the Yerkes Laboratory chimpanzees Ross, Bula, Kambi, Bimba, and Alpha. First, each chimpanzee was individually taught to pull a rope inside its cage, which drew toward it a heavy box outside the cage, with a piece of orange on it. When the box was close enough, the chimpanzee was able to extend its hand to get the orange. Then the box was made too heavy for a single chimpanzee to pull it in. Two ropes were attached, one to each corner, and two chimpanzees were placed together in the cage. In the new situation, each animal first discovered that it was not strong enough to pull the load alone; moreover all the relevant features of the problem situation were visually available to the subjects, and there were two pieces of orange one on either side of the weighted box near the rope. It would seem to be a situation where an insightful solution could typically occur. However, out of the five chimpanzees involved, no two of them ever achieved their rewards through cooperative teamwork. "Typically, one animal would pull, while the other watched or played about the cage. When the first finished pulling, the other would take the rope, often the same one, and pull while the first one did something else."

Although Crawford was able, by long and laborious training, to teach the chimpanzees, by stages, to pull together on the ropes, we are not so interested in this chapter in the results of specific training procedures on ape performance. What we are really interested in is the extent to which apes spontaneously show natural abilities in situations demanding intelligent and adaptive behavior. And on the test demanding ability to cooperate, Crawford's chimpanzees failed miserably. The observations of Köhler tend to conform with Crawford's findings. For many of the tests, such as box building or stick use, several of the chimpanzees were presented with the problem as a group. Usually the animals all worked individually for themselves, taking boxes off a neighbor's pile or fighting to climb on a construction to get the prize. As Köhler wrote, "Mutual obstruction is more frequent than mutual co-operation."

But on one observed occasion something like a cooperative effort occurred, almost by accident, though the animals concerned were undoubtedly working each for its own interest. Grande realized that one way to reach the prize was to bring over a large cage standing in a corner. It was very heavy:

She shook it to and fro, to turn it over and roll it towards the objective, but could not move it. Rana forthwith came up, and laid hold of the cage in the most adequate way, and the two were in the act of lifting and rolling it, when Sultan joined them and, seizing one side of the cage, 'helped' with great energy. Alone, none of the three could have stirred the cage from its place, but under their united efforts—which were timed together perfectly —it rapidly approached the goal.

Sultan then leaped onto it and took the fruit.

The above seems to be a unique occurrence in chimpanzee behavior. Apart from this, however, Sultan was known to help other chimpanzees he was watching, if they could not solve their problems. He sometimes passed sticks through the bars to them, and on one occasion joined two sticks together for Chica, who was unable to do it, and gave the extended stick back to her. Sultan, obviously an unusually intelligent and perceptive chimpanzee, seemed to be really interested in problem solution for its own sake.

Taken as a whole, the evidence appears to indicate that chimpanzees do have enough understanding of some situations to be able to cooperate, but that they rarely do so, because it is not a natural thing for them to do. Cooperative teamwork probably evolved as a specifically human attribute in response to the ecological pressures of life on the savannahs.

Another experiment, again on chimpanzees, has shown that they have the ability to acquire motives and to learn tasks on the basis of these acquired motives, an essentially human way of behaving. For if we think about it, very few of our activities are performed for the purpose of directly obtaining satisfaction of a primary drive such as hunger, sex, or defense of territory. Most of what we do is to achieve a stage in a whole chain of motives, many of which are acquired, some on the basis of attachment to a primary drive such as our daily work, to get money to buy food; others are motives purely socially induced by imitation or ambition, such as the motive to have the newest or fastest model of car. Whether this ability to acquire motives is to be used as an indication of intelligence is an uncertain point, but it is certainly typical of humans, and as such it is interesting to find the seeds of the same behavior in chimpanzees. Wolfe and, later, J. T. Cowles of the Yerkes Laboratories trained their subjects to use small colored disks to operate a raisin-vending machine. After a while the chimpanzees came to value the disks, much in the same way as we do money. So much so that the animals worked on choice problems set them, though the only immediate rewards were the disks. They would go to the vending machine to redeem them for raisins. No chimpanzees, however, were reported to become misers, hoarding away the disks for their own sake, and being reluctant to turn them into goods.

Among the more imaginative ways in which the mental abilities of the apes have been explored are some of the activities of the 6571st Aeromedical Laboratory in New Mexico, where Ham and Enos, the space chimps, were trained. Perhaps the most spectacular was the success achieved in getting chimpanzees to play ticktacktoe (noughts and crosses) (see Plate 88). Each of the two players sat in its own cubicle, and in each cubicle there was a display panel showing the results of its own performance and that of the opponent. After a time, the apes got the idea that to win (and get a reward) they had to get three of their own symbols in a row.

A unique observation made by Mrs. Hayes on her home-raised chimpanzee Viki indicated that Viki indulged in purely imaginary make-believe play much as a two to three-year-old human child may do. Viki was accustomed to going to the bathroom where her potty was kept, when it was about time for her to use it. While she was waiting, however, she was allowed to play in the bathroom. It was during one of these waiting periods that Cathy Hayes noticed Viki trailing her hand behind her in an odd way, and looking back at it from time to time. Then she began to do hauling movements, hand over hand. It was the same kind of movement she made when playing with one of her pulltoys on a string. On a later occasion, Viki ran round and round the bathroom furniture, and seemed to get the imaginary string all tangled up, for she fiddled about for some time, and when Cathy Hayes offered to undo it for her, and made the appropriate movements of untangling string, Viki heaved a sigh of relief. Taken on its own, this observation is difficult to interpret, but when added to what we know from an earlier chapter on home-raised apes, on their ability to paint aesthetically pleasing pictures, and their seeming understanding of human misery or illness, it all seems to indicate that the "higher" mental processes of imagination, creativity, and sympathy are present in apes at least in simple form.

So far, in our discussion of their capabilities, it has appeared that the apes, in particular chimpanzees upon which by far the greatest part of the work has been done, show in less developed form most of the mental processes that are often assumed to be the prerogative of man. They show ability to weigh a problem situation by taking into account relevant features of the surroundings, and act purposefully toward a solution; faced with any task, even one where they do not comprehend all the factors, apes tend to form hypotheses as to the correct solution, and act on the basis of each one until it is proved wrong, rather than tackle it by trial and error. They show a high learning potential; they show flexible rather than stereotyped responses; they have ideas, concepts, plans, and imagination; and they can work on the basis of acquired motives. But, after all, they are demonstrably not so intelligent as humans (on human-devised tests), so what are their limitations—why have they not mastered the earth? Some of their failures, such as the lack of spontaneous cooperation, or their inability to understand how one box can be made to balance on another, are clearly due to their own particular environmental adaptations—as predominantly forest-living vegetarians. Close cooperation between humans in a group, for a common purpose, was probably evolved in response to the pressures of seasonal savannah life, and the need for the hunting of larger game by emergent man. A vegetarian primate forages for his food individually, and there is very little advantage to organized cooperation in the food quest.

But in other problems set for apes, failure was due to a different reason. Julius cannot get the idea "second from the right," although he can understand "leftness"; Köhler's chimpanzees need all relevant objects within visual range if they are to solve the problem; Congo fails to realize the difference between "apple to left of stick" and "apple to right of stick." It is obvious that the apes are limited by their lack of that powerful aid to logical thinking—*speech*.

The question of why the apes have never evolved even rudimentary speech is a puzzling one, though even here the answer must lie in the nature of the selection pressures of the environment. Of course, all apes, and monkeys too, do have a complex vocal repertoire of calls, expressions, and postures whereby they communicate their mood, their intentions, or their status to one another. This "language" extends to man to a great extent, in features such as crying, or glowering, or using a particular tone of voice. But all the calls of apes are involuntary expressions, communicating anger, threat, fear, surprise, sympathy, hunger, maternal authority, social excitement. There is no start in the direction of the identification of specific arbitrary sounds with particular objects, movements, or concepts, made voluntarily and without emotional content.

The difference in mental organization is seen not only in the lack of speech but also in the low degree of *comprehension* of human words spoken to the ape. There is evidence that in responding to human commands the ape takes into account the total cues of the situation rather than associating particular sounds with particular objects. For although the Kelloggs showed that at sixteen months the chimpanzee Gua could respond to ninety-five phrases, most of these occurred in particular situations predisposing the ape to do a certain thing, such as "Hand me your bib"; "Open your mouth"; "Show me the shoe." Cathy Hayes pointed out that chimpanzee Viki's response to certain words was dependent upon what stage of a routine she was at. For example "Give me a pin" always followed her being placed on a clean diaper. "Would you like to go to a show?" was responded to blankly in mid-morning, but greeted with wild excitement after dark. Some words were understood, however, irrespective of supplementary cues. Mrs. Hayes estimated there were about fifty of these when Viki was three years old. Some of them proved that Viki was in fact capable of grasping the specific identity of an object with a sound, if she was familiar enough with it. She could "go get the dog" even if it was in another room; she could turn on the water or switch on the light when asked. Soon, however, another limitation of Viki's neural organization became apparent. New *combinations* of perfectly understood items had to be learned as if they were new words. For example Viki knew "Kiss me" and "Bring me the dog" very well indeed. But "Kiss the dog" was not understood. Viki appeared to learn this as a new phrase, after the Hayeses had demonstrated the meaning.

The Hayeses' greatest effort was put into trying to teach Viki to talk, for at the outset of their experiment it seemed reasonable that an intelligent chimpanzee, obtained at birth and brought up in an encouraging and stimulating environment, should be able to learn this. Only two previous attempts were known from the literature, one of a performing chimpanzee that could say "Mama," the other of an orang taught to say "Papa" and "cup." Early in Viki's development the Hayeses noticed a significant difference between her and a human baby. During her first three months, Viki produced most of the instinctive chimpanzee calls, such as the scream of distress, the *coo-oo* of misery, *uh-uh-uh* of greeting, bark of anger. All these were reflex sounds made in response to certain situations. Otherwise Viki lay silent in her cot. At about three months a human infant begins to *babble,* playing with consonants and vowels, repeated on and on. Quite spontaneously the human baby in this way practices the motor skills of speech, for use some months later when his brain matures sufficiently for him to attempt to reproduce the sounds he hears. But Viki did not prepare herself in this way. She did make a few experimental sounds, but so rarely that they were big events. And at four months even these ceased altogether. "Now at this age, when the human child begins making every conceivable sound, Viki grew increasingly silent." It became obvious that Viki would not learn to speak spontaneously. So the Hayes undertook to teach her.

The first stage of active training was the hardest—to get Viki to utter any sound at all *to order,* that is, to control her own vocalization. "She was five months old the day I first held out a portion of milk and said "Speak!" She looked at the milk, and then at me, and of course said nothing. I waited for fifteen minutes and then rose to leave. As I moved away, worried little "oo oo's" broke the silence and I quickly rewarded her for making the sound." This went on for five more months, with no further progress. Then Viki got the idea. "Suddenly one day when she was ten months old, she began making a very strange new sound. The first time we heard it we were surprised and vaguely displeased for it was an ugly sound, hoarse and strained. It was like someone whispering 'ah' as loudly as possible and with great effort. When Viki said it her face contorted while her eyes assumed the tense preoccupied stare of a stutterer. Then from her lips burst this rasping tortured 'ahhhhhhh.'" This achievement was immense for a chimpanzee, a purposeful sound. Viki used this voluntary utterance from this time on as her "asking sound": asking for food, to be got up out of bed, to be taken off her potty, to be given a toy. When this had gone on for another four months, the Hayes began to try to get Viki to form consonants. "When Viki was fourteen months old Keith began this training at her morning meal. Holding her on his lap he slipped his hand around her head so that his thumb was on her upper lip and his other fingers cradled her chin. In this position he could work her lips open and shut to form the m." In this way Viki was made to say "Mama." Eventually Viki's lips learned to form the *m's* unaided, and "Mama" was her first real word. In later months she learned to say "Papa" and "cup."

As Viki's capacity to reproduce human words was obviously extremely limited, in later years the Hayeses reversed the procedure and began to try to build up a communications system based on sounds that Viki naturally made herself. They gave meanings to her sounds, and Viki was able to learn a larger vocabulary of self-expression by this more sensible method. But the basic difference between the ape and a human child remained: "Viki readily imitates our production of her mouth sounds and learns meanings we assign to them. . . . However, unlike the human child who has just begun to speak, Viki uses her words only for the practical purpose of getting what she wants. She does not engage in purely sociable conversation, or ego-centric expression."

It follows from all this that, however intelligent an ape may be in other ways, it lacks something quite essential in the organization of its brain, which in the human motivates and develops speech. It lacks the ability to describe objectively features of its environment. It appears only to be able to express ideas concerning *feelings*, wanting food or drink, and basic social needs. This is one of the apes' greatest limitations, and forms a crucial difference between them and man.

For it is a fact that until the age of speech development in human children, the juvenile ape learns faster and develops motor skills more quickly than does the human child. For example, the home-raised chimpanzees Viki and Gua were given each month the Gesell Tests for Preschool Children. They were both equal to, or slightly ahead of, the average performance of a child of the same age. At 18 months, Cathy Hayes reported of the chimpanzee Viki,

she was turning in results typical of this age. At the most recent testing she had solved the three-hole form-board. She built impressive towers of six or seven blocks. She could draw a straight line in imitation, changing to a scribble as the tester did so. She could feed herself with a spoon, inhibit forbidden acts on command, open doors, wave bye-bye, turn the pages of her picture books, and was showing some promise in washing and dressing herself.

Chimpanzee Gua was tested in comparison with the boy Donald, and at 16 months she passed 15 of the Gesell tests, while Donald at 15½ months had passed 16.

The Kelloggs wrote:

There are a number of learned tasks in which the ape has shown herself to be actually above the average human as old or even older than herself. Examples of superior behaviour of this sort consist of her "telling" the experimenters in bladder and bowel training, her unusual progress at eating with a spoon, and her striking advancement in opening doors. There are other quite obvious respects in which Gua is inferior to normal humans of her own age. Instances of this are her retardation in picking up the pellet with the thumb-and-finger reaction of the child, her apparent inability to make any progress towards inhibiting the hand-to-mouth reaction, and her lack of speech development.

Thus it appears that Gua, an infant chimpanzee, did very well in general on tests designed for infant humans. For comparison, the Kelloggs also tested both chimpanzee and child on the kind of intelligence tests chiefly designed for *apes*. And in these too, Gua at 14½ months did better than Donald at 17 months.

One such test was called the "suspended cookie test," and was identical in design to Köhler's box-and-banana experiment. The only difference was that the subjects Gua and Donald were given three practice trials with the chair already in position under the suspended cookie. Then the chair was placed elsewhere in the room. Gua succeeded on trial 1 in pushing the chair beneath the cookie and obtaining it. Donald failed for the first three trials. Gua's method showed her up to advantage too, for she always looked at the cookie, and pushed the chair straight toward it. Donald, however, only rarely glanced at the cookie, but followed a "more or less stereotyped series of movements which eventually put the chair in the right place."

On a test similar in design to Köhler's stick-and-banana test, neither managed very well at first. They looked through a wire screen across a doorway toward an apple out of reach beyond. A *T*-shaped rake lay with the apple enclosed on the near side. Like the monkeys, Gua and Donald both pulled it in immediately. But, like the monkeys again, their troubles started when the apple was placed a little to one side of the rake. Both were then given weeks of trials on this test, interspersed with the easy ones where the apple could be drawn in, in order that their motivation should remain high. After over a hundred trials, the Kelloggs demonstrated how the rake could be moved to the right to get the apple. The infants learned this, and then, like the gorilla Congo, when the apple was placed on the left side, they still moved the rake to the right. In all, both required about 500 trials to learn the coordinated manipulation of the rake as an implement. The prolonged process of the early learning of such skills confirms Schiller's results on captive chimpanzees at the Yerkes Laboratory, reported earlier in this chapter. He found that up to four years of age, young chimpanzees did not respond with insight to the stick problems, but "just learn to do something to the stick before obtaining food." His results showed that there is "an important maturational element in the adaptive use of a stick as a rake by chimpanzees." And in humans there is too, as Donald's performance shows.

Gua's performance with the chair on the suspended-cookie test seems exceptional for a fourteen-month-old ape. Her progress here may be due to the stimulating environment of the human household, with its opportunity to manipulate and experiment with objects, in her play.

The operation of a rich environment on the development of problem-solving ability in the chimpanzee is well demonstrated by Cathy Hayes. For she gave a series of tests to Viki when the animal was three years of age, to another three-year-old chimpanzee called Frans reared in the Yerkes Laboratory, and to a little girl of three, called Chrissie. The first problem was a small wire tunnel, containing a gaily wrapped prize. Nearby was a long stick. None of the subjects was able to figure it out for himself, so each was given one demonstration of how he could poke out the prize with the stick. Viki and Chrissie then did it successfully after a little experimental behavior. Frans was unable to achieve success, being totally unfamiliar with the use of a stick. In further tests the same relationship held. Viki and the little girl of three performed equally well, while Frans was at an enormous disadvantage owing to the meager opportunities of his limited environment.

By way of summary we can say that in comparison with monkeys and other animals, apes are certainly more intelligent; they can solve problems of far greater complexity than any other species except man; they can, in the case of chimpanzees and orangs, discover spontaneously the use of implements to manipulate their environment; in problems requiring the use of their natural abilities, their methods of solution resemble those of humans in the same situation, in that their actions eventually show purpose, and insight into the nature of the problem. The development of the infant chimpanzee, which is known in the greatest detail, proceeds faster than that of the human infant, and the ape shows great learning power and ability to profit from a complex environment. Later, at the age when the human child starts to use language to aid him in his thought processes, the ape begins to show at a disadvantage. It seems to be the lack of underlying neural organization that in the human motivates the communication of specific information about the environment, and leads to the formation of symbolic concepts, that chiefly limits the intellectual powers of the apes.

It may be, however, that we have got it all wrong and that the apes are more intelligent than we think. For some African tribes traditionally believe that apes can talk but that they will not allow humans to know this, lest the humans put them to work. So perhaps the apes refuse to talk, preferring to remain outside the terrible human "rat race." Köhler, in fact, provides some circumstantial evidence that the apes' great fear is being made to work, for he reports how he once tried to get Sultan, the most intelligent of his chimpanzees, to go round in the evening after they had all been fed, collecting the fruit skins, and putting them in a basket. "He quickly grasped what was required of him, and did it—but only for two days. On the third day he had to be told every moment to go on; on the fourth he had to be ordered from one banana skin to the next, and on the fifth and following days his limbs had to be moved for every movement, seizing, picking up, walking, holding the skins over the basket, letting them drop, and so on, because they stopped dead at whatever place they had come to, or to which they had been led."

I am sure that Sultan was intelligent enough to know that that was the best way to get Köhler to do the dirty work himself.

CHAPTER **10**

Some Modern Myths

PEOPLE, IT SEEMS, need to believe in monsters. The long struggle of our ancestors against the natural elements, the big wild animals, and perhaps other manlike types later to become extinct may have something to do with it—possibly we need to re-create frightening creatures that we can then defeat in order to test our conviction that we are masters on earth. No one knows why, but monsters are as popular today as they ever were in medieval times, or in ancient Greece and Rome. One of the best-known popular monsters is a giant ape—often a gigantic gorilla.

In Chapter 2 we traced the progress of zoologists in finding the "Pongo" of Battell, describing its anatomy and behavior, and classifying it as a new kind of great ape. Science put the lowland gorilla on the map in 1847 and the mountain gorilla in 1902. One might think that, having entered the journals and textbooks of the academics, the gorilla would no longer be fair game for the world of fantasy. There was no more doubt about its existence; stuffed specimens and, later, live ones were to be seen in the museums and zoos of Europe and America; it

[[225

was just a big ape. In classical times, monsters were invariably put in unknown and unexplored parts of the world—"the Indies," for example. When "the Indies" and other unknown parts were explored in the Renaissance, and the old monsters could not be found, it was easy enough for scientists such as Tulp and Tyson to discredit them. In a few centuries nearly the whole world was known, and most if its fauna described. No dragons, no sphinxes, no giants, no "mantichoras," no griffins, no goat-footed Pans and satyrs were found. And so the myths associated with them, which had thrived in the darkness of the ages past, breathed their last. Except for the gorilla.

For some reason, increased knowledge of the facts about the gorilla has had no effect on the original myth of the gigantic hairy manlike monster of huge proportions and terrible power hinted at in the classics and clearly described in medieval times.

At the same time, three English bestiaries from this period, all of which still exist, portray a huge manlike creature from "the East," which feeds on man. This creature is described as follows: "huge men with legs twelve feet long: bodies seven feet broad, black in color, 'whom we rightly call enemies, for whomever they catch they quickly devour.'" Another description runs: "Men of three colours, lion-headed, twenty feet long, with huge mouths. If pursued, they flee and sweat blood." Many fabulous creatures occur in bestiaries, and there is no guarantee that they are even based on living species. Perhaps these tales relate to the large apes, but it is just as likely, perhaps more so, that they have their origins in earlier tales of giants, and, like the monster Grendel in *Beowulf,* are expressions of a deep-set human fear of something bigger and more brutal than he is himself.

The twentieth century has shown how few people really want the truth, when it is dull, and when a dramatic alternative exists that may not be the truth but is so much more exciting. All those who set out to destroy the image of an evil, murderous ape achieved no more than paper victories. The public cherished its myth.

The first author to draw on this myth to make a powerful story was Edgar Allan Poe. His short story "The Murders in the Rue Morgue" first appeared in 1841, and was widely read (Plate 89). The narrator of this sordid horror story starts off with a quotation from a Paris newspaper giving details of a sensational double murder. At 3:00 A.M. the people of the Saint-Roch district were awakened by shrieks issuing from the fourth story of a house in the Rue Morgue, which was occupied by Madame L'Esplanaye and her daughter Camille. Neighbors made their way in:

The apartment was in the wildest disorder . . . on a chair lay a razor, besmeared with blood. On the hearth were two or three long and thick tresses of grey human hair, also dabbled with blood, and seeming to have been pulled out at the roots. . . . Of Madame L'Esplanaye no traces were here seen, but an unusual quantity of soot being observed in the fireplace, a search was made in the chimney, and (horrible to relate!) the corpse of the daughter, head downward, was dragged therefrom. . . . Upon the face were many severe scratches, and, upon the throat, dark bruises, and deep indentations of finger nails, as if the deceased had been throttled to death. . . . The party made its way into a small paved yard in the rear of the building, where lay the corpse of the old lady, with her throat so entirely cut that, upon an attempt to raise her, the head fell off. . . .

Reports of witnesses followed. There was no clue to the murderer or how he might have escaped. The narrator and his friend Dupin take an interest in the case, which the police are handling without imagination.

Dupin eventually finds some nonhuman hair in the old lady's grasp, and shows that the fingermarks on the girl's throat are not those of a human hand. He finds in Cuvier a description of the "large fulvous Ourang-Outang of the East Indian Islands. The gigantic stature, the prodigious strength and activity, the wild ferocity, and the imitative propensities of these mammalia are sufficiently well known to all."

Dupin has an idea. He puts an advertisement in the paper, claiming to have caught an orang. This is a trap, to see if anyone has lost one. A sailor turns up. After a long inquiry, he tells how, on the night of the murder, the pet orang had burst into his room and was trying to shave itself in imitation of its master. He tried to retrieve the razor, but the orang escaped and fled. The sailor followed and climbed up to the window into which he saw his pet disappear.

"As the sailor looked in, the gigantic animal had seized Madame L'Esplanaye by the hair (which was loose, as she had been combing it), and was flourishing the razor about her face, in imitation of the motions of a barber." It killed her first, then the girl. Then it saw its master's face at the window, so it tried to hide its deeds—pushing the girl up the chimney, and throwing the woman out of the window. The sailor fled, and so did the orang.

Thus ended the tale of the Rue Morgue. Two features of the orang's behavior stand out: its imitativeness—the quality for which monkeys have been famous since antiquity—and its great strength and dangerously uncontrollable behavior when excited. This was a new element, and one that relied on widespread knowledge of the great size of these apes, and belief in their violent nature, for its credibility.

It is not surprising that Poe took the orang and not the gorilla for his model, because he would have been ignorant of the latter. His story was a powerful boost to the popular idea of the violent ape. Most later authors looked to Africa rather than to Borneo for their model, basing themselves more directly on the stories of Du Chaillu (see Chapter 6) and his predecessors and followers.

Ironically, Du Chaillu himself was one of the first to deny some of the tales about the gorilla's violent nature. He denied that gorillas drag passersby up into the trees to kill them; he denied that gorillas attack elephants; he denied that these big apes carry off and ravish native women. Even for Du Chaillu, the gorilla was not so evil as that. Yet these very tales are current in the civilized world today, and if Du Chaillu could not dispose of them I very much doubt whether any one will.

One of the most exciting stories our century has known is the story of Tarzan (Plate 90). Tarzan is the hero of more than a dozen books by Edgar Rice Burroughs. This remarkable man was born in Chicago in 1875, and, after being discharged from the army as under age, worked as a cattle drover, a gold dredger, and a railway detective before he turned to writing. The character he created—Tarzan—was the gold he had sought: over 25 million copies of his Tarzan books were sold. Their hero is a strong, muscular white man, a man of action, not of words, who lives in the jungle. Most of us know Tarzan from the screen rather than from books, and a variety of film makers has portrayed him in a variety of ways, from an almost wordless long-haired savage (as Johnny Weissmuller played him) to (alas!) a nambypamby lovelorn Hollywood lout.

But the real Tarzan persists, despite Hollywood's ravages. And the real Tarzan is the Tarzan of Burroughs's first and most exciting book—*Tarzan of the Apes,* published in New York in 1914. It recounts the story of Tarzan's birth and his experiences as he grew up to maturity.

Tarzan's father, John Clayton, Lord Greystoke, a noble Englishman, was traveling in 1888 to a foreign appointment with his beautiful wife, Alice, when mutiny occurred aboard their ship, the *Fuwalda,* and the lord and lady were dumped unceremoniously on the African coast and abandoned to their fate. Inland, everywhere, was the jungle. Lord Greystoke set to and made a hut; for his wife, to add to the complications, was pregnant. The jungle fiends—leopards and malignant apes —kept close watch on the intruders. One day an ape attacked.

It was approaching through the jungle in a semi-erect position, now and then placing the backs of its closed fists upon the ground—a great anthropoid ape, and, as it advanced, it emitted deep guttural growls and an occasional low barking sound.

Clayton warned Alice, with a shout, but the ape closed on him:

The ape was a great bull, weighing probably three hundred pounds. His nasty, close-set eyes gleamed hatred from beneath his shaggy brows, while his great canine fangs were bared in a horrid snarl as he paused a moment before his prey . . . with an ugly snarl he closed upon his defenseless victim, but ere his fangs had reached the throat they thirsted for there was a sharp report. . . . [Alice had shot him!] Screaming with rage and pain, the ape flew at the delicate woman, who went down beneath him to merciful unconsciousness.

When Alice recovered consciousness, she had become insane, and she never recovered. That night her baby was born. She thought she was at home in London, and loved her son. A year later, she died.

Kerchak was a fierce king ape living nearby, who would kill any other ape, male or female, if he was in a temper. One day he killed the female Kala's ape-baby. Kerchak now wanted to kill the man Clayton, get his gun, and see his hut. He crept into the hut and did the deed. Kala snatched the babe from its cradle, to replace her own loss.

The baby was slow to develop, but Kala had patience. Tublat, her husband said "He will never be a great ape . . . let us leave him." But Kala held on. They called him Tarzan, which means "White-Skin."

Tarzan developed. He noticed the difference between himself and the apes. And he was more intelligent: "In Tarzan's clever little mind many thoughts revolved, and back of these was his divine power of reason."

At the age of ten, Tarzan entered the hut. He saw the skeletons, found a knife, and a child's illustrated alphabet, with pictures of beings like himself. He learned to use the knife, becoming a great hunter and killer; he also taught himself to read and write, but not to speak.

So Tarzan grew up knowing only the violent loves and the violent hates of ape society and the riddles of the hut. Life in the treetops had made him strong, and besides his understanding of jungle lore he soon came to prove his superior intelligence in many ways, earning a position of leadership and making enemies of the most violent old males, who had hitherto ruled by brute force alone. Tarzan fought and won many fights, but his closest tie was always with Kala, his adoptive mother. He took part in the secret midnight rite called the "Dum-Dum" when the apes gathered in a moonlit glade and danced round and round their victim—a captured enemy ape from a neighboring tribe—uttering wild howls and shrieks and, at the height of the orgy, devouring their prisoner. Tarzan devoured some too, as intoxicated as the other apes by the noise of "those strange earthen drums which the anthropoids build for the queer rites, the sounds of which men have heard in the fastnesses of the jungle, but which none has ever witnessed."

One day Tarzan's mother was killed by a mysterious thing, an arrow. Tarzan tracked the killer and saw his first man, and killed him. He had often been back to the hut, and now he knew that both he and this other creature were men.

In the course of time, Tarzan found a mate. A party of whites arrived, led by the son of the then Lord Greystoke, Tarzan's cousin. With the party was a lovely American girl, Jane Porter. Tarzan saw her, and immediately fell in love. "For the girl he had a strange longing which he scarcely understood."

Then an ape attacked her. It was Terkoz, who had been expelled from the ape tribe because of his brutality, and had "turned, foaming with rage, into the jungle. . . . It was then that the horrible, man-like beast, swinging from tree to tree," came upon Jane.

One piercing scream escaped her lips as the brute hand clutched her arm. Then she was dragged toward those awful fangs which yawned at her throat. But ere they touched that fair skin another mood claimed the anthropoid.

The tribe had kept his women. He must find others to replace them. This hairless white ape would be the first of his new household, and so he threw her roughly across his broad, hairy shoulders and leaped back into the trees, bearing Jane Porter away toward a fate a thousand times worse than death.

Tarzan gave chase, and caught up with the pair. He attacked Terkoz:

Jane Porter—her lithe young form flattened against the trunk of a great tree, her hands tight pressed against her rising and falling bosom, and her eyes wide with mingled horror, fascination, fear and admiration—watched the primordial ape battle with the primeval man for possession of a woman—for her.

Tarzan won the battle, and with it the love of Jane. But her conscience intervened, and he took her back to her party, and she sailed away. Tarzan followed her to Baltimore in the end, and saved her from a forest fire and the hand of the feeble but rich young man who was bent on marrying her. At the end of the book, a telegram arrives, pronouncing him the true Lord Greystoke.

I have recounted the Tarzan story at length because it is exciting and also because it combines so many features of other more ancient myths—strange circumstances of birth and upbringing, the emergence of superior qualities, heroic battles against huge odds, great moral integrity of the hero, in contrast with the evil enemy—in a new and entirely modern setting: the African ape-infested jungle. Such a setting, with the ape as the terrible foe, is a direct product of earlier popular and scientific writings. Let us see whence Burroughs got his ideas.

Burroughs never went to Africa. His knowledge of the forest and its inhabitants was derived solely from conversations and his reading. Unfortunately, we do not know how extensively he read. Possibly he had seen T. H. Huxley's essay on the natural history of the manlike apes, in which the author drew attention to a mistranslation by Buffon. The passage concerned is the one from Purchas that we have already quoted on page 43. Purchas stated that Battell had told him that "one of these *Pongos* [gorillas] tooke a *Negro* boy of his, which liued a moneth with them." Buffon had translated this as: "un pongo lui enleva un petit nègre qui passa un an entier dans la société de ces animaux." Buffon had stretched the period from a month to a year; perhaps Burroughs extended it further. But it seems unlikely that Burroughs would have read Huxley.

Another possible origin also, oddly enough, involves a mistake. Boccaccio, the great Italian storyteller of the fifteenth century, related a tale, derived from classical sources, of how Vulcan was ejected from Olympus by Jupiter when still a boy, and landed on earth among a tribe of apes, which brought him up. Scholars have pointed out that Boccaccio was working with a medieval text in which had been miscopied the name of the folk who brought up Vulcan. In the original, classical versions, they were a tribe of people called the "Sintii." The version used by Boccaccio, however, had them down as the "simii"—

apes. We do not know, of course whether Burroughs ever read Boccaccio in some popular English version; but once again, it seems unlikely. It is our duty to search for origins, but there is no reason at all why Burroughs should not have independently invented the idea of a boy being brought up by a horde of apes.

Tarzan's apes are definitely violent, and dangerous to man. They are, indeed, portrayed in a more violent way than they ever were in Battell's account or those of Du Chaillu and the others. Burroughs let his imagination feed on the earlier tales of the savage ape. For Burroughs, quite clearly, the idea that male apes, including the gorilla, could be gentle creatures was anathema. For his purpose they had to be cruel. The travelers had stressed that it was only the adult males that were so malignant. Burroughs adopted this idea, and his females, especially Kala, are loving and fiercely possessive rather than cruel.

Burroughs, as we saw in the quotation above, made good use of the "Dum-Dum" to bring out the "cannibalistic" nature of the apes. He drew the idea of the "Dum-Dum" directly from the reports of travelers in Africa. Thomas S. Savage, the missionary, in his 1844 report to the Boston Natural History Society on the chimpanzee specimen, had described the way chimpanzees "occasionally assemble in large numbers in gambols . . . not less than 50 engaged in hooting, screaming and drumming with sticks on old logs." Livingstone, the missionary, wrote in his *Last Journals* of 1874 of how chimpanzees "beat hollow trees as drums with hands, and then scream as music to it." Burroughs may have read this. But more probably he based his "Dum-Dum" on the "kanjo," or "carnival," as described much later by R. L. Garner, in 1896 (see quotation in Chapter 5, p. 114). Garner described the clay "drum" of the chimpanzees and their habit of assembling and dancing around it on carnival nights: an ample "factual" basis for Burroughs's imagination to work on.

Burroughs did not flinch at combining the most suitable features of the gorilla with those of the chimpanzee into his own brand of "apes." No one had described the chimpanzee as terrifying, and no one attributed the wild "carnivals" to gorillas. Garner was unsure while he was in Africa whether the shrieking and hooting and drumming he heard was made by chimpanzees or gorillas; and although he later decided it was chimpanzees, we can perhaps find in his doubt some basis for Burroughs's merging of the characteristics of chimpanzee and gorilla. But just as probably Burroughs took what he wanted from each and did a conscious job of combining the most dramatic aspects of each species into his own brand of "apes." Burroughs's apes—Tarzan's apes—are neither gorillas nor chimpanzees, but a mixture of both.

To Burroughs and his readers, these nearest relatives of man were the incarnation of man's brutal characteristics, unrelieved or perhaps unburdened by his intellectual and moral capacities. As such, they proved to have a magnetic attraction for civilized people. Another ape story to fire the public imagination was (and still is) that of King Kong. In one scene from the film *King Kong*, we see the giant gorilla Kong in a dawn-age world, defying the Pteranodon, a great prehistoric glider, in its attempt to seize Ann Darrow, a hapless but lovely girl whom Kong has in his power. The story and stills from the film appear quite often in magazines in the 1960's. There are many of these "monster" magazines on sale, mainly in the United States of America; and while they go in for monsters of all sorts, the huge hairy ape has a firm niche among them. These magazines are an offshoot of the film industry, and today it is films rather than books that have come to express and transmit the monster myths. The maker of monster films has a great variety of trick methods at his command, and he can create in visual form the huge beasts and terrible events that for so long have remained in man's imagination or in the printed pages and static illustrations of books. King Kong and other ape-monsters are exaggerated versions of the violent gorilla. And the theme of all these tales is fundamentally the same: Puny but beautiful woman is the prize the ape seeks, while puny but courageous man is the hero who must save her from its terrible embrace.

The idea of the film *King Kong* was conceived in 1932 by Merian C. Cooper, motion-picture producer, and the story was written by himself and Edgar Wallace. It was to be a "Lost World" setting, in which dinosaurs and pterodactyls survived alongside the most terrible monster of them all—a gigantic gorilla called Kong. Living on an unknown island, Kong had its human inhabitants enslaved to him; they lived in fear behind a wall at one end of the island. From time immemorial, whenever a maiden of unusual beauty grew to maturity in the village, she was sacrificed to the monster, who, in return, left the people in peace.

One day a group of whites arrived at the island, led by an adventure-film producer, Carl Denham. They brought with them the lovely Ann Darrow. She was promptly captured by the savages, and carried off to the sacrificial altar. Kong entered and surveyed his prize.

He was fifty feet tall. He picked her up in his hand and gazed at her—
she was pure white, with lovely golden hair. She screamed and
struggled. He was enraptured. With a mighty roar, he headed inland
toward his lair.

The white men were now in pursuit, especially Jack Driscoll, who
was in love with Ann. Following Kong's trail, they ran into trouble
with giant reptiles. When they caught up with Kong, he promptly
killed them all (except Denham and Driscoll), hurling them into a
chasm. Ann, in the meantime, was in danger from a Pteranodon, with
which Kong now fought a terrible primordial battle.

Here Kong was fighting in defense of his prize. Later he did so
again, with the Pterodactyl. Oddly enough, this puts us on his side.
Also, he was gentle with her, even to the point of falling in love with
her. He did not molest her in any way. And so his rage was the greater
when Driscoll caught up and made off with her. He finally charged the
whites, to be met by a gas bomb that knocked him out. Denham took
him back to New York for exhibition, but he broke his bonds, caused
panic and terror, and at last got hold of Ann again (Plate 91). Kong
was killed by airplane attacks atop the Empire State Building. As
Denham said, it was a victory of Beauty over the Beast.

This story is essentially a development of one aspect of the Tarzan
story, which we met most clearly with Terkoz—the sexual interest of
the ape in lovely woman. But there was nothing new about this theme;
on the contrary the Tarzan story was new, and King Kong is a new
version of a very ancient myth.

Among the earliest tales containing the various elements of this
story are the legends of the "satyrs" of the ancient Greeks. As we saw
in Chapter 1, most Greeks and Romans believed in satyrs. To give an
example, here is how the Greek writer Pausanias described them in his
Description of Greece, written around the end of the second century
B.C.:

Wishing to know better than most people who the Satyrs are I have in-
quired from many about this very point. Euphemus the Carian said that on
a voyage to Italy he was driven out of his course by winds and was carried
into the outer sea, beyond the course of seamen. He affirmed that there were
many uninhabited islands, while in others lived wild men. The sailors did
not wish to put in at the latter, because, having put in before, they had some
experience of the inhabitants, but on this occasion they had no choice in the
matter. The islands were called Satyrides by the sailors, and the inhabitants
were red haired, and had upon their flanks tails not much smaller than those

of horses. As soon as they caught sight of their visitors, they ran down to the ship without uttering a cry and assaulted the women in the ship.

The "ape" continued through medieval Christian times to be associated with ideas of sexual lasciviousness, and with the printing of travel books the tale of "ape rape" was common in the seventeenth and eighteenth centuries. For instance, Francesco Guazzo, in his *Compendium Maleficarum* of 1608, related a story of a woman who was deported to an island populated by "apes," one of which took her to a cave, brought her fruit, and then ravished her. In 1641, Pierre Gassendi, in his *Life of Peiresky*, related a story of ape rape, and Tulp gave his hearsay account of this behavior by the "orang-outang" (see page 46) together with a picture of the culprit. Tyson, in 1699, disagreed, but the story lived on. Buffon, in 1812, mentioned no less than four recent authors each of whom related that apes ravished women. As for our own century, Plate 92 shows an English political cartoon of 1910, in which Britannia is about to be assaulted by an ape. A final example: on November 11, 1964, I noticed a report in an English newspaper concerning the case of a nineteen-year-old youth, sentenced to life imprisonment for robbery, rape, and violence. Summing up, the judge said he had "no more control of himself than a young gorilla." The myth, it seems, is ever with us. And it has never been so successfully put across as in *King Kong*.

The unique element of the Kong story is a post-Christian strand—romantic love—woven into the old tale. Kong's response to lovely woman is inhibited and noble, gallant and chivalrous. In that sense he is a hero, not a monster, and his death is a tragedy, with power to move us. This is where the Kong story departs from ancient myths. Kong was innocent because he came from a world before the dawn of intelligence and morality. Kong's love for Ann was, in his time, the highest emotion a beast ever experienced. While, as in all versions of this theme, the sexual element is ever present and not to be denied, there is more to it in the case of Kong. He *falls for* Ann, as Jack Driscoll had done. He loves her. As the airplanes dive in for the kill, Kong puts Ann on a ledge, out of harm's way, and dies.

A score of other films has been made on the theme of the bestial attraction of the ape toward woman, and in nearly all of them the girl is rescued by a vigorous, heroic young man. Magazines and books on the subject are equally abundant.

It is obvious that for many people the ape is the ideal beast to play this role. Doubtless there are many reasons for this. The ape's half-human appearance and subhuman intelligence make it an ideal object on which to project our "animal instincts." Its close kinship to ourselves gives it a sufficiently human nature for us to accept its interest in our own species. Man has beaten the ape in the evolutionary race for supremacy; rejected and forced into retreats in the jungle, the ape envies man, and makes the most of any chance to exploit its superior strength by abducting women, who cannot fight and are an easy prey. But they are more than easy prey. Just as, for man, they are sexually exciting, so for the ape they are doubly so, because the ape is more carnal by being more animal, and more so still by having a member of the higher species for its love object.

These explanations are nonsymbolic. Once we let symbolism in, a new flood of interpretations offers itself. The woman can be seen as a fertility symbol, the ape as the enemy or forces of destruction. The young hero is the tribe's militia. In this case, the tale repeats the old saga of wars long past.

Or an "oedipal" explanation can be used: the ape is father; the girl is mother; the hero is son. Only by killing off father can son achieve union with mother.

Maybe this projection of violent and sexual appetites onto apes is a peculiarity of our own culture, dating from classical times. Certainly among Africans we find a more matter-of-fact attitude toward them. In the land of the gorilla and the chimpanzee, there is less talk of ape rape than outside.

A few reports occur of African women who told their white questioners that they had had sexual relations with apes. Buffon quotes one such case from M. de la Brosse: "I knew a Negress at Loango who remained three years with these animals" (chimpanzees), and Winwood Reade has another: "A woman was brought to me, who stated that she herself had excited the passion of a gorilla and had hardly escaped him." But we know nothing of the circumstances in which these tales were told. In neither case does it appear that the ape actually abducted the woman by force.

There is an indigenous story of a violent gorilla, called "The Boy Kinneneh and the Gorilla," which Stanley heard in the Congo and reported in his book *My Dark Companions and Their Strange Stories* in 1893. This gorilla was a man-killer, and he killed by squeezing his victims—men and women—to death. He carried off a woman and squeezed her to death (Plate 93). But he did not rape his female victims; indeed, his main interest was in stealing and eating bananas, for which he had an insatiable greed. Bananas, in the end, were his undoing, for Kinneneh kept removing his supply, and eventually he died of hunger. The emphasis is on *food* in the African tale, as opposed to *sex* in the tales of most Europeans—evidence, perhaps, of a different focus of interest in these two cultures.

While I was in Uganda, a tracker named Xavier once told us about the chimpanzees' drum. He did not describe the drum, but told us that the chimps took it around with them, each group having its own drummer-chimp, who brought up the rear as they made their way through the forest. The chimpanzees were very careful, he said, not to let people see the drum, and no one had ever seen it. Xavier also told us another "fact" about the chimps; namely, that normally they walk upright and that is how you first see them. But when they know a human being is watching them, they go down on all fours and run off like any other animal. This idea—that apes pretend to be less capable than they really are—occurs in the ancient African story, told by Richard Jobson in 1623 among others, that they could in fact speak if they so wished, but choose not to do so, lest they be put to work.

In Stanley's book, the chimpanzee hardly features at all. It comes into the stories only once, when recognition is accorded by the animals to its phenomenal climbing ability. The tortoise wants revenge on the crane, which has killed its mother. He wants a rattan climber tied to the crane's nest so that he can climb up to it. Soko the chimpanzee agrees to tie one, for the price of "a potful of good nuts, ten bunches of ripe bananas, one hundred eggs, and sundry other trifles." He can charge this exorbitant fee because he is the only one in the forest who can climb the branchless trunk up to the crane's nest. Stanley's illustrator drew the scene (see Plate 94).

In Stanley's tale of the violent gorilla and the boy Kinneneh, the emphasis is on the greed of the gorilla, and its moral is that human cunning can triumph over brute force. Another tale about the gorilla in Stanley's book explains why the people of the Black River region are friends of the gorillas. One day, a fisherman from the Black River above Basoko town met a big gorilla—"Gorilla Father"—in the forest. The gorilla offered him food, and then told him that man must not quarrel with the gorilla. He told him the gorillas' password, "Tu-wheli, tu-wheli!" Later the man's village went on a gorilla hunt, but this fisherman let the gorillas through the line of hunters so that they escaped. The villagers were angry with him. Later on, he met a gorilla in the woods who showed him which of the forest foods were good to eat. He returned to the village and told the people about the foods. They were grateful to the gorillas for this knowledge, and vowed never again to hunt them. So the Black River people and the gorillas are mutual friends.

As for the way in which apes came into being, Stanley heard vaguely of a terrible eruption, which caused all the surrounding peoples to flee, whereupon the adults were converted into apes, and the children into monkeys. And Du Chaillu heard a story that men who leave their village in anger may turn into gorillas, in which case they are most savage.

A story accounting for the behavior of the African apes is this one, first recorded in 1911, and also printed in G. B. Schaller's book *The Year of the Gorilla*. It is a Bulu story, from Cameroun. It tells how God had five children: the gorilla, chimpanzee, elephant, pygmy, and man. He gave to each three things—fire, seeds, and tools—and told them to go out into the world and settle down. The gorilla, the chimpanzee, and the elephant all let their fires go out while they were busy eating fruit. The pygmy kept his fire, and man did best of all. When God went out to see how his children had fared, he told the apes and the elephant that, because they had not done so well, they would never again be able to face man, but must always flee from him.

Although the apes have no fire, two reports state that they are interested in it. Battell's account tells us that the "Pongos" (gorillas) come to abandoned fires. And Lord Monboddo has told (of the "chimpenza") that "they take a stick out of the black man's fire."

There are various other oddments of gorilla lore in the literature—that gorillas cover their dead with the branches of trees, that the gorilla will not attack a hunter who drops his spear, and that a fetish of gorilla's brain makes a man brave.

Most of the tales I have found concerning the orangutan are about its strength. A. R. Wallace, in 1890, told two tales which he had heard from old Dyak chiefs in Borneo. Each has the same theme: that the orang is the strongest of the animals. The first story is as follows:

No animal is strong enough to hurt the Mias (orang-utan), and the only creature he ever fights with is the crocodile. When there is no fruit in the jungle, he goes to seek food on the banks of the river, where there are plenty of young shoots that he likes, and fruits that grow close to the water. Then the crocodile sometimes tries to seize him, but the Mias gets upon him, and beats him with his hands and feet, and tears him and kills him.

The second story is as follows:

The Mias has no enemies; no animals dare attack it but the crocodile and the python. He always kills the crocodile by main strength, standing upon it, pulling open its jaws, and ripping up its throat. If a python attacks a Mias, he seizes it with his hands, and then bites it, and soon kills it. The Mias is very strong; there is no animal in the jungle so strong as he.

According to C. Hose and W. McDougall, writing in 1912, the Kenyahs and Kayans, two peoples of Borneo, fear the orang. Kayan women avoid seeing one, for they believe that it might affect the appearance of their child.

Some modern stories reported by Gaun anak Sureng, an inhabitant of Sarawak, tell of encounters between man and orang. Sometimes the man flees, sometimes the orang. If the two fight, it is a serious business for the man. Perhaps the most interesting is the story of a girl who alleged she had been caught by an orang. Here is the climax of the story:

When I reached the spot where I had seen the *nendak* bird, there I was suddenly embraced by a maias, who came from my rear. I fell down to the ground. My basket also was dropped to the ground—and all the cucumbers poured out. These at once attracted the maias who freed me to pick the cucumbers. These it took up unto a tree top.

Later, men came and killed the orang.

These tales are not folklore so much as "true stories" of the kind people tell one another about recent events. Nevertheless, they reflect attitudes. It is interesting that, as in the African gorilla story, the orang was ultimately more interested in food than in the girl. It is not stated why it attacked her.

Tom Harrisson has found that orang folklore rather sadly indicates the decline of the orang in Borneo. Those tribes—the Dusun, Land Dayaks and Sea Dayaks—in whose folklore the orang features live in areas where a few orangs survive today; not all that long ago, they were common there. Among the inland tribes there is little or no orang mythology. And along the northwest coast of Borneo, where his archaeological researches have brought to light evidence that orangs once lived and were preyed upon by man, there is no trace of them in the folklore memory of the present day.

Of the gibbon and siamang, I have discovered only a few fragments of lore. Carl Bock, in 1881, said of the siamang that "the popular belief among the Malays is that the animal is descended from a woman who had turned her son away from home, and was punished by being transformed into an animal."

Of the gibbon, C. R. Carpenter found a similar reincarnation idea in Burma in his field study in 1937. This time the gibbons were believed to be the reembodiments of disappointed lovers. Doubtless the mournful wailing calls of these apes are connected with this theory.

The idea of the gibbon as a human reincarnation was also found in Borneo among the Ibans. Hose and McDougall tell the story of why one Iban would not kill the gibbon:

He will not kill the gibbon because the *ngarong* of his grandfather, who died twenty years ago, was a gibbon. Once a man came to his grandfather in a dream and said to him, "Don't you kill the gibbon," and then turned into a grey gibbon. This gibbon helped him to become rich and to take heads, and in all possible ways. On one occasion, when he was about to go on the warpath, his *ngarong* came to him in a dream and said, "Go on, I will help you," and the next day he saw in the jungle a grey gibbon which was undoubtedly his *ngarong*. When he died he said to his sons, "Don't you kill the gibbon," and his sons and grandsons have obeyed him in this ever since.

What happened when the Iban—whose name was Anggus—was ordered to kill his tabooed animal, is related in the next paragraph:

Anggus himself once shot a gibbon when told to do so by one of us. He first said to it, "I don't want to kill you, but the *Tuan* who is giving me wages expects me to, and the blame is his. But if you are really the *ngarong* of my grandfather, make the shot miss you." He then shot and missed three times, and on shooting a fourth time he killed a gibbon, but not the one he had spoken to.

A neat compromise in a difficult situation!

CHAPTER **11**

Ape-keeping Today

T H E R E M A Y W E L L be as many apes in research laboratories in America, England, and Russia as there are in captivity in zoos. It is of course inevitable that this should be so. Most of the laboratory apes are chimpanzees.

This century has seen an enormous expansion of research in medicine, psychology, biochemistry, and latterly space research, and for these it is often necessary to use a man-substitute in the experimental stages. For many areas of investigation, a rhesus monkey is quite suitable, and this species is the one most frequently found in primate institutions. But the chimpanzee is much closer to man, and can catch and be cured of most of his diseases.

I list a few of the diseases in which research is being helped by apes: malaria, poliomyelitis, diphtheria, common cold, syphilis, whooping cough, heart disease, and cancer. In addition, one of the newest and potentially greatest uses for ape subjects is in the field of organ transplantation. Already chimpanzee kidneys have been used to replace a diseased human kidney, though as yet this technique is in its infancy, and has not had any long-term successes. This is a rapidly expanding medical field, however, and it is a reasonable prophecy that, by the end of this century, there will be many people alive only by virtue of the chimpanzee kidneys and hearts within their bodies; or people who have regained their sight by the grafting of chimpanzee corneas into their eyes. Chimpanzees may even be used to bring to term an implanted human fetus. Other fields of physiological research using apes include investigations of the effects of low temperatures, work on blood groups and immunological reactions of the serum, reproduction and artificial insemination and drug tolerance.

In the field of space exploration, chimpanzees have been used extensively in laboratory tests on acceleration, deceleration, rotation, simulated weightlessness, and loss of atmospheric pressure. Two apes, Ham and Enos have made brief but important space flights, which established that launching, acceleration, weightlessness, and reentry were safe for a man. On January 31, 1961, Ham, a 37½-pound chimpanzee, made a 16-minute trip 156 miles up into space and down again into the sea. He traveled in a Mercury capsule mounted at the nose of a Redstone rocket, and reached a speed of 5,800 miles an hour (Plate 95). He was weightless for 6½ minutes, and experienced an acceleration rate of 17g's. Through the flight, his temperature, breathing rate, and heartbeat were recorded, and he carried out a series of actions (for which he had undergone preflight training), pulling levers in response to flashing lights (Plate 96). All his actions and expressions were recorded on film. His experience left him with only one minor injury, a bruised nose. And it indicated strongly to the American space scientists that the conditions met with could be tolerated by a man and that the capsule's environmental and recovery systems were efficient, which was what they needed to know.

The third great exploiter of laboratory apes is the psychologist. As we have seen in a previous chapter, much work has been done on the problem of intelligence in apes. But psychologists are also interested in how the process of learning operates; how mechanical skills are developed; in right- and left-handedness; in the effects of maternal deprivation, and in the effects of the social play of juveniles; in communication by facial expression, gesture, and speech; in memory, imagination, and symbolism; in the effects of early motor restriction or perceptual isolation on later development; in the effects of drugs on behavior, and in drug addiction; and in the effects of brain lesions, removal of certain brain areas, or electrical stimulation of the brain. In all these fields, and in many more, chimpanzees may be used as human substitutes. In his attempts to provide hygienic and controlled conditions for his subjects, the psychologist invariably houses his apes in small bare cages, often in solitude; it is a common practice to remove every infant from its mother at birth.

There is, of course, an ethical problem involved. Are we justified in exposing these near-human apes to such procedures, giving them malignant growths, removing their frontal lobes? Or depriving them of their emotional comfort? This is only part of the wider question of the justification of this type of experiment on any animal, and most rational people argue, rightly, that if such experiments lead to a breakthrough in the prevention or cure of some disease that at present kills human beings, or to an understanding of abnormal behavior, then it is justifiable, for if we accept the principles of evolution by natural selection, we must be logical and preserve our own species before any other.

However, we do know, from ample personal and scientific studies, that the senses of apes equal our own, that they feel pain as we do, that they have similar emotions of fear, love, hatred, and jealousy in similar situations. Thus I think that all would agree that experiments involving mental or physical suffering in primates, in particular the apes, ought to be kept to a minimum, and carried out with all the safeguards which apply to operations on human beings.

I would suggest that in the chief countries concerned, possibly by international agreement, a code of rules be set up for the treatment of laboratory apes. These rules would set certain humane standards, such as stating a minimum necessary living space per ape; enforcing the provision of bedding and climbing frame; and encouraging the practice of leaving infants with their mothers, unless there were exceptional circumstances against it. In addition, it might be advisable for special licenses to be required before experiments involving operative techniques, drugs, or disease induction were performed on apes. Such licenses would be granted only if the necessity of using apes was reasonably justified.

Another manner in which apes, in particular chimpanzees once more, are exploited for profit, is by their use as performers in the entertainment industry, especially circuses. Such shows provide hilarious delight for the audience, although some individuals feel strongly that the natural dignity of the animals is insulted by their being made to wear silly hats, and to be trained to carry out crude imitations of human activities, for us to mock or wonder at.

But in my opinion, young chimpanzees trained to perform are often happier and more motivated than those sitting bored and unstimulated in zoo or laboratory cages. There is invariably a close relationship between the trainer and his animals, such that the chimpanzees want to win his approval. Chimpanzees even in the wild are given to periodic jamborees of excited jumping and dancing about and wild shouting in a merry chorus, and to some extent the ritual of circus performances, and the feedback of the roared applause of the audience, provide a not unnatural experience. Certainly chimpanzees seem to look forward to their performances, and to enjoy taking the limelight. Often a chimpanzee does something quite spontaneous during an act, showing that it is not for him a fearsome ritual performed to escape punishment. In fact punishment is rarely used in the successful training of chimpanzees. For example, a famous trainer, Rudi Lenz of Bertram Mills Circus in England, stresses the value of imitation in initial training. A chimpanzee watching another ride a tricycle will want to do the same himself. If he then succeeds or makes a good attempt, he will gain a small reward of a piece of banana or a lump of sugar. This indicates to him that he has won the approval of his master. Mr. Lenz sometimes gets the idea for a new routine from something an animal does quite spontaneously in an act; and he does not punish if an animal refuses to do something he has been trained to do as there is probably a good reason. This case illustrates that young performing chimpanzees, with a good relationship with their trainer and their daily routine filled up with the excitement of their act, can be better off than in other forms of captivity. But of course there comes a time when every performing chimpanzee reaches puberty and becomes too strong and intractable, and has to be finally placed in a zoo.

This leads us to a consideration of zoo conditions. How ought apes to be kept in zoos?

We can distinguish two opposed schools of thought on this subject, which have emerged quite clearly over the recent years in the world's zoos. The first I shall call the *hygiene* school, and the second the *natural* school. In the first the emphasis is on keeping the apes in the most hygienic way possible in order to protect their physical health; in the second, the emphasis is on providing them with the most natural conditions possible both socially and environmentally, in order to keep them occupied and content. In the former, cages tend to be small, made of materials such as glazed tiles that can be easily washed down and will harbor no bacteria, and glass-fronted to avoid breath from the public reaching the apes. The environment is thus made as sterile as possible. A problem is what to do with the apes' excreta, and in some cases these are washed away four to six times a day. Underfloor heating may be provided to keep a constant temperature, and there may also be humidity control. All these artificial devices are aimed at giving the apes the healthiest possible home.

The natural school has very different ideas on how to keep apes healthy. It emphasizes primarily the need for a paddock or field for the apes to run in, trees for them to climb, plenty of fresh air, a shallow moat with electric fence to prevent their escape, and it prefers to see a large group living together than single individuals or pairs. It emphasizes the provision of nesting materials, and drumming boards, swings, climbing bars and so on, to keep the apes occupied. It makes no claims to provide sterile conditions, but believes that the exercise and well-being resulting from field conditions will more than compensate for this in keeping the animals healthy, alert, and in breeding condition.

There are two obvious problems facing the natural school—the space they require may not be available and the climate may be too hot, too cold, or too wet for part of the year. If there is no space available to house the apes in adequate accommodation then it is questionable whether they should attempt to keep apes at all. If the climate is seasonally unsuitable, then thermostatically regulated indoor accommodation must be provided adjacent to the open area.

The problems facing the hygiene school are less obvious but no less real. Often they find, to their distress, that their bored and deprived apes develop neurotic symptoms such as prolonged rocking, self-biting or stereotyped displays. Or the apes develop very strong hierarchies, friendships, and enmities—all of which are problematic in the long run when changes to the group composition have to be made. Finally, they may fail completely to breed, although this is not always so.

Ideally the ideas of both schools of thought should be combined with regard to accommodation, so that the apes have a clean temperature-controlled indoor home, adjoining a large exercise paddock. Chimpanzees do need a big space to roam in, particularly in the case of the big, adventurous adult male chimpanzee, who is such a wanderer in the wild. Failing a paddock adjoining the cage, older apes should be "retired" to a big paddock elsewhere in the zoo, or at another zoo. Young apes can be kept in less space, especially if with their mothers. Field studies have shown that mothers and their offspring are far less mobile than males. And young, tractable apes can be used in training programs, circus-style, to brighten their lives and amuse the public (Plate 97). There is absolutely no reason why zoos should be shy of using circus techniques. These may result in healthier animals and greater subsequent breeding success, and zoos should embrace them as a valuable management aid.

Another way to alleviate boredom is to situate the apes' enclosure where the animals can look out onto an area where something is usually going on, such as the road outside the gardens or a busy part of the zoo. Another idea is to install TV in the vicinity of the cage, as the Bronx Zoo in New York has done with its gorillas!

Chester Zoo, in England, has a fine series of balanced ape enclosures (see Plate 98). The fine-looking, active, motivated gorillas, orangs, and chimpanzees at Chester make that zoo a model for the world (Plates 99 and 100). These apes all have grass paddocks. Grass is better, I think, than concrete. The large indoor cages have sloping concrete floors and are rather bare, but the apes can wander in and out at will, except during the coldest times of winter when they must stay indoors. An interesting point in the case of Chester is that the chimpanzee accommodation is makeshift and inexpensive, and yet provides a greater draw to the visiting public than many shiny new architect-designed zoo buildings elsewhere. Chester's two female breeding chimpanzees, Babu and Meg, have had thirteen infants between them since 1956.

More recently, a very large and extremely fine chimpanzee enclosure has been built at the Holloman Air Force Base in New Mexico (Plate 101). This was completed, and received its first inhabitants, in 1966, and I was present at the initial release of the animals and was able to study their responses to the new environment. The Holloman area is known as a "consortium." A large building with two main rooms provides feeding and housing facilities, for use in hot or cold weather. This building abuts a circular area of no less than 30 acres, surrounded by a moat, over which the apes are free to roam. The vegetation is sparse, owing to the low rainfall in New Mexico, but a number of tree trunks have been erected in the consortium to enable the apes to climb. Irrigation ditches provide moisture for the soil, thus improving conditions for plant growth and keeping the area from becoming too dusty. It is hoped that this consortium will provide better living space for the adult chimpanzees in the Holloman colony and that they may eventually breed there more readily than they have done in the past in their normal, more typical cages (Plates 102 and 103).

Unfortunately, this century has not always seen apes housed in more and more satisfactory conditions—often the reverse has been true. The pioneer of ape housing was Mme. Rosalia Abreu, whose work is described in Yerkes' book, *Almost Human.* Early in this century she set up an ape station at Quinta Palatino, Havana, Cuba, in which her animals had fine, big cages, a very suitable climate, and a sympathetic and painstaking staff looking after them. By 1930, she had reared seven chimpanzees there from birth (Plate 104). Yerkes himself conducted some early experiments there, and later took over the colony, moving it to Florida, where it continued to thrive. Apes were also, however, being kept more and more in town zoos. If apes were kept in small cages it was often because everything was in small cages. That is the stage most of the world's town zoos are still at, unable to expand in any direction, unwilling to favor any given species at the risk of losing or overcramping others.

All the apes have in fact bred in captivity except the mountain gorilla, of which there are only about twelve in captivity. But the breeding has rarely been consistent, or sufficient to keep the zoo's stock up to strength. Lowland gorilla births are still comparatively rare (Plate 105), although there were 148 specimens in captivity in sixty zoos in 1962. Orangs breed occasionally, here and there. An exceptional orang record is that of the single female, Guarina, at Philadelphia Zoo, who gave birth to nine offspring. In the case of chimpanzees, an average of sixteen zoos had breeding successes each year during the years 1959–1962. Pygmy chimpanzees have bred once only in captivity, as far as I know, and that was at Frankfurt Zoo, on January 22, 1962 (Plate 106). Gibbons are not often born in zoos, but Adelaide Zoo had had ten births by 1954, and a second-generation gibbon was born that year. New York Zoological Park has a pair of gibbons that had produced seven young by 1963, but unfortunately most of them died in accidents before reaching maturity. A technique that may one day help toward breeding apes is artificial insemination, and research is currently going forward in this field. Accurate figures for the numbers of apes in the world's zoos are slowly becoming available, as agencies, such as the *International Zoo Yearbook,* compiled at London Zoo, gather information from far and wide, and books such as Crandall's *Management of Wild Mammals in Captivity* synthesize zoo data. We need to know how the number of apes being reared in captivity compares with the number of deaths and replacements by imports from the wild.

One of the problems in the breeding of apes in captivity is that in many cases the mother ape does not seem to know how to care for the infant, and may reject it completely, or else hold it to her in such a position that it is unable to suck the nipples. This happens in females which have been in captivity from their own infancy, and have been kept without companions for much of the time. It seems that the experience of normal social relationships with the mother and with playmates is a necessary factor in the development of normal maternal responses in apes, and in monkeys too. In these cases, even when a much-wanted ape infant has been born, the zoo management is faced with the problem of finding a full-time home and nurse for it for many months. However, it sometimes happens, as in the case of Achilla, the mother of the famous Goma at the Frankfurt Zoo, that the mother behaves perfectly with her later infants.

Epidemics are an ever-present danger in the keeping of captive apes in zoos. For example, Rotterdam Zoo imported four orangs in 1949–1951. These produced no less than nine offspring up to 1963, a fine record for an endangered species. Then in December 1964 a tragedy occurred. Some apparently healthy anteaters developed a rash, which two of the young orangs caught. They died within three days, and during the next two months all the others, with the exception of two old females and one young orang, died of the disease.

Medical techniques for the treatment of sick apes have been developing in recent years, mainly due to the availability of modern relaxing and tranquilizing drugs, which of course are a great aid in catching and treating the ape. Such drugs can be given by syringe or orally, say in a mixture of grape juice. There is nothing new in using drugs on apes—Yerkes was using these techniques in the 1930's—but safer drugs are now available, and dosages more exactly known. Surgical techniques are also in more widespread use today than before, and new successes are being reported. A chimpanzee recently gave birth to a healthy offspring by Caesarean section at Friedrichsfelde animal hospital, East Berlin. The *International Zoo Yearbook* has reported several cases of surgery on apes, including removal of the appendix in an orangutan at the Rotterdam Zoo, and repair of an um-

bilical hernia in a gorilla at the London Zoo. The provision of facilities
for surgery in zoo hospitals is to be encouraged where apes are kept,
and minor checkups should be routine (see Plates 107, 108).

As man develops increasing skill in ape management, an improvement in the rate of breeding of captive apes can be expected. In
the end, however, lack of space will always be the ape-keeper's
greatest enemy. The problem will thus be greatest for zoos, especially
town zoos. In the next chapter I shall discuss the best possible way to
keep apes, but it is one no zoo could afford, in money or space. To end
this chapter, I shall describe a "model" zoo enclosure, of a kind that
should, I think, be satisfactory for a group of apes, including adults, in
a conventional zoo.

All the apes live among trees in their natural habitat, therefore trees
are a first essential of any ape enclosure. The trees should be big and
sturdy, and although they will probably die from stripping and
overuse, they should remain. The trees should be situated outdoors in
a grassy paddock. Providing the paddock is big enough, the apes will
not kill the grass (the Chester Zoo's fine ape paddocks prove this). The
paddock should be surrounded by a moat, with an electric wire slung
above it. If it can be divided by outcrops of rock into two or three
separate areas, then natural groupings of friends can form, and individuals can avoid enemies or find solitude. These rock divisions can be
built, if need be, by plastering cement on a steel framework, in the
style of artificial landscaping devised and built by Carl Hagenbeck at
Hamburg Zoo at the beginning of this century. There should be cave-
like rain shelters at the foot of the rocks. A regular supply of fresh-cut
branches should be supplied for nest construction in the case of
gorillas, orangs, and chimpanzees, and they will certainly make use of
such materials to the interest of onlookers. In a large enough space, the
inclusion of different species of ape together, and possibly monkeys as
well, could provide a focus of attraction.

At one end of the enclosure, in all but the most favorable climates,
there would have to be an indoor house. This should be enlivened with
plenty of climbing materials, tree trunks, climbing frames, swings, or
bamboo constructions like the fine ones at Zurich Zoo, and plenty of
dry straw for nest play and comfort. The door from the indoor to the
outdoor enclosure should be open nearly all the time, so that the apes
feel they are where they are by choice, and do not feel trapped. If they
are healthy, they will probably want to go outdoors briefly even in
cold weather, and to go indoors in hot weather from time to time. Such

a design of paddock and indoor quarters should ensure that the apes could vary their surroundings and their companions in something approaching their natural way in the wild. Their social interactions, and their use of materials for climbing, nest building and play should ensure that they provide a much more interesting spectacle for zoo-goers than is usual in the caged conditions.

Some kind of prepared food biscuits should be available from hoppers throughout the day and night, in addition to their regular feeds of fruit and greens, etc. For the apes' natural feeding routine is to forage for most of the day, and without this interest, they become bored, tend to eat things lying around, and may develop coprophagy.

Such an ape house is not expensive, but requires sufficient space. This surely we owe to such manlike creatures, in return for their lives at our service and profit. The worst chimpanzee accommodation I have ever seen was in a large zoo on the West coast of the U.S.A. Three adult males were caged, singly, in small wire cells. All showed symptoms akin to catatonic schizophrenia in their motionless postures and staring eyes. I enquired of a keeper why there were no females, and he replied that the management thought their sexual swellings would be an embarrassment to the public. He said that one of the males had been caged alone for thirteen years. This particular zoo was in many other respects a very good zoo—it was just the chimpanzees that were suffering.

CHAPTER **12**

The Future: Conservation

CONSERVATION is not a new idea; it is a very old one. When man domesticated dogs, horses, and cattle, he was already engaged in conservation. The primary lesson we can learn from this is that only if keeping a species alive serves some purpose useful to man will he conserve it.

Unfortunately, man does not always know, or even want to know, where his best interests lie. The case of the blue whale shows this. Ever since the 1930's, when a study by A. H. Laurie showed conclusively that more blue whales were being caught than the stock could support, the factory ships have continued to take their toll. As a result, the annual catch, which was 30,000 in the mid-1930's, was barely a hundred in 1964. For man, this hunting to the verge of extinction has meant not merely an economic loss but also the loss of an animal of great scientific interest. It is the same with the apes—short-term interests are eroding populations whose existence we ought to be taking the very greatest care to preserve. Only the conservationists have fully realized this.

[[251

Many authorities today believe the apes to be in grave danger. The orang's lifetime in the wild is expected to end before the close of this century, after which the remaining captive specimens will linger on for a few years. The mountain gorilla may survive beyond the twentieth century if it is lucky, but its wild population is already too dependent on human protection to give comfort. The lowland gorilla population is unknown, but is undoubtedly overexploited. Most zoo gorillas are lowland, because protection is less effective than for the mountain form. Only the chimpanzee looks as though it will survive until, say, the middle of next century, and then it, too, will probably succumb to the pressure of exploitative, demanding man. The large apes will then be extinct. That will leave the gibbons, which will assume great importance, being the last of the apes. Slowly, by erosion, they will be eliminated. For the gibbons, too, the next century may be their last.

In modern times, conservation has become a much broader field than it ever was before. The progress of serious zoological studies and the spread of their discoveries has led to a general emphasis on the value of animal life, and a feeling, among all interested in animals, that no species should be unduly depleted by man and that steps must be taken to prevent the extermination of even those species that have no immediate usefulness.

Many active conservationists in this century have been former hunters themselves. An extreme example of this is the case of William Hornaday, killer of forty-three orangs on his trip to Borneo (in the interests of science), and later founder of the conservation movement in the United States of America. His book *Two Years in the Jungle*, written in 1885, in which he describes and fairly gloats over his orang-shooting exploits, makes a strange contrast with his book *Wild Life Conservation in Theory and in Practice*, published in 1914, which is an eloquent plea for the protection of much of North America's wildlife from hunting. Perhaps Hornaday knew better than most how easy it is to deplete a species. In the latter book he wrote: "It is natural for man to believe that the resources of nature are inexhaustible. The wish is father to the thought. The theory is comforting because it helps to salve the conscience of the man who commits high crimes against wild beasts, and birds and forests." Later, that conscience would not be stilled, and much good for the wildlife of America was the result, for Hornaday's Permanent Wild Life Protection Fund became a rich and powerful organization that eliminated much of the random slaughter of birds such as ducks and geese, and put many species of deer (and the American bison) back on their feet again.

In the case of the apes today, it is the orangutan that is the primary object of concern. A very great deal has been written and said about it, and the most active part in trying to reduce orang exploitation has been taken by Tom and Barbara Harrisson in Borneo. They and Schaller have drawn up maps showing the distribution of orangs in Sarawak, which is now limited to a few areas. Figure 6, page 68, based on the report of the Maias (orangutan) Protection Commission, published in 1960, shows the distribution of orangs during 1950–1960 in Sarawak, on the basis of reports of orang individuals being seen. Orangs occur in certain areas in Sabah, North Borneo, as shown in Figure 7, page 69. In Sumatra their distribution is slowly becoming better known, thanks to the early work by Carpenter and later studies (see Figure 8, page 70). In addition, there are orang areas in Indonesian Borneo (Kalimantan), but their size is not known. The latest estimate of the total surviving wild population is:

Sabah (North Borneo)	approx.	2,000
Sarawak	"	700
Indonesian Borneo	"	1,000
Sumatra	"	1,000
TOTAL:	less than	5,000

This would be a seriously low figure even if the population were well constituted. Unfortunately, it is not. For half a century collectors have concentrated on shooting mothers to obtain their infants, and so the remaining population contains an excess of males. This must seriously affect the rate of breeding. In addition, orangs naturally have a loose, scattered population, more like that of chimpanzees than that of gorillas. This scattered population is less well organized for breeding than a more compact one would be. Assuming that orangs are like the other large apes in their breeding rate, females probably can have an infant every three or four years, on average. Infant mortality probably accounts for some 30 percent or 40 percent of these. Thus, in theory, a female could give birth to about 6 infants in her 30-year life-span (24 or so reproductive years, with a baby every 4 years) and of these, 3 or 4 might survive. This would be fine. But the reality is different—the lives of many mothers are cut short, and their infants are removed from the population. A major problem these days is the presence in orang areas on the Sarawak-Kalimantan and Sabah-Kalimantan borders and in Sumatra of Indonesian soldiers who have automatic weapons and can pass on captured infants to smugglers. Shotguns are common possessions among all the longhouse men of Sarawak, and the presence of soldiers has only increased a problem that has existed for years. As Tom Harrisson has recently written, "he who can shoot a mother and catch her baby . . . and smuggle it out to an agent, can secure his family's diet and health for years in one gesture." With such an incentive near to hand, small wonder that the orang trade goes on. It is the presence of this golden opportunity in a land of poverty that makes Borneo a bad place for the orang to be. It cannot long survive in its natural home. Efforts to set up protected areas of great size will not eliminate poaching, judging from the experience of national parks in Africa, where, for example, there is widespread illegal poaching of rhinoceros horn, which is a lure comparable to that of the orang. Well-guarded areas must therefore be of manageable size, and cannot house a big population of orangs. Even well-guarded areas may succumb in the event of political upheaval.

A different kind of threat to the orang is "the accelerating rate and changing techniques of massive timber extraction . . . obliterating some of the world's largest remaining virgin jungles, no longer tree by tree but at the rate of square miles a day. Timber is the largest single revenue source for Borneo as a whole" (Tom Harrisson, 1965). Felling breaks up the forest canopy and, if on a large scale such as we have in Borneo, makes arboreal travel, the normal orang method of moving around, difficult or impossible. Barbara Harrisson has pointed out the absence of orang nests in areas where the forest has been heavily exploited, indicating the absence of orangs. And she has stressed that modern silvicultural techniques have another weapon, deadlier to the orang than the saw, and that is the poisoning of "undesirable" tree species after logging. This may remove the orang's food supply, by killing off the fruit trees. It is a problem that I found, independently, in Africa, and I shall discuss it later in this chapter in the context of the chimpanzee.

Having been caught by a hunter, the orang infant is next crated in a small box, fed on rice and bananas, and then taken on a long journey to the coast, sometimes taking several months. During this time, malnutrition and infestation with worms take their toll. Next, a coastal agent, who pays little, smuggles the orang to an established animal dealer in the region, for a large profit. This dealer now arranges the details of final export, and fakes the necessary papers.

Here is a typical example, which Barbara Harrisson wrote to me about. A two-year-old male orang had been bought by a British Army sergeant "who wanted a pet." He had paid Straits $60 for it, to an agent who had already paid another agent who had paid the hunter who caught it about Straits $5 to $10. This sergeant kept his pet well, but did not realize that it was very sick. However, it weakened, and when he discovered it was a protected species, he handed it over to the Sarawak Museum, where Mrs. Harrisson cured it of worms and finally, after a long convalescence, arranged for its transfer to a zoo.

Had this animal been smuggled to Singapore, it would have been worth Straits $800 (sick) or $2,000 (healthy) to an overseas dealer, and if it had reached the U.S.A., it would have doubled its value.

Having been caught by a hunter, the orang infant is next crated in a small, easy-to-hide box, fed a little rice from time to time, and then taken in secret to an agent who buys it for a small sum. The agent transfers it to a smuggler with a boat for a handsome profit. The smuggler now has to take it to a port where a large vessel will take it on to Europe or the United States of America. In the last four months of 1963, 84 orangs left Borneo. The receiving ports normally used were Hong Kong, which tightened up on orang control in 1962–1963, and Singapore, which tightened up in 1964–1965. The Harrissons have calculated that "for 1946–64 not fewer than 2,000 orang utans passed through Chinese, Indian, Eurasian and American dealers based there" (Singapore). Bangkok remains a port for aerial smuggling, but the traffic is lighter than by boat. Now, with better relations between Indonesia and the Netherlands, the flow has been from Indonesia itself, via the Netherlands, to other European countries and America. Like any smuggling route, the orang route is a constantly shifting one, ever sensitive to new openings. There is little hope that this smuggling can ever be controlled.

Once orangs reach the West, they have to be brought into certain countries that have import restrictions, such as the United Kingdom. Most of them have faked papers. The Animals (Restriction of Importation) Act 1965, which became effective in January, 1965, prohibits the importation of *"Pongidae"* (and certain other species, mainly primates but also rhinoceroses and tortoises) except under license, and such a license cannot normally be obtained by private individuals or animal dealers, being confined to reputable zoos or institutes with breeding facilities. If private individuals try to bring apes into the U.K., they are likely to be confiscated (see Plate 109). Unfortunately, the working of this Act is likely to be hampered by the fact that the species prohibited are all listed by their Latin names, and not every customs official is a zoologist! This is certainly an error, and I hope the common names will be put in in later editions of the Act.

Whether its entry is illegal or not, the young orang has obviously got to be given the greatest possible care and attention if it is to recover, be cured of the diseases contracted en route and survive. For the most part, however, the whole job is still left to animal dealers, who advertise quite openly (see Plate 110), when they have orangs for sale. Then the final transaction is reached—a private person, zoo, or laboratory buys the animal. The orang may now have many years of bored captivity. Or it may quickly succumb to some disease, and die. Most infants in fact die before arrival at their destination.

This haphazard trading in orangs could, and should, be entirely eliminated. The illegality of the whole business, especially at the point of origin in the Far East, has the result of reducing the number of baby orangs that survive. However, if trafficking were legalized, it might increase, as long as the demand remains high. Demand will remain high, in Europe and America, unless orang keeping is made totally illegal for everybody, including most laboratories and zoos. This, I think, would be a good thing, and should now be done. Perhaps the easiest way to achieve this would be to issue orang-purchasing licenses only to those zoos whose orang-breeding history shows them to be likely to breed again. For example, Cheyenne Mountain Zoological Park, in Colorado, has a highly organized orang-rearing routine, and has had seven orang births in recent years, of which five have survived.

So far in this chapter I have concentrated almost entirely on the orangutan. The reason for this is that there has been grave concern over it for many years, and therefore much information has been collected. Now I should like to consider the other apes. None of the species of gibbons is currently believed to be in danger of extinction, although very little is known about the precise distribution of some of them. The one with the smallest distribution range (see Figure 9) is *Hylobates klossii*, the pygmy gibbon, but its population numbers are unknown.

Of the gorillas, the lowland form is not well known. It has a fairly

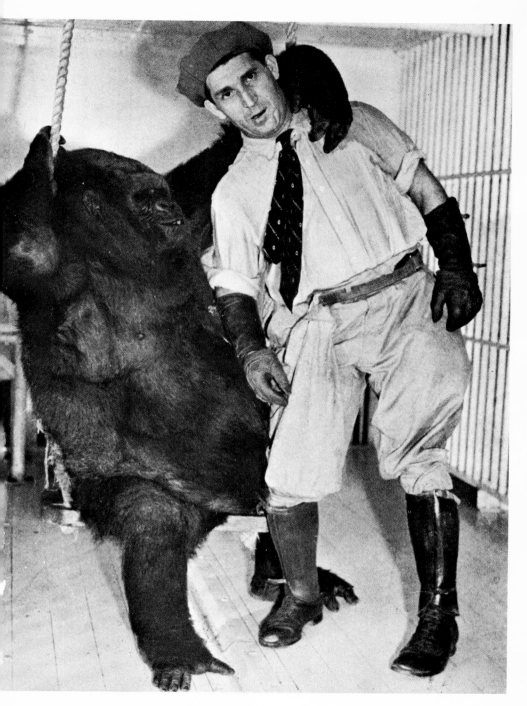

Plate 83. Toto and her caretaker Tomas, en route to meet Gargantua.

Plates 84 and 85.
Wolfgang Köhler's
chimpanzees at Tenerife,
trying to solve the banana
and boxes problem.

Plates 86 and 87. *Above:* Apparatus for testing chimpanzee performance. *Below:* A typical test panel. The top window shows one of the four symbols shown below, and the subject must press on the matching window to obtain a reward in the food box at lower left.

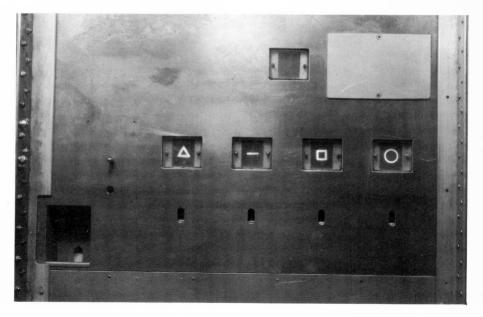

Plate 88. Chimpanzee playing ticktacktoe (noughts and crosses).

Plate 89. Arthur Rackham's illustration for Poe's "Murders in the Rue Morgue."

Plate 90. Tarzan, ape, and snake.

Plate 91. King Kong.

Plate 92.   An old myth in the setting of twentieth-century politics.

Plate 93. Illustration to the African tale of the greedy gorilla.

Plate 94. Another African tale, celebrating the tree-climbing abilities of the chimpanzee.

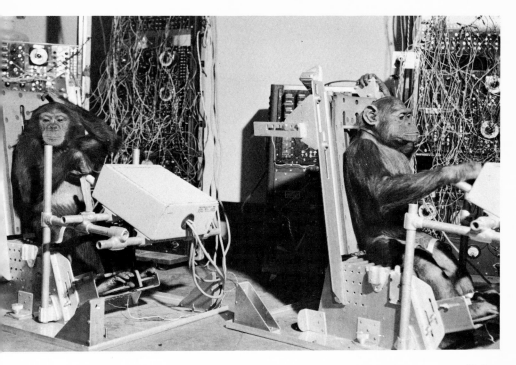

Plates 95 and 96. *Above:* Chimpanzee in test box designed for space flight. *Below:* Ham and Enos at practice: both later flew in space.

Plate 97. William Peckitt, head keeper of London Zoo, with four of the zoo's chimpanzees.

Plate 98. Chester Zoo's chimpanzee enclosure.

Plate 99. Chimpanzees at Chester Zoo.

Plate 100. Orangs at Chester Zoo.

Plate 101. Aerial view of the 30-acre chimpanzee enclosure at Holloman Air Force Base, New Mexico, in course of construction.

Plate 102. Indoor section of two-part chimpanzee cage: the doorway to the open air is at lower right.

Plate 103. The familiar view: ape and steel mesh. ▶

Plate 104.   Cucusa and Anuma, at Mme. Abreu's ape colony in Cuba.

Plate 106.   Pygmy chimpanzee mother and young, at Frankfurt Zoo.

Plate 105.   Achilla and Jambo, at Basel Zoo.

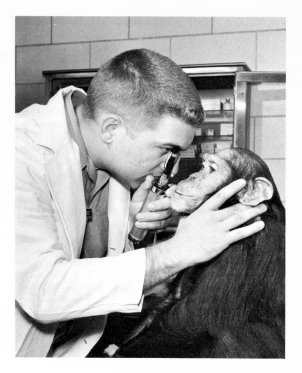

Plate 107. Veterinarian examining chimpanzee's eye.

Plate 108. Veterinarian examining chimpanzee's heart.

Plate 109. Two young chimpanzees at London Zoo. They were confiscated from their owner because of illegal entry into the United Kingdom.

Plate 110. Apes, even those on the brink of extinction, are advertised quite openly at the present time. This advertisement appeared in *International Zoo News,* October-December, 1963.

FOR SALE

Adult male

ORANG UTAN

175 lbs - US $ 3,000,00

Write for photo or details to:

RAYMOND BIDDLE
328 Manheim Street
PHILADELPHIA 44
Pa.   U.S.A

extensive range (Figure 4) in West Africa, and may be holding its own, being a rather secretive forest dweller. A sanctuary for it is currently being established in Rio Muni, West Africa, where its distribution is being studied. In 1961, a census revealed the presence of 119 lowland gorillas in captivity outside Africa. There is a slow, but continuing, trade in them, and the occasional lowland gorilla still turns up for sale in a pet shop. In England, such gorillas will from now on be routed into establishments capable of looking after them properly. Whether the demand is reducing the wild population is not known, but lowland gorillas are subject today to very similar pressures to those they have had to face in the past (hunting by local Africans, collecting by agents of the white man, disease), and none of these pressures is known to be increasing at an alarming rate. Their natural rain-forest habitat is not being depleted by sawmill operations to any great extent. However, in view of the fact that we lack information on the size of the population, there is an urgent need for a census, and distribution maps. In addition, it is a pity that records are not kept of the numbers of lowland gorillas leaving African ports, and the numbers being imported into countries outside Africa.

Much is known about the status of the mountain gorilla in the wild, thanks to the work of J. T. Emlen and G. B. Schaller who, in 1960, reported its numbers and distribution after an intensive on-the-spot survey. They found that its range covered an area of about 35,000 square miles, within which most of the gorillas were concentrated in about 60 more or less isolated tracts of 10 to 200 square miles each. The area occupied by gorillas was about 7,500 to 8,000 square miles, that is, only about 21 to 23 percent of their total range area (see Figure 5). They estimated the total population of mountain gorillas to be not less than 5,000 and not more than 15,000. This is a very low population, and it is fortunate that the mountain gorilla is not subject to the same exploitation as the orang. But it is not, and several reasons can be given for this.

During the early part of this century, hunting the mountain gorilla was fine sport for zoo and museum collectors and private sportsmen. Then came Carl Akeley and the setting up of the Albert National Park. Gorillas were now wholly protected and, within the park at least, *protection was enforced*. From the 1930's on, it was impossible for collectors of any kind to gain admittance to the park, and even scientists were generally refused permission to disturb the gorillas. Poaching had never operated on a workable scale here, doubtless because of the difficulties of transporting a baby gorilla from the heart of Africa to a port. The thorough protection given, and the difficulty of poaching, succeeded in conserving the population in the park. But the park occupies only a fraction of the mountain gorilla's range. Elsewhere, in the lowland forests where most of the mountain gorillas live, the story is the same as for the lowland gorillas—local Africans continue to hunt them, on a small scale, and they can probably hold their own against this. Why numbers had fallen so low in the first place, even before the hunters arrived, we do not know. The main thing the conservationists achieved was the elimination of further hunting, and it is perhaps safe to guess that during the last thirty years the population has been stable or has even increased.

Besides hunting, there has always been that other threat to wildlife: destruction of habitat. In the case of the gorillas, it is not so much logging (as in Borneo) but the encroachment on gorilla habitat by agriculturalists and pastoralists with their herds of cattle that provides the menace. Such people were successfully kept out by the Belgian and British authorities until the revolution in the Congo in 1960.

With independence for the Congo, there were fears that hunting would begin again, the Albert Park would cease to exist, and humans and their cattle would spread up into the gorilla areas. These fears have not been justified. The biologist at the Albert Park, Jacques Verschuren, and many of his wardens, have kept the park going, and the new government continues to protect the gorillas. On the Uganda side of the Virunga volcanoes, gorillas have become scarcer, and it is possible that they have been killed in some numbers in Ruanda, for the travels of many of the Uganda volcano gorillas take them into Ruanda. Further into Uganda, the Kayonza Forest gorillas are quite safe at present.

The population remains, however, very low, and so it is necessary to keep a constant watch to ensure that this, the most impressive of the apes, is not endangered in the future. Threats at the moment come from two main quarters—the pastoral African tribes whose lands border on the gorillas' habitat and who threaten constantly to spread into it as their herds increase in size; and the demands of the world's zoos, circuses, and medical institutions, which, for the most part, would dearly like to have a mountain gorilla. In 1963, a census showed that there were only twelve live mountain gorillas in zoos outside Africa (seven males and five females in six zoos). This low figure was partly, if not wholly, the outcome of the work of the conservationists. Only constant watchfulness can prevent it from rocketing up.

The pygmy chimpanzee is the least well known of the large apes. Its distribution was plotted by Harold Coolidge in 1933, on the basis of all the specimens that had been collected by that date, and his map was improved on by G. Vandebroek in 1959, who plotted the distribution as shown in Figure 3. It is generally agreed that the pygmy chimpanzee, or bonobo, is confined to the forested regions south of the Congo River and north of the Kasai River. But how common it is in this vast region is not known, and no estimate of its total population is possible at present. Nor do we know whether the population is stable or in decline or rising. We do know that it is not leaving Africa in great numbers, for in 1964 there were only some seventeen pygmy chimpanzees in zoos (six males and eleven females in six zoos). This ape doubtless has to contend with African hunters, a few local agents, and the invasion of its habitat by agriculturalists, but these pressures are not known to be on the increase. The need for a study of this species, beginning with a census, is great. However, in the present state of political upheaval in the Congo Republic, such a survey may not be possible for some time to come.

From the least familiar we pass to the most familiar of the apes, the common chimpanzee. This is, happily, still plentiful in some areas, and it may be asked why it is included in a chapter on conservation when it is manifestly succeeding in looking after itself so well. There are two reasons. First, it is not managing at all well in some parts of its range. Second, the case of the chimpanzee well illustrates the complexity of the situation in which silvicultural demands are in conflict with those of the conservationist.

The chimpanzee occurs in a truly vast range of tropical forest and surrounding woodland, from east-central to western Africa (Figure 2). No census has ever been made that covers the whole of this area. However, we can derive some information from the studies that have been made at the eastern and western ends of the range, from brief reports about the number of chimpanzees in specific areas, and from the recent study of a fairly large area in West Africa by Adriaan Kortlandt.

It is generally agreed that chimpanzees do not occur evenly over their entire range in the Congo rain forest. Some areas of forest appear to be wholly lacking in chimpanzees. In the case of the mountain gorillas, Emlen and Schaller found that only about 21 to 23 percent of the total area of the range was actually inhabited. Since this is the only figure available for a species in any way comparable to the chimpanzee, it may serve as an indication of how much of the range may in fact be inhabited by chimpanzees. Within the inhabited areas, population density is known to vary considerably. In the area I studied, the Budongo Forest, several different methods of calculating the density of our study area all produced the same result—about ten chimpanzees to the square mile. But our study area was specially selected by us as being favored chimpanzee habitat. Elsewhere in the Budongo Forest the density was almost certainly lower. And in other forests we visited, in Uganda, the density was probably lower than this. To the south, in a woodland zone in Tanzania, Jane Goodall studied a population of chimpanzees that were 3.3 to the square mile of habitable country. This indicates a lower density in woodland than in rain forest. Kortlandt's recent survey of chimpanzees in West Africa led him to believe that they are more often found in semiopen country than in rain forest. If this is so, the number of chimpanzees living in the Congo rain-forest belt may be lower than appears from a glance at the distribution map. Unfortunately, accurate surveys or censuses in the Congo rain forest are extremely difficult to make, and at the present time of political unrest, impossible.

In some, perhaps many, areas of the Congo, chimpanzees are eaten, being caught most often by means of guns or spears and nets. This predation by man is a threat they have always had to face. Modern threats are the same as with the other apes—collecting on the one hand, and destruction of habitat on the other. In the case of such a widely dispersed animal, these corrosive agents have been able to take their toll in parts of West Africa, while hardly affecting some more easterly districts. By far the most vicious of the two is the former. Collecting has been in vogue throughout this century, for the usual reasons: zoos, circuses, and scientific institutions want apes. In addition, of course, some chimpanzees are taken to be pets. As with the other apes, the conventional way of obtaining chimpanzees is by destruction of the mother, and only a third to a quarter (or, according to Kortlandt, a much smaller fraction) of the catch survives to reach its destination.

In the past, chimpanzees have been hunted primarily in West Africa, where the forest abuts the coastal trading centers, and a baby ape can soon be got rid of to an agent for a good price. One channel of chimpanzee supply for laboratories was the Pasteur Institute in Guinea, which had been an export route for chimpanzees, primarily to America, ever since the pioneering study there by H. W. Nissen in 1931. With the independence of Guinea in 1958, the new government laudably put a stop to this trade, which they rightly regarded as a colonial phenomenon, and gave chimpanzees full protection. As a result, in 1964 Kortlandt found a new, revived population of unterrified chimpanzees, and considers Guinea to be a good study area at the present time.

In Sierra Leone, chimpanzee exploitation has gone on for many years unabated until, in 1962, in a report in *Oryx,* the number of chimpanzees reported to be leaving the country was put as high as 100 to 200 babies per annum, involving the sacrifice of 300 to 400 chimpanzees each year, a rate no ape population could survive for long. According to information collected by Kortlandt for the northwestern half of Sierra Leone, chimpanzees are "practically never heard nor seen anymore" there. He found that at present 150 export licenses are granted annually for chimpanzees captured in Sierra Leone—far more than the population can withstand. In neither Guinea nor northwestern Sierra Leone are chimpanzees eaten by man—the depletion of the apes is a direct result of collecting for export. In Dahomey, chimpanzees have apparently been exterminated in recent years. In French Cameroun they have almost been exterminated, and in Liberia they are depleted, partly for export, partly by local armed meat seekers. In Nigeria, chimpanzees are on the decline; they still occur sporadically in certain areas of the south and east.

Toward the center of the continent, chimpanzees become progressively less liable to human interference, partly because of the difficulty of getting them to the coastal traders and partly because fewer Africans possess guns. However, airports in the Congo provide potential trading foci, and will doubtless take their share of the trade when the West Coast dries up as a source of supply. In East Africa (western Uganda and Tanzania) chimpanzees are already very well protected by efficient game departments, and permits to take specimens are not readily issued. This is an excellent situation, and I hope that when pressure is put on these countries to act as sources of chimpanzee supply, they will refuse to do so, for if they do not, the fate of the chimpanzee will be sealed.

There is another threat that faces the chimpanzees at the present time, and this is the effects of modern tree felling and silvicultural techniques on their habitats. Conventional, age-old agricultural methods have always involved the clearance of patches of forest, in order to allow light to penetrate to the ground and ripen the crops. Such forest or swidden farming occurs all over the world, including the area occupied by the African apes. F. G. Merfield and G. B. Schaller have shown that gorillas, lowland and mountain, prefer areas that have been exploited by man, relishing the dense secondary vegetation that grows while the forest is recovering. T. S. Jones and A. J. E. Cave have shown that chimpanzees adapt well to secondary forest in Sierra Leone, and there is no doubt that the same is true in many other areas, perhaps chiefly because in the profusion of varieties of species that grow in open, disturbed forest, there is a good percentage of light-loving trees whose fruit they eat, such as figs. Thus, natural human forest felling and apes can co-exist very well.

In Uganda, however, as in Borneo and elsewhere, forest felling does not take this simple form. In Borneo, one problem noted by the Harrissons is large-scale mechanized timber felling, which makes the canopy unsuitable for habitation by orangs. This does not occur in Uganda as far as I know, where trees are selectively felled according to species and girth of trunk. But one feature of exploitation in Uganda, which also occurs in Borneo, is the poisoning off of unwanted "weed" trees. A "weed" tree is one that will not yield useful timber. It is, therefore, to the silviculturist, of no value in the forest, and should be replaced by a timber tree. In the Budongo Forest we noticed that among the weed trees that were being poisoned off were several species that provide the chimpanzees with a major food source for part of the year. Figs, for example, are "weeds," and are currently being eliminated from the Budongo Forest, as well as other chimpanzee forests in Uganda. For several months during our study, we observed chimpanzees feeding avidly on ripe figs, which appeared to be their chief food source at the time. It was therefore with some alarm that we discovered that man is slowly but surely depriving the apes of one of their favorite food supplies.

I have personally been in correspondence with the Uganda Forest Department for three years now, in an attempt to bring about some reduction of the poisoning program, where it affects chimpanzee food sources. The Forest Department is itself concerned with the welfare of the chimpanzees that live in this forest, according to its own Working Plan, which, in Paragraph 76, states that one of the objects of management is to give "rare species such as the potto, chimpanzee, dwarf forest antelope and birds . . . a reasonably undisturbed area." With our present knowledge of the widespread use the chimpanzees make of the forest, roaming several miles each day in their search for food, the idea of leaving aside a small "nature reserve" for them is clearly inapplicable. A higher density of chimpanzees has been found in Budongo than anywhere else (ten per square mile), and to maintain this superb population, their food supply must not be cut.

To this end I recently suggested to the Forest Department that if they could spare the lives of no more than sixty trees of the species *Ficus mucuso* (the chimpanzees' favorite fig) in each square mile of forest, this would be of great benefit to the apes. Calculations showed that this would mean a reduction of no more than 0.5 percent of the crop, that is, the timber yield—a negligible loss. Shortly after submitting this recommendation, I received a reply in which doubt was expressed that the poisoning program was affecting the chimpanzees, but promising to keep a close watch on the results. The poisoning of figs, therefore, continues, and we shall have to await the results of later surveys before any effects can be seen.

I have dwelt on the problem of silvicultural side effects for two reasons—first, it is rather complex and unspectacular, and hence often overlooked, and second, it is a threat that will continue to grow in importance over the years, as more and more of the tropical forest comes under control for systematic timber production. We should keep the perspective right, however. At the present time, the greater danger is definitely the actual removal of apes for export. In one way the two threats are related, for the opening up of forest that accompanies timber extraction and refinement also enables animal catchers to pursue their quest more efficiently. So there are many issues and side issues in the equation; but ultimately it all boils down to the question Can the apes adapt? And the honest answer is that we do not know.

There are other things we do not know. No accurate figures are available on the number of chimpanzees at present in captivity, but there must be several thousands. Most of the world's zoos can afford a chimpanzee or two (cost at the time of writing: about $600, as opposed to $3,000 for an orang or $6,000 for a gorilla). And, as was discussed in the previous chapter, there is the demand of research institutions. The evidence is that this demand will continue to grow faster than the supply will satisfy it, and that certain key supply areas such as Sierra Leone, Liberia, Ivory Coast, Nigeria, and Cameroun will not long be able to meet it. We know from the orang story that nothing can be done to stop a lucrative animal from being caught and sold into near-extinction.

And these animals are lucrative, at all levels, not only to the natives that catch them and the dealers that pass them on but also to the zoos and laboratories and circuses that keep them. They double or even triple their value yearly, providing they become established in their new home and remain healthy and tractable. Much money has to be spent to keep them in good condition. Their diet must be of the best. They must have regular health checks, and any symptoms discovered must be treated. Expensive surgery may be required, and ape keepers must be prepared for this eventuality. The high value of what is known as a "prime" animal reflects the cost of all this care. One American institution, which may not be atypical, values its "prime" chimpanzees at $25,000 each. Later, their value declines, as they become less tractable, less attractive, and as their life expectancy and breeding potentiality are reduced. What can be done? The only long-term answer is that demand must be met from animals bred in captivity, and not imported from the wild.

I should like to see the setting up of two or more "Apelands" on the lines of the "Marinelands" so successfully established in the U.S.A. in recent years. Each Apeland would consist of a large moated or island area of suitable habitat—tropical or subtropical forest—with artificial food sources around the perimeter. It is important that there should be a sufficient area of forest to avoid its destruction by the apes; at least a square mile for each small colony. The species could be represented together. Wardens would make daily tours of the apeland forest areas, to check for fallen trees and ensure that the electric wire running along the moat was functioning. They, too, would be the only people permitted into the forest areas, where they would supervise the clearing of the numerous paths crisscrossing the forest, and make regular censuses of the number of apes present.

By the side of the forest would be the laboratories, where all work of scientific importance would be conducted. The apes used in this research would come direct from the forest, being caught at their feeding places some time before being required, and housed in the laboratory to enable them to adjust for some weeks or months before being used. After their experimental lives were over, they would be returned to the forest, if possible.

Another whole sector of the Apeland would be devoted to the sole purpose of entertaining the public. Every day a number of young apes, especially selected and trained, and housed apart from the forest in special enclosures, would give performances of the "tea party" and "intelligence test" type for the public. After they grew too old, they would be added to the free colony or used to set up a new one. As apes in general become scarcer, this would prove an ever-increasing attraction, and the gate money collected might very well pay for the running of the Apeland.

The siting of the Apelands presents difficult problems. On the one hand, all the apes live naturally in warm, moist tropical forests. On the other hand, the tropical areas of the world are not the ideal location, because they are too far from the visiting public and from the medical institutions which need to work on the apes. Also, they are often subject to political upheaval. The most enterprising venture in this direction has been the recent release of several erstwhile captive chimpanzees on an island in Lake Victoria, Tanzania, by Dr. Bernhard Grzimek, the director of the Frankfurt Zoo. The first reports indicate that the colony immediately adapted to its freedom and will no doubt provide a healthy and expanding population in future years. This of course was an altruistic and nonprofit-making enterprise.

Florida is a very suitable location for an apeland, although even Florida is subject to occasional periods of subzero temperatures in winter, and while the apes might well survive this, many tropical fruit trees would probably be killed off. Climatically better places, such as Central America (Yucatán, Mexico, or any of the countries farther south as far as Panama), or the West Indies, are all less convenient than a site in the United States would be, even though they would satisfy the requirement for tropical vegetation. A mainland site in the United States is essential in order to attract sufficient visitors, and so Florida, southern Georgia, southern Alabama, southern Mississippi, or Louisiana would be the best places for the Apelands to be sited. Research should indicate which are the most suitable trees.

Another crucial issue is: Where are the citizens of Apeland to come from? Taking the orang first, we run into a whole set of problems. Should we deplete yet further the tiny wild population to stock the Apelands? If possible, we should not. Can the existing captive population provide the stock? There were known to be 134 males and 146 females in 92 zoos in 1962 (of which 13 males and 15 females were captive-born). This is an average of 3 orangs per zoo. Although this degree of dispersion of orangs is the worst possible thing from the breeding standpoint, it is probably impossible to do anything about it, because zoos are likely to hold on to their orangs tenaciously. They could, however, be invited to donate orangs to the Apelands, even though they might not wish to do so. The only safe way to stock the Apelands would be to ensure that all orangs arriving in the West were routed to them, and to make all other purchase of them illegal. The same would apply to other apes. It would certainly be best to begin collecting apes at home—by confiscating new arrivals and taking unwanted stock before going into the field.

And collecting trips to the field need to be of a rather different kind in future from the hit-miss kind of trip we have known hitherto, where the collector went out with a species and a number in his mind and looked around until, somewhere or other, he got what was wanted.

In future, a series of "feeder reservations" should be set up in ape habitats in Africa and Asia, to which apes would be routed after capture and in which they would be kept and cared for. These apes would be studied by veterinarians and others, to determine their natural intestinal flora and parasites, and treat any naturally occurring disease. They could also be used in other kinds of research, where such research could be conducted away from civilization. Their main purpose, however, would be to provide the animals needed by the world's research laboratories. They would be released to accredited institutions for a given period of time, for use (except in most unusual circumstances) in nonterminal experiments, after which they would be returned to their reservation. The owners and managers of these ape reservations should be paid by the countries interested in using their apes, and compensation would be heavy for each animal not returned in good condition at the end of the period. This system would emphasize that these apes belong in their native country, and are only abroad on a temporary basis.

Having established one Apeland in the United States of America and one or two feeder reservations, we should then quickly proceed to establish a few more, simply to avoid catastrophic loss in the event of an epidemic.

I hope that the idea of Apelands will one day not too far off be taken up by a competent government institution. In the meantime, a much closer watch must be kept on the trade in apes than is done at present. We lack, for most African countries, annual reports on the numbers of gorillas and chimpanzees leaving along export routes, and we lack internal data on their abundance or scarcity except for the mountain gorilla and the chimpanzees in certain areas of West and East Africa. Our knowledge of the orang is more complete. As for gibbons, we do not even know how many types there are, or their range of habitats. A basic study is badly needed here. All ape imports into "civilized" countries should be reported to a central authority—none exists. And there is no check at present on prices paid for apes; such a check would provide a sensitive barometer measuring the pressure on these species.

Anyone who doubts that urgent action is necessary to save the large apes is under a misapprehension. Anyone who doubts that it is worth the effort involved in saving them is blind to the future needs of mankind. The gorilla, the orang, the chimpanzee, and their lesser cousin the gibbon, have a right to survive. We, their deadliest enemy, have the power to save them. Most of us, indeed, want to save them. We simply lack the organized machinery of control to do so. Must we watch gloomily while our nearest relatives in the animal world are slowly exterminated by our more exploitative fellowmen?

Postscript: Some Implications for Man

IN THIS LAST chapter, I want to show how some of the findings of studies of apes can help us to understand man and the human way of life. They enable us to look at our own species more objectively and to see how the universals of human social behavior may have evolved out of an apelike system tens of millions of years ago.

The large apes are our nearest relatives. This means that our genetic inheritance has developed from the same stock that produced the large apes. In our chapter on the evolution of the apes, we saw that man's common ancestor with the large apes was living, in all probability, in the Oligocene period, and that the gibbon line had already diverged from the main ape stock by the middle of the Oligocene; we saw too that the hominid line is not directly related to the monkey line, which was also distinct in the Oligocene. The hominid line must have become distinct toward the late Oligocene or very early Miocene, at much the same time as the forerunners of chimpanzees and gorillas were differentiating too.

The field studies of the 1960's have now provided us with enough information about the way present-day apes live in the wild to enable us to formulate some general principles about the social life of the large apes. We can see at once big differences between them and the monkeys. The apes (meaning for the purposes of this chapter chimpanzees, orangs, and gorillas, and excluding the gibbon) do not live in closed groups. Rather, they live in what can be termed "communities." Even in the case of gorillas, which do maintain a fairly stable group membership, different groups sometimes meet and mingle with each other, and individuals appear to be free to join or leave a group at will. When two gorilla groups meet, they do not behave aggressively, but appear to recognize each other, and to join up or go their separate ways depending on past experiences. In chimpanzees (and in orangs, as far as we can tell from the rather sketchy data), the society is loosely structured. Group membership is always fluctuating, and groups or individuals can roam widely through the forest without encountering hostilities. In all three apes there is nothing resembling the "ranges" found in monkey groups. Monkeys, in particular open-country-dwelling species, have closed groups which forage within a defined range; ranges of neighboring groups may overlap but the groups will avoid meeting in the common area by having routine movements within their ranges, which keep them apart. Even at water holes, where different groups have to come in contact, it is rare for monkeys to change from one group to another when they separate. Apes, in contrast, seem to recognize a nexus of relationships beyond the group they happen to be with, and join up and make new partnerships. Chimpanzees in particular belong to different kinds of groups according to their prevalent motivation; for example, an adult male may one day join up with a group of females because he is interested in a sexually receptive female; another day he may be off exploring for new fruit trees with a band of other males; and another day he may return for a while to his mother and her younger offspring and forage with them for a while.

This capacity of the ape to be part of different types of social groupings on different occasions, and for different purposes, and his ability to recognize relationships with other individuals over time and space, is in my opinion the most important behavioral tendency which we have inherited from our common stock, and may be responsible for preadapting the human line for its successful colonization of the savannahs.

Looking at the social organization of man, we can see immediate resemblances to the pongid pattern. Hominids, throughout most of their evolution, have been predominantly foragers who supplemented their vegetable diet with some meat, opportunistically caught or scavenged. It is only during the last two or three million years, at the longest estimate, that they have taken to organized hunting, and even then, except in areas very rich in game, their diet has consisted, to a greater or lesser extent, of vegetable matter. Modern studies of aborigines, Bushmen, and other hunting and gathering societies have shown that the bulk of the diet is vegetable matter, usually collected by the women, while the men are off in search of game. When a big kill is made, there is plenty of meat for all, but such occasions are not part of the daily routine.

The social groupings which hunting and gathering societies typically form tend to resemble closely those found in the most widespread and adaptable of the large apes—the chimpanzee. As with chimpanzees, humans join up into different groups for different activities. The hunting bands of adult males parallel the food-finding bands of exploratory chimpanzee males; as chimpanzee mothers and infants tend to remain in one feeding area for some time, so the women forage in the vicinity of the temporary camp; the children form play groups among themselves as do chimpanzee infants; from time to time, usually at a period of abundance of food, all the groups in the vicinity join up to drum and dance in communal festivity, just as noisy gatherings of large numbers of chimpanzees congregate in areas of plenty of fruit; as with apes, individuals or small groups of humans are free to travel about and join up with other communities, where they have a friend or relation. Nomadic hunting tribes do not have defended hunting territories, although there is usually a region to which each community feels itself attached, while many of the individuals or families living there may have originally belonged to other communities in other regions. This comes out clearly in modern studies of existing hunter-gatherer societies from all over the world—the Northwestern Canadian Indians, the Eskimos, the Western American Shoshoni Indians, the East African Hadza, the Bushmen of the Kalahari, the Pygmies of the Congo, the Birhor of India, and even, contrary to earlier reports, the Australian aborigines. I am sure that it was a tendency to flexible community structure, such as is seen in the large apes, that preadapted the first hominids to develop successful colonization of the Tertiary savannahs along quite different behavioral lines from those of other primate species which also "came down from the trees." The first tool cultures were, as a result, diffused over huge areas, and there is evidence throughout hominid evolution of open communities with constant intermixing and contact with neighboring populations.

During the late Paleolithic, some human populations developed highly complex hunting technologies, and highly organized societies. Finally, little more than ten thousand years ago, some populations began to experiment with the domestication of animals and the cultivation of plants. These people began to give up the nomadic hunting way of life, and settle in one place. We should note what a recent development this is in the evolution of man, twenty million years an intelligent ape, three million years a nomadic hunter and gatherer, a few thousand years only a settled agriculturalist. Everything we accept as civilization has happened since then. The agricultural revolution was probably the most important factor determining the direction of development of human civilizations. Man has come to rely on agriculture as his primary source of nutrition, and he remains, nearly everywhere in the world, primarily a vegetarian, in that the bulk of his diet consists of vegetable foods. Meat is now, as it always was, a luxury.

The effects of the transition from a nomadic hunting and gathering economy to settled agricultural living were vast, and caused a revolution in human society. Productive land became a possession that needed defending. For the first time, a man placed his food where he wanted it, and waited for it to grow. A community could not move off, or split up into bands, or accept the presence of too many visitors. This was probably when complicated systems of kinship relationships became institutionalized, in order to specify just who were kin, and could share food and hospitality, and who were not.

When families or groups "owned" stretches of land, rights of inheritance had to be controlled. Man became home-based, not as a species, and not innately, but due to economic dependence on particular land for his survival. And while individual plots, or village land as a whole, might be defended against strangers, no human populations are as utterly territorial as many animal species. For the individual, even in agricultural societies, has always recognized a wide nexus of friends and kin to which a family's home and land are ever open. This is one of the most important aspects of our apelike behavioral inheritance, and one which, I am sure, is in some measure responsible for the achievements of human societies.

I have inferred that, in my view, aggression between groups began with settled agricultural living and economic dependence on land. Although there is a little evidence of hostility before this time, it can usually be traced to economic dependence on land for some other reason. For example, cave paintings in Spain and France dating from the late Paleolithic depict warriors fighting. These are seasonal areas, where the population lived in caves and rock shelters as winter protection. Thus they must have been dependent for many months on the products of the surrounding country to satisfy their needs.

There was a way of life that developed alongside agriculturalism, more in keeping with man's nomadic instincts: pastoralism. With the taming of the aurochs, the horse, the reindeer, goats and sheep, the pastoralists moved around, as some still do today, exploiting the available grazing land. We know from historical sources such as the Bible that such groups have always been in conflict with settled agriculturalists, in their constant search for fertile plains.

Whereas the nomadic life of hunters and gatherers kept the group population in balance with environmental resources, the development of more efficient means of food production, such as pastoralism and agriculture, of more adequate and permanent shelters, and of less strenuous traveling, produced the effect that the population could increase, bringing the need for more land.

Within the community, too, the necessity of keeping together as a group, with a common source of livelihood, required internal changes and controls in social organization. A colony of apes kept in captivity develops jealousies, enmities and a hierarchy of dominance; human settlement brought about hierarchies of authority structure, the institutionalization of kinship relationships, regulations imposed on sexual behavior, and an awareness of group solidarity. All this is necessary for the survival of the group under the conditions of shared economic dependence, but it causes pressures and frustrations in the individual that need not occur in hunter-gatherer communities.

Latterly, I think man has developed a partial solution to the problems of settled living, in the form of cities, and this helps to account for their success. Cities attract people, especially adults at the peak of their mental and physical development.

What is the source of the appeal of city life? It offers an excitement and a faster tempo than villages in the countryside. There is a surfeit of social interaction, a constant stream of new faces to look at. There seems ample opportunity to make new social relationships with members of this vast population, to join new groups. There is the anonymity of the crowd—gone is the close scrutiny of the tight-knit little village community. There is (apparently at any rate) plenty of scope for self-assertion, for sexual relationships, or for withdrawal into peaceful obscurity. But especially there is the big, fascinating manmade world all around, offering novelty every day—an unceasing array of opportunities for exploration.

This is back to the hunter-gatherer environment, and back beyond that, to the nomadic ape. Gone is the oppressive atmosphere of the small-scale, settled peasant community. Now, in his giant cities, man has achieved a remarkable combination: he can be, and is, a good human citizen and a good instinctive ape.

References

Key to Abbreviations

Act. Soc. linn. Bordeaux—Actes de la Société linnéenne de Bordeaux
Amer. Anthrop.—American Anthropologist
Am. J. Phys. Anthrop.—American Journal of Physical Anthropology
Anat. Rec.—Anatomical Record
Ann. Mag. Nat. Hist.—Annals and Magazine of Natural History
Ann. Soc. Roy. Zool. Belg.—Annales de la Société Royale Zoologique de Belgique
Arch. Néerl. de Zool.—Archives Néerlandais de Zoologie
Bull. Geol. Soc. Am.—Bulletin of the Geological Society of America
Bull. Hist. Med.—Bulletin of the History of Medicine
Bull. Soc. Roy. Zool. d'Anvers—Bulletin de la Société Royale Zoologique d'Anvers
Comp. Psych. Mon.—Comparative Psychology Monographs
Human Biol.—Human Biology
Int. Zoo Yearbook—International Zoo Yearbook
J. Anat.—Journal of Anatomy
J. Comp. Phys. Psych.—Journal of Comparative and Physiological Psychology
J. Comp. Psych.—Journal of Comparative Psychology
J. Geol.—Journal of Geology
J. Mammal.—Journal of Mammalogy
J. Morph.—Journal of Morphology
Malayan Nature J.—Malayan Nature Journal
Proc. Amer. Phil. Soc.—Proceedings of the American Philosophical Society

[[275

Proc. Int. Symp. Bone Marrow Therapy—Proceedings of the International Symposium on Bone Marrow Therapy
Proc. Nat. Acad. Sci.—Proceedings of the National Academy of Sciences
Proc. Zool. Soc. Lond.—Proceedings of the Zoological Society of London
Psych. Bull.—Psychological Bulletin
Psych. Rev.—Psychological Review
Sarawak Mus. J.—Sarawak Museum Journal
S. Afr. J. Sci.—South African Journal of Science
Southwestern J. Anthrop.—Southwestern Journal of Anthropology
Symp. Zool. Soc. Lond.—Symposia of the Zoological Society of London
Trans. Linn Soc. Lond. Zool.—Transactions of the Linnean Society of London
Zeit. f. Säugetierkunde—Zeitschrift für Säugetierkunde
Zeit. für Tierpsychologie—Zeitschrift für Tierpsychologie
Z. Morph. Anthrop.—Zeitschrift für Morphologie und Anthropologie
Zool. Gart., Leipzig—Der Zoologische Garten, Leipzig

Chapter 1   The "Ape" in Ancient Times

Aesop. Fables. Translated by J. J. Gent. Theo Tebb and Thos. King, London, 1715 ed.
Agatharchides (quoted by Photius and Diodorus, ed. Müller). Geographi Graeci Minores, 2 vols. Paris, 1855–1861.
Aristotle. History of Animals. English translation by D'Arcy Wentworth Thompson, Oxford University Press, London and New York, 1910.
Ashley Montagu, M. F. "Knowledge of the Ancients Regarding the Ape." Bull. Hist. Med., Vol. 10 525–543, 1941.
Brandon, S. G. F. Creation Legends of the Ancient Near East. Hodder and Stoughton, London, 1963.
Brentjes, B. "Die älteste Darstellung des Gorillas." Säugetierkundliche Mitteilungen, Vol. 13, pp. 14–22 (1965).
Galen, C. Claudii Galenii . . . de anatomicis administrationibus, libri ix Joanne (Guinterio) Andernaco interprete. Luyduni, 1551.
Gervais, F. L.P. Histoire des mammiferes, Vol. 1. L. Curmer, Paris, 1854.
Gesner, K. Historiae animalium. Vol. I, De Quadrupedibus viviparis. Tiguri, 1551–1587.
Graves, R., and R. Patai. Hebrew Myths—The Book of Genesis. Doubleday, New York, 1963.
Hanno. The Voyage of Hanno, Translated, and Accompanied with the Greek text . . . by Thomas Falconer. London, 1797.
Janson, H. W. Apes and Ape Lore in the Middle Ages and the Renaissance. Warburg Institute, London, 1952.
Layard, Sir A. H. Nineveh and Its Remains, Vol. II. John Murray, London, 1853.
MacDermott, W. C. The Ape in Antiquity. Johns Hopkins, Baltimore, 1938.
Mackay, E. J. H. Further Excavations at Mohenjo-Daro, 2 vols. See especially Vol. 1, pp. 293–294, and Vol. 2, Plate LXXX. Arthur Probsthain, London, 1938.
Plinius Secundus. The Natural History of Pliny. Translated by J. Bostock and H. T. Riley. London, 1848.
Pliny. The Historie of the World. Translated into English by Philemon Holland. London, 1601.
Topsell, E. The History of Four-footed Beasts and Serpents. London, 1658 ed. (1st ed. 1601).

Tyson. E. *A Philological Essay Concerning the Pygmies, the Cynocephali, the Satyrs and Sphinges of the Ancients.* David Nutt, London, 1794 ed.

Wendt, H. *Out of Noah's Ark.* Translated by M. Bullock. Houghton Mifflin, Boston, 1959.

Yerkes, R. M. and A. W. *The Great Apes,* a study of anthropoid life. Yale University Press, New Haven, 1929.

Chapter 2   Finding the True Apes

Aldrovandus, U. *De quadrupedibus digitatis viviparis* . . . Bonon, 1637.

Ashley Montagu, M. F. *Edward Tyson, M.D., F.R.S., 1650–1708, and the Rise of Human and Comparative Anatomy in England.* American Philosophical Society, Philadelphia, 1943.

Audebert, J. B. *Histoire naturelle des singes et des makis.* Desray, Paris, 1800.

Battell, A. In S. Purchas. *Hakluytus posthumus, or Purchas his pilgrimes.* W. Stansby, London, 1613.

Bewick, T. *A General History of Quadrupeds.* S. Hodgson, Newcastle-upon-Tyne, 1791 ed.

Bontius, J. *Historiae naturalis & medicae Indiae Orientalis,* Bk VI, pp. 84–85. L. and D. Elzevirios, Amsterdam, 1658.

Buffon, Georges-Louis Leclerc, Comte de. *Histoire naturelle.* Vol. 35, *Des Singes.* Paris, 1802.

Cuvier, Baron George. *Le Règne Animal distribué d'apres son organisation* . . . 4 vol. Paris, 1817.

Geoffroy-Saint-Hilaire, E., and F. Cuvier. *Histoire Naturelle des Mammifères,* Vols. II, III. Musée d'Histoire Naturelle, Paris, 1824.

Gray, J. E. "Zoological Notes on Perusing M. Du Chaillu's 'Adventures in Equatorial Africa.'" *Ann. Mag. Nat. Hist.,* 3rd ser., 7, pp. 463–470. London.

Hill, J. *An History of Animals.* pp. 535–537. Thos. Osborne, London, 1752.

Hoppius, C. E. "Anthropomorpha." *Amoenitates academicae* (Linné), Erlangae, 1760.

Huxley, T. H. *Evidence as to Man's Place in Nature.* Williams & Norgate, London, 1863.

Jardine, Sir W. *The Naturalist's Library,* I, 56–66, W. Lizars. Edinburgh, 1833.

Linnaeus, C. *Regnum Animale,* pp. 20–24. British Museum (Natural History), London (facsimile of Vol. 1 of 10th ed., 1758).

Loisel, G. *Histoire des ménageries de l'antiquité à nos jours,* 3 vols. Octave Doin et Fils, Paris, 1912.

Maunder. S. *The Treasury of Natural History.* pp. 125–126. Longman, Green, Longman, and Roberts, London, 1862 ed.

Nordenskiöld, Erik. *The History of Biology.* Tudor, New York, 1928 ed.

Ogilby, J. *Atlas Japannensis.* From the original by A. Montanus, 1670. See p. 160.

Pennant, T. *History of Quadrupeds.* London, 1793 ed.

Raffles, T. S. "Descriptive catalogue of a zoological collection, made on account of the Honourable East India Company, in the Island of Sumatra and its vicinity." *Trans. Linn. Soc. Lond. Zool.,* 13, 239–243 (1822).

Richardson, Sir J., and others. *The Museum of Natural History,* I, Wm. Mackenzie.

Scherren, H. "Old Pictures of Apes." *Proc. Zool. Soc. Lond.* 2, 298–302.

Schweinfurth, G. *The Heart of Africa,* 2 vols. Sampson Low, London, 1873.

Smith, Rev. T. *The Naturalist's Cabinet.* Vol. 1, Chap. 5. James Cundee, London, 1806.

Stiles, C. W. "The Zoological Names *Simia, S. satyrus*, and *Pithecus*, and Their Possible Suppression." *Nature* (1926), 118, 49.

Tulpius, N. *Observationum medicarum libri tres*, pp. 274–279. Amsterdam, 1641.

Tyson, E. *Orang-Outang, sive Homo Sylvestris: or, the Anatomy of a Pygmie compared with that of a monkey, an ape, and a man.* T. Bennett and D. Brown, London, 1699.

Vosmaer, A. *Description de l'espèce de singe aussi singulier que très rare, nommé orang-outang, de l'île de Borneo.* Amsterdam, 1778.

Yerkes, R. and A. *The Great Apes.* Yale University Press, New Haven, 1929.

Chapter 3   The Apes: Their Basic Structure and Behavior

Bereznay, Y. "Composition du sang des singes anthropoïdes par rapport au sang humain." *Bull. Soc. Roy. Zool. d'Anvers* (1959), 10, pp. 1–57.

Biegert, J. "The Evaluation of Characteristics of the Skull, Hands and Feet for Primate Taxonomy." In S. L. Washburn (ed.), *Classification and Human Evolution*, pp. 116–145. Aldine Publishing Co., Chicago, 1963.

Bierens de Haan, J. A. "Discrimination of Musical Tempi by a Young Chimpanzee." *Arch. Néerl. de Zool.* (1951), 8, p. 393.

Brandes, G. *"Das Heranwachsen des Schimpansen,"* IV, 115–132. *Zool. Gart.,* Leipzig, 1931.

Coon, C. S. *The Origin of Races.* Alfred A. Knopf, New York, 1962.

Crandall, L. S. *The Management of Wild Mammals in Captivity.* University of Chicago Press, Chicago, 1964.

Ducrotay de Blainville, H. *Ostéographie ou description iconographique comparée.* Vol. 1 and Atlas 1. J. B. Baillière & Fils, Paris, 1839.

Elder, J. H. "Auditory Acuity of the Chimpanzee." *J. Comp. Psych.* (1934), Vol. 17, No. 2, pp. 157–183.

———, and R. M. Yerkes. "The sexual cycle . . ." *Anat. Rec.* (1936), 67, pp. 119–143.

Ellis, R. A., and W. Montagna. "The Skin of Primates. VI. The Skin of the Gorilla (*Gorilla gorilla*)." *Am. J. Phys. Anthrop.* (1962), 20, No. 2, pp. 79–94.

Fiedler, W. "Uebersicht über das System der Primates." In *Primatologia*, I, pp. 1–266. Ed. by H. Hofer, A. H. Schultz, and D. Starck. S. Karger, Basel and New York, 1956.

Finch, G. "Chimpanzee Handedness." *Science* (1941), Vol. 94, pp. 117–118.

Forster, M. C. *Temporal Relations of Behavior in Chimpanzee and Man as Measured by Reaction Time.* Yale University reprint, New Haven, 1935.

Gavan, J. A. "Growth and Development of the Chimpanzee." *Human Biol.* (1953), 25, 2, pp. 93–143.

Goodman, M. "Man's Place in the Phylogeny of the Primates as Reflected in Serum Proteins." In S. L. Washburn (ed.) *Classification and Human Evolution*, pp. 204–234. Aldine Publishing Company, Chicago, 1963.

Gregory, W. K., ed. *The Anatomy of the Gorilla.* Columbia University Press, New York, 1950.

Grether, W. F., and R. M. Yerkes. "Weight Norms and Relations for Chimpanzees." *Am. J. Phys. Anthrop.* (1940), Vol. 27, No. 2, pp. 181–197.

Groves, C. P."Ecology and Taxonomy of the Gorilla." *Nature* (1967), Vol. 213, No. 5079, pp. 890–893.

Grzimek, B. "Beobachtungen an Gorillas und Schimpansen in Span.-Guinea." *Zool. Gart.* (1957), Leipzig, 23, p. 249.

Harrisson, B. "A Study of Orang Utan Behaviour in Semi-wild State, 1956–60." *Malayan Nature J.* (1962), 16, 1 and 2.

Hartmann, R. *Anthropoid Apes.* Kegan Paul, Trench, Trübner & Co. Ltd., London, 1904 ed.

Hauser, F. "Goma, das Basler Gorillakind." *Documenta Geigy* (1960), No. 4.

Hooton, E. A. *Up from the Ape.* The Macmillan Company, New York, rev. ed., 1961.

Hornaday, W. T. *Two Years in the Jungle.* Charles Scribner's Sons, New York, 1885.

Johnston, Sir H. "On the Nomenclature of the Anthropoid Apes." *Proc. Zool. Soc. Lond.* (1905), No. 2, pp. 70–74.

Kellogg, W. N. and L. A. *The Ape and the Child.* McGraw-Hill, London, 1933.

Kirschshofer, R. "Beobachtungen bei der Geburt eines Zwergschimpansen (*Pan paniscus Schwarz* 1929)." *Zeit. für Tierpsychologie* (1962), 19, 5.

Klinger, H. P., J. L. Hamerton, D. Mutton, and E. M. Lang. "The Chromosomes of the Hominoidea." In S. L. Washburn (ed.), *Classification and Human Evolution*, pp. 235–242. Aldine Publishing Company, Chicago, 1963.

Mayr, E. *Animal Species and Evolution.* Harvard University Press, Cambridge, Mass., 1963 ed.

Napier, J. R. "The Human Thumb." *Panorama*, December, 1963.

Nissen, H. W. "A Field Study of the Chimpanzee. Observations of Chimpanzee Behaviour and Environment in Western French Guinea." *Comp. Psych. Mon.* (1932), Vol. 8, No. 36, pp. 1–122.

Piveteau, J. *Traité de Paléontologie*, VII. Masson et Cie., Paris, 1957.

Portmann, A. "Goma, das Basler Gorillakind." *Documenta Geigy* (1960, 1961), Nos. 3 and 8.

Reynolds, V. and F. "Chimpanzees in the Budongo Forest." In Irven DeVore (ed.), *Primate Behavior: Field Studies of Monkeys and Apes*, pp. 368–424. Holt, Rinehart and Winston, Inc., New York, 1965.

Riesen, A. H. and E. F. Kinder. *Postural Development of Infant Chimpanzees.* Yale University Press, New Haven, 1952.

Rode, P. *Les Primates de l'Afrique.* Librairie Larose, Paris, 1937.

Schaller, G. B. *The Mountain Gorilla: Ecology and Behavior.* University of Chicago Press, Chicago, 1963.

Schenkel, R. "Zur Ontogenese des Verhaltens bei Gorilla und Mensch." *Z. Morph. Anthrop.* (1964), 54, 3, pp. 233–259.

Schmitt, J. "Blood groups in Anthropoid Apes." *Int. Zoo. Yearbook* (1962), IV, 147–148.

Schultz, A. H. "Die Körperproportionen der erwachsenen catarrhinen Primaten, mit spezieller Berücksichtigung der Menschenaffen." *Anthropologischer Anzeiger* (1933), x, pp. 154–185.

————. "Observations on the Growth, Classification, and Evolutionary Specialization of Gibbons and Siamangs." *Human Biol.* (1933), Vol. 5, Nos. 2–3, pp. 212–428.

————. "Genital Swelling in the Female Orang-utan." *J. Mammal.* (1938), Vol. 19, No. 3, pp. 363–366.

————. "Growth and Development of the Chimpanzee." *Contributions to Embryology* (1940), No. 170, pp. 1–63. Carnegie Institution, Washington, Publication no. 518.

————. "Growth and Development of the Orang-utan." *Contributions to Embryology* (1941), Vol. 29, No. 182, pp. 57–110. Carnegie Institution, Washington, Publication No. 525.

————. "Age Changes and Variability in Gibbons." *Am. J. Phys. Anthrop.* (1944), Vol. 2, n.s., No. 1, pp. 1–129.

————. "Morphological Observations on Gorillas." In *The Anatomy of the Gorilla*, Part V. Columbia University Press, New York, 1950.

————. "Postembryonic Age Changes." In *Primatologia*, I, 887–964 (1956).

————. "The Occurrence and Frequency of Pathological and Teratological Conditions and of Twinning Among Non-human Primates." In *Primatologia*, I, 965–1014 (1956).

————. "Die rezenten Hominoidea." *Menschliche Abstammungslehre*, pp. 56–102. (G. Heberer ed.). Stuttgart, 1965.

————. "Changing Views on the Nature and Interrelations of the Higher Primates." *Yerkes Newsletter* (1966). Vol. 3, No. 1, pp. 15–29.

Selenka, E. *Studien über Entwickelungsgeschichte der Tiere*, II, IV. Wiesbaden, 1898.

Simons, E. L. "Early Relatives of Man." *Scientific American*, July, 1964.

Sonntag, C. F. *The Morphology and Evolution of Apes and Man*. J. Bale & Co., London, 1924.

Spence, K. W. "Visual Acuity and Its Relation to Brightness in Chimpanzee and Man." *J. Comp. Psych.* (1934), Vol. 18, No. 3, pp. 333–361.

Thomas, W. T. "Observations on the Breeding in Captivity of a Pair of Lowland Gorillas." *Zoologica* (1958), Vol. 43, pp. 95–104.

Tinklepaugh, O. L. "Sex cycles and other cyclic phenomena in a chimpanzee during adolescence, maturity and pregnancy." *J. Morph.* (1933), 54, pp. 521–547.

Urbain, A., and P. Rode. *Les Singes anthropoïdes*. Paris, 1948.

Washburn, S. L. (ed.). *Classification and Human Evolution*. Aldine Publishing Company, Chicago, 1963.

Wiener, A. S., J. Moor-Jankowski, and E. B. Gordon. "Blood Groups of Apes and Monkeys. II. The A-B-O Blood Groups." *Am. J. Phys. Anthrop.* (1963), n.s., Vol. 21, 3.

Yerkes, R. M. *Chimpanzees: A Laboratory Colony*. Yale University Press, New Haven, 1943.

Yerkes, R. M. and A. W. *The Great Apes*. Yale University Press, New Haven, 1929.

Young, W. C., and R. M. Yerkes. "Factors Influencing the Reproductive Cycle in the Chimpanzee." *Endocrinology* (1943), 33, No. 3, pp. 121–154.

Zuckerkandl, E. "Perspectives in Molecular Anthropology." In S. L. Washburn (ed.), *Classification and Human Evolution*, pp. 243–273. Aldine Publishing Company, Chicago, 1963.

Zuckerman, S., and J. F. Fulton. "The Menstrual Cycle of the Primates. Part VII. The Sexual Skin of the Chimpanzee." *J. Anat.* (1934), 69, pp. 38–46.

Chapter 4 Evolution of the Apes

Ankel, F. "Der Canalis sacralis als Indikator für die Länge der Caudalregion der Primaten." *Folia primatologica* (1965), 3, pp. 263–276.

Arambourg, C. "Continental Vertebrate Faunas of the Tertiary of N. Africa." In F. C. Howell and F. Bourlière (eds.), *African Ecology and Human Evolution*, pp. 55–64. Aldine Publishing Company, Chicago, 1963.

Avis, V. "Brachiation: The Crucial Issue for Man's Ancestry." *Southwestern J. Anthrop.* (1962), 18, 2, pp. 119–148.

Bishop, W. W. "The Later Tertiary and Pleistocene in Eastern Equatorial Africa." In F. C. Howell and F. Bourlière (eds.), *African Ecology and Human Evolution*, pp. 246–275. Aldine Publishing Company, Chicago, 1963.

Brooks, C. E. P. *Climate Through the Ages.* E. Benn, London, 1926.

Chaney, R. W. "A Tertiary Flora from Uganda." *J. Geol.* (1933), Vol. 41, pp. 702–709.

————. "Tertiary Forests and Continental History." *Bull. Geol. Soc. Am.* (1940), Vol. 51, pp. 469–488.

Clark, W. E. L. *History of the Primates*, 8th ed. British Museum (Natural History), London, 1962.

————. *The Antecedents of Man.* Edinburgh University Press, 1962.

————, and L. S. B. Leakey. "The Miocene Hominoidea of E. Africa." No. 1 of *Fossil Mammals of Africa.* British Museum (Natural History), London, 1951.

Colbert, Edwin H. *Dinosaurs: Their Discovery and Their World.* E. P. Dutton & Company, New York, 1961.

Cole, S. *The Prehistory of East Africa.* The Macmillan Company, New York, 1964.

Cornwall, I. W., and M. M. Howard. *The Making of Man.* Phoenix House, Ltd., London, 1960.

Darlington, P. J. *Zoogeography: the Geographical Distribution of Animals.* John Wiley & Sons, New York, 1957.

Devore, I., and S. L. Washburn. "Baboon Ecology and Human Evolution." In F. C. Howell and F. Bourlière (eds.), *African Ecology and Human Evolution*, pp. 335–367. Aldine Publishing Company, Chicago, 1963.

Fiedler, W. "Uebersicht über das System der Primates." *Primatologia*, pp. 1–266. I. S. Karger, Basel and New York, 1956.

Goodman, M. "Man's Place in the Phylogeny of the Primates as Reflected in Serum Proteins." In S. L. Washburn (ed.), *Classification and Human Evolution*, pp. 204–234. Aldine Publishing Company, Chicago, 1963.

Harrisson, Tom. "The Threat to Rare Animals in Borneo." *Malayan Nature J.* (1962), No. 16, Nos. 1 and 2, p. 7.

Howells, W. *Mankind in the Making.* Doubleday, New York, 1960.

Mayr, E. *Animal Species and Evolution.* Harvard University Press, Cambridge, Mass., 1963 ed.

————. "Taxonomic Categories in Fossil Hominids." *Cold Spring Harbor Symposia on Quantitative Biology* (1950), New York, 15, 109–117.

Moreau, R. E. "The Distribution of Tropical African Birds as an Indicator of Past Climatic Changes." In F. C. Howell and F. Bourlière (eds.), *African Ecology and Human Evolution*, pp. 28–42. Aldine Publishing Company, Chicago, 1963.

Napier, J. "The Locomotor Functions of Hominids." In S. L. Washburn (ed.), *Classification and Human Evolution*, pp. 178–189. Aldine Publishing Company, Chicago, 1963.

————. "Brachiation and Brachiators." *Symp. Zool. Soc. Lond.* (1963), No. 10, pp. 183–195.

Neaverson, E. *Stratigraphical Paleontology.* Oxford, Clarendon Press, 1962 ed.

Pilbeam, D. R. and E. L. Simons. "Some Problems of Hominid Classification." *American Scientist* (1965), Vol. 53, No. 2,

Piveteau, J. *Traité Paléontologie*, Vol. 7, *Primates.* Paris, 1957.

Remane, A. "Palëontologie und Evolution der Primaten, besonders der Nicht-Hominoiden." *Primatologia*, pp. 268–378. I, S. Karger, Basel and New York, 1956.

Robinson, J. T. "Adaptive Radiation in the Australopithecines and the Origin of Man." In F. C. Howell and F. Bourlière (eds.), *African Ecology and Human Evolution*, pp. 385–416. Aldine Publishing Company, Chicago, 1963.

Romer, A. S. *Vertebrate Paleontology*. University of Chicago Press, Chicago, 1945 (2nd ed.).

Schultz, A. H. "Age Changes, Sex Differences and Variability as Factors in the Classification of Primates." In S. L. Washburn (ed.), *Classification and Human Evolution*, pp. 85–115. Aldine Publishing Company, Chicago, 1963.

———. "Changing Views on the Nature and Interrelations of the Higher Primates." *Yerkes Newsletter*, (1966), Vol. 3, No. 1, pp. 15–29.

Simons, E. L. "New Fossil Apes from Egypt and the Initial Differentiation of the Hominoidea." *Nature* (1965), 205, pp. 135–139.

———, and D. R. Pilbeam. "Preliminary Revision of the Dryopithecinae (Pongidae, Anthropoidea)." *Folia Primatologica* (1965), No. 46, pp. 1–70.

Simpson, G. G. "The Meaning of Taxonomic Statements." In S. L. Washburn (ed.), *Classification and Human Evolution*, pp. 1–31. Aldine Publishing Company, Chicago, 1963.

Straus, W. L. "The Classification of *Oreopithecus*." In S. L. Washburn (ed.), *Classification and Human Evolution*, pp. 146–177. Aldine Publishing Company, Chicago, 1963.

Suess, E. *The Face of the Earth*, II, translated by H. B. C. Sollas. Oxford, Clarendon Press, 1906.

Wadia, D. N. *Geology of India* (3rd ed.), pp. 367–371. London, Macmillan & Company, 1957.

Washburn, S. L. "Behavior and Human Evolution." In S. L. Washburn (ed.), *Classification and Human Evolution*, pp. 190–203. Aldine Publishing Company, Chicago, 1963.

Chapter 5   The Natural Life of Chimpanzees

Bolwig, N. "A Study of the Nests Built by Mountain Gorilla and Chimpanzees." *S. Afr. J. Sci.* (1959), Vol. 55, No. 11, pp. 286–291.

Garner, R. L. *Gorillas and Chimpanzees*. Osgood McIlvaine & Co., London, 1896.

Goodall, J. "Feeding Behaviour of Wild Chimpanzees." *Symp. Zool. Soc. Lond.* (1963), No. 10, pp. 39–47.

———. "Chimpanzees of the Gombe Stream Reserve." In *Primate Behavior*, I. DeVore (ed.), pp. 425–473. Holt, Rinehart and Winston. New York, 1965.

———. *My Friends the Wild Chimpanzees*. National Geographic Society, Washington, 1967.

Kortlandt, A. "Chimpanzees in the Wild." *Scientific American* (1962), 206, 5, pp. 128–138.

———. Some Results of a Pilot Study on Chimpanzee Ecology (unpublished).

———, and M. Kooij. "Protohominid Behaviour in Primates." *Symp. Zool. Soc. Lond.* (1963), No. 10, pp. 61–88.

Livingstone, D. *The Last Journals of David Livingstone in Central Africa*. John Murray, London, 1874.

Nissen, H. W. "A Field Study of the Chimpanzee. Observations of Chimpanzee Behavior and Environment in Western French Guinea." *Comp. Psych. Mon.* (1932), Vol. 8, No. 36, pp. 1–122.

Pitman, C. R. S. *A Game Warden Takes Stock*. London, Nisbet & Co., 1942.

Reynolds, V. "An Outline of the Behaviour and Social Organisation of Forest-living Chimpanzees." *Folia Primatologica* (1963), 1, pp. 95–102.

———. *Budongo: A Forest and Its Chimpanzees*. Natural History Press, New York, 1965.

———. "Some Behavioral Comparisons Between the Chimpanzee and the Mountain Gorilla in the Wild." *Amer. Anthrop.* (1965), Vol. 67, No. 3, pp. 691–706.

———, and F. Reynolds. "Chimpanzees of the Budongo Forest." In *Primate Behavior*, I. DeVore (ed.), pp. 368–424. Holt, Rinehart and Winston, New York, 1965.

Chapter 6 The Natural Life of Gorillas

Akeley, C. E. *In Brightest Africa.* London, Heinemann, 1924.

———, and M. L. J. Akeley. *Lions, Gorillas and Their Neighbours.* London, Stanley Paul & Co., 1933.

Bingham, H. C. *Gorillas in a Native Habitat.* Carnegie Institution of Washington, Publication No. 426, 1932.

Bolwig, N. "A Study of the Nests Built by Mountain Gorilla and Chimpanzee." *S. Afr. J. Sci.* (1959), Vol. 55, No. 11, pp. 286–291.

Donisthorpe, J. "A Pilot Study of the Mountain Gorilla (*Gorilla gorilla beringei*) in South-West Uganda, February to September 1957." *S. Afr. J. Sci.* (1958), 54, 8, pp. 195–217.

Du Chaillu, P. *Explorations and Adventures in Equatorial Africa,* J. Murray, London, 1861.

Emlen, J. T. "The Display of the Gorilla." *Proc. Amer. Phil. Soc.* (1962), 106, 6, pp. 516–519.

Ford, H. A. "On the Characteristics of the Troglodytes Gorilla." *Proc. Nat. Acad. Sci. U.S.A.* (1852), 6, 30–33.

Garner, R. L. *Gorillas and Chimpanzees.* Osgood, McIlvaine & Co., London, 1896.

Osborn, R. "Observations on the Behaviour of the Mountain Gorilla." *Symposia of the Zoological Society of London* (1963), No. 10, pp. 29–37.

Pitman, C. R. S. *A Game Warden Among His Charges.* London, Nisbet & Company, 1931.

Reynolds, V. "Some Behavioral Comparisons Between the Chimpanzee and the Mountain Gorilla in the Wild." *Amer. Anthrop.* (1965), Vol. 67, No. 3, pp. 691–706.

Sabater Pi, J. "Beitrag zur Biologie des Flachlandgorillas." *Zeit. f. Säugetierkunde* (1960), 25, pp. 133–141.

———, and L. de Lassaletta. "Beitrag zur Kenntnis des Flachlandgorillas." *Zeit. f. Säugetierkunde* (1958), 23, pp. 108–114.

Schaller, G. B. *The Mountain Gorilla: Ecology and Behavior.* University of Chicago Press, Chicago, 1963.

———. *The Year of the Gorilla.* University of Chicago Press, Chicago, 1964.

———. "The Behavior of the Mountain Gorilla." In *Primate Behavior*, I. DeVore (ed.), pp. 324–367. Holt, Rinehart and Winston, New York, 1965.

Chapter 7 The Natural Life of Gibbons and Orangs

Carpenter, C. R. "A Field Study in Siam of the Behavior and Social Relations of the Gibbon (*Hylobates lar*)." *Comp. Psych. Mon.* (1940), 16, 5.

Davenport, R. K., Jr. "The Orang-utan in Sabah." *Folia Primatologica* (1966), No. 4, pp. 247–263.

Ellefson, J. O. Territorial Behavior in the Common White-handed Gibbon (*Hylobates lar*) (pre-publication), 1965.

Harrisson, B. *Orang-Utan*. Collins, London, 1962.
Hornaday, W. T. *Two Years in the Jungle*. Charles Scribner's Sons, New York, 1885.
Schaller, G. B. "The Orang-utan in Sarawak." *Zoologica* (1961), 46, 2, pp. 73–82.
Wallace, A. R. *The Malay Archipelago*. Macmillan & Co., London, 1890.

Chapter 8   Living with Apes

Benchley, B. J. *My Friends, the Apes*. Little, Brown & Co., Boston, 1942.
Harrisson, B. *Orang-Utan*. Collins, London, 1962.
Hayes, C. *The Ape in Our House*. Harper & Brothers, New York, 1952.
Hess, L. *Christine, the Baby Chimp*. G. Bell and Sons, Ltd., London, 1954.
Hoyt, A. M. *Toto and I: A Gorilla in the Family*. J. B. Lippincott Company, Philadelphia, 1941.
Johnson, M. *Congorilla*. G. Harrap, London, 1932.
Kellogg, W. N., and L. A. *The Ape and the Child*. McGraw-Hill, New York, 1933.
Lang, E. M. "Goma, das Basler Gorillakind." *Documenta Geigy* (1960–1961), Nos. 1, 3, and 8.
———. *Goma the Baby Gorilla*. Gollancz, London, 1962; Doubleday, New York, 1963.
———, and R. Schenkel. "Goma, das Basler Gorillakind." *Documenta Geigy* (1961), Nos. 6 and 7.
Morris, D. *The Story of Congo*. Batsford, London, 1958.
Schenkel, R. "Goma, das Gorillakind." *Documenta Geigy* (1960), Nos. 2 and 5.
Yerkes, R. M. *Almost Human*. Century Co., New York, 1925.

Chapter 9   The Abilities of Apes

Benchley, B. J. *My Friends, the Apes*. Little, Brown & Co., Boston, 1942.
Birch, H. G. "The Role of Motivational Factors in Insightful Problem-solving." *J. Comp. Psych.* (1945), 38, pp. 295–317.
———. The Relation of Previous Experience to Insightful Problem-solving." *J. Comp. Psych.* (1945), 38, pp. 367–383.
Boutan, L. "Le pseudo-langage. Observations effectuées sur un anthropoïde: le gibbon (*Hylobates leucogenys* Ogilby)." *Act. Soc. Linn. Bordeaux* (1913), 67, pp. 5–80.
Cowles, J. T. "Food Tokens as Incentives for Learning by Chimpanzees." *Comp. Psych. Mon.* (1937–1938), 14, No. 71.
Crawford, M. P. "The Co-operative Solving of Problems by Young Chimpanzees." *Comp. Psych. Mon.* (1937–1938), 14, No. 68.
Douglas, J. W. B., and C. W. M. Whitty. "An Investigation of Number Appreciation in Some Sub-human Primates." *J. Comp. Psych.* (1941), 31, pp. 129–143.
Drescher, K., and W. Trendelenberg. "Weiterer Beitrag zur Intelligenzprüfung der Affen," *Zeitschrift für vergleichende Physiologie* (1927), 5, pp. 613–642.
Ferster, C. B. "Arithmetic Behavior in Chimpanzees." *Scientific American*, May, 1964.
Finch, G. "The Solution of Patterned String Problems by Chimpanzees." *J. Comp. Psych.* (1941), 32, pp. 83–90.
Guillaume P., and I. Meyerson. "Le problème du détour," and "L'intermédiaire lié à l'objet." *Journal de Psychologie* (1930), 27, pp. 177–236 and pp. 481–555.

Hayes, C. *The Ape in Our House,* Harper & Brothers, New York, 1952.

Hayes, K. J. and C. "The Intellectual Development of a Home-raised Chimpanzee." *Proc. Amer. Phil. Soc.* (1951), 95, pp. 105–109.

——. "The Cultural Capacity of Chimpanzees." *Human Biol.* (1954), 26, pp. 288–303.

Kellogg, W. N. and L. A. *The Ape and the Child.* McGraw-Hill, New York, 1933.

Köhler, W. *The Mentality of Apes.* Humanities Press, New York, 1956.

Morris, D. *The Biology of Art.* Alfred A. Knopf, New York, 1962.

Nissen, H. W. "Individuality in the Behavior of Chimpanzees." *Amer. Anthrop.* (1956), 58, pp. 407–413.

Riesen, A. H., B. Greenberg, A. S. Granston, and R. L. Fantz. "Solutions of Patterned String Problems by Young Gorillas." *J. Comp. Phys. Psych.* (1953), 46, pp. 19–22.

Rumbaugh, D. M., and C. McCormack. "The Ontogeny of Object-quality Learning Set in the Lowland Gorilla." Paper delivered to the Western Psychol. Assoc., 1965.

——, and C. P. Rice. "Learning Set Formation in Young Great Apes." *J. Comp. Phys. Psych.* (1962), 55, pp. 866–868.

Schiller, P. H. "Innate Constituents of Complex Responses in Primates." *Psych. Rev.* (1952), Vol. 59, No. 3, pp. 177–191.

Spence, K. W. "Experimental Studies of Learning and the Higher Mental Processes in the Infra-human Primates." *Psych. Bull.* (1937), 34, pp. 806–850.

Yerkes, R. M. "A New Method of Studying Identical and Allied Forms of Behavior in Man and Other Animals." *Proc. Nat. Acad. Sci.,* U.S.A. (1916), Vol. 2, pp. 631–633.

——. "Ideational Behavior of Monkeys and Apes." *Proc. Nat. Acad. Sci.,* U.S.A. (1916), Vol. 2, pp. 639–642.

——, and A. W. Yerkes. *The Great Apes.* Yale University Press, New Haven, 1929.

Chapter 10   Some Modern Myths

Bock, C. *The Head-hunters of Borneo.* Sampson Low & Co., London, 1881.

Boullet, J. "*La Belle et la Bête.*" Le Terrain vague, Paris, 1958.

Burroughs, E. R. *Tarzan of the Apes.* A. L. Burt Company, New York, 1914.

Carpenter, C. R. "A Field Study in Siam of the Behavior and Social Relations of the Gibbon (*Hylobates lar*)." *Comp. Psych. Mon.* (1940), 16, 5.

Du Chaillu, P. B. *Explorations and Adventures in Equatorial Africa.* John Murray, London, 1861.

Hose, C., and W. McDougall. *The Pagan Tribes of Borneo,* 2 Vols. Macmillan & Company, London, 1912.

Heuvelmans, B. *On the Track of Unknown Animals.* Rupert Hart-Davis, London, 1958.

James, M. R. (ed.). *Marvels of the East* (*Tractatus de diversis monstris quae sunt in mundo*). Oxford University Press, New York, 1929.

Poe. E. A. *Tales of Mystery and Imagination.* G. Harrap & Company, London, 1935.

Reade, W. W. *Savage Africa.* Smith, Elder & Co., London, 1863.

Reynolds, V. *Budongo: A Forest and Its Chimpanzees.* Natural History Press, New York, 1965.

Schaller, G. B. *The Year of the Gorilla.* University of Chicago Press, Chicago, 1964.

Stanley, H. M. *My Dark Companions and Their Strange Stories.* Sampson Low, London, 1893.
Wallace, A. R. *The Malay Archipelago,* 2 Vols. London and New York, 1890 ed.
Yerkes, R. M., and A. W. *The Great Apes.* Yale University Press, New Haven, 1929.

Chapter 11 Ape-keeping Today

Crandall, L. S. *The Management of Wild Mammals in Captivity.* University of Chicago Press, Chicago, 1964.
Day, P. W., J. Fineg, and D. C. Van Riper. "Anaesthetic Techniques for Chimpanzee Restraint." ARL-TR 65-18, Holloman AFB, New Mexico, 1965.
Farrer, D. N., and J. E. Warrell. "Chimpanzee Performance During Sustained Transverse Acceleration." ARL-TR-65-2, Holloman AFB, New Mexico, 1965.
————, and F. A. Young. "The Refractive Characteristics and Intraocular Tensions of Colony Chimpanzees." ARL-TR-65-23, Holloman AFB, New Mexico, 1965.
Fineg, J., W. C. Hanley, J. R. Prine, D. C. Van Riper, and P. W. Day. "Isoniazid Therapy in the Chimpanzee." ARL-TR-66-1, Holloman AFB, New Mexico, 1966.
Fisher, J. *Zoos of the World.* Aldus Books, Ltd., London, 1966.
Gall, L. S. "The Influence of Diet on the Normal Fecal Flora of the Chimpanzee." ARL-TR-65-21, Holloman AFB, New Mexico, 1965.
Graham-Jones, O. "Surgical Repair of an Umbilical Hernia in a Gorilla (*G. gorilla*)." *Int. Zoo Yearbook* (1961), Vol. 3, pp. 109–110.
Hediger, H. *Wild Animals in Captivity.* Butterworth's Scientific Publications, Ltd., London, 1950.
Kirchshofer, R. "The Birth of a Dwarf Chimpanzee at Frankfurt Zoo." *Int. Zoo Yearbook* (1962), Vol. 4, pp. 76–78
Kortlandt, A. "Can Lessons from the Wild Improve the Lot of Captive Chimpanzees?" *Int. Zoo. Yearbook* (1960), Vol. 2, pp. 76–80.
Lang, E. M. "Survival of Animals in Zoos." *Int. Zoo Yearbook* (1962), Vol. 4, pp. 63–65.
Mottershead, G. S. "Experiments with a Chimpanzee Colony at Chester Zoo." *Int. Zoo Yearbook* (1960), Vol. 1, pp. 18–20.
Reynolds, V., and F. "The Natural Environment and Behaviour of Chimpanzees, and Suggestions for Their Care in Zoos." *Int. Zoo Yearbook* (1965), Vol. 5, pp. 141–144.
Riopelle, A. J., and O. J. Daumy. "Care of Chimpanzees for Radiation Studies." *Proc. Int. Symp. Bone Marrow Therapy* (1962), pp. 205–227.
Rohles, F. H., R. E. Belleville, and M. E. Grunzke. "Measurement of Higher Intellectual Functioning in the Chimpanzees and Its Relevance to the Study of Behavior in Space Environments." *Aerospace Medicine* (1961), Vol. 32, pp. 121–125.
D. M. Rumbaugh. "The Birth of a Lowland Gorilla at the San Diego Zoo." *Zoonooz* (1965), Vol. 38, No. 9, pp. 12–17.
Van der Bergh, W. K. "The Zoological Garden—Noah's Ark of Future Generations." *Int. Zoo Yearbook* (1962), Vol. 4, pp. 61–62.
Vervat, D. "Appendicitis in Orang-utan at Rotterdam Zoo." *Int. Zoo Yearbook* (1961), Vol. 3, p. 112.
Young, F. A., G. A. Leary, and D. N. Farrer. "Ultrasound and Phakometry Meas-

urements of the Primate Eye." ARL-TR-65-5, Holloman AFB, New Mexico, 1966.

Chapter 12   The Future: Conservation

Anonymous. *Report of the Maias Protection Commission.* Government Office, Sarawak, 1960.

———. *Animals (Restriction of Importation) Act,* Chap. 61, pp. 1–3. Her Majesty's Stationery Office (1964).

Carpenter, C. R. "A Survey of Wild Life Conditions in Atjeh, North Sumatra, with Special Reference to the Orang-Utan." Commn. No. 12, Neth. Committee for Int. Nat. Prot., Amsterdam, 1938.

Dart, R. A. "Memorandum on the Preservation of the African Great Apes." *S. Afr. J. Sci.* (1960), 56, 1, pp. 1–4.

Emlen, J. T. "Current Field Studies of the Mountain Gorilla." *S. Afr. J. Sci.* (1960), 56, 88–89.

Harrisson, B. "Orang-utan: What Chances of Survival?" *Sarawak Mus. J.* (1961), 10, No. 17–18 (n.s.), pp. 238–261.

———. Report on Recent Investigations in North Borneo on Behalf of the World Wildlife Fund Project 21. Typescript report, 1962.

———. "Education to Wild Living of Young Orang-utans at Bako National Park, Sarawak." *Sarawak Mus. J.* (1963), 11, No. 21, pp. 220–258.

Harrisson, T. "A Future for Borneo's Wildlife?" *Oryx,* (1965), Vol. 8, No. 2, pp. 99–104.

Hornaday, W. T. *Two Years in the Jungle.* Charles Scribner's Sons, New York, 1885.

———. *Wild Life Conservation in Theory and Practice.* Yale University Press, New Haven, 1914.

Jones, T. S., and A. J. E. Cave. "Diet, Longevity and Dental Disease in the Sierra Leone Chimpanzee." *Proc. Zool. Soc. London* (1960), 135, pp. 147–155.

Laurie, A. H. "The Age of Female Blue Whales and the Effect of Whaling on the Stock." *Discovery Reports* (1937), 15, pp. 223–284.

Merfield, F. G. with H. Miller. *Gorillas Were My Neighbours.* Longmans Green & Co., London, 1956.

Milton, O. "The Orang-utan and Rhinoceros in North Sumatra." *Oryx* (1964), 7, pp. 177–184.

Schaller, G. B. "The Orang-utan in Sarawak." *Zoologica* (1961), 46, 2, pp. 73–82.

———. *The Mountain Gorilla: Ecology and Behavior.* Chicago University Press, Chicago, 1963.

Vandebroek, G. "Notes écologiques sur les anthropoïdes." *Ann. Soc. Roy. Zool. Belg.* (1958), 89, pp. 203–211.

INDEX

Abreu, R., 79, 115, 168, 169, 177, 247
adult weight, comparison with human, 73
Aegyptopithecus, 97, 103, 105
Aeolopithecus, 96, 104
Aesop, 28, 29, 36
aggression, human, 272–73; in infant apes, 170–72; in wild chimpanzees, 132; in wild gibbons, 154, 155; in wild gorillas, 146, 149; in wild orangutans, 159–60
agile gibbon, 60, 61
agricultural revolution, 272
Akeley, C., 140–46
albino, 61
Amphipithecus, 93
anatomy, comparative, 46, Chapter 3 *passim*
ancestral ape stock, behavior, 105–107; fossils, 97–105
Animals (Restriction of Importation) Act, 255

"Apelands," 264–66
Apidium, 97–98, 102
appearance, of chimpanzee, 60–61; of pygmy chimpanzee, 61; of gibbons, 61–62; of siamang, 62; of gorillas, 61; of orangutans, 61
Aristotle, 29
artistic records, 26–29, 36, 38
Asai, Rikiso, 189
auditory acuity, 82
Augustine, St., 36

Barbary ape, 26, 28–30, 34
Battell, A., 42, 43, 238
Benchley, B., 178, 206–208, 214
Beringe, O. von, 57
Bingham, H., 142–45, 206
bipedal walking, in ancestral apes, 106; in chimpanzees, 123, 130; in

[[289

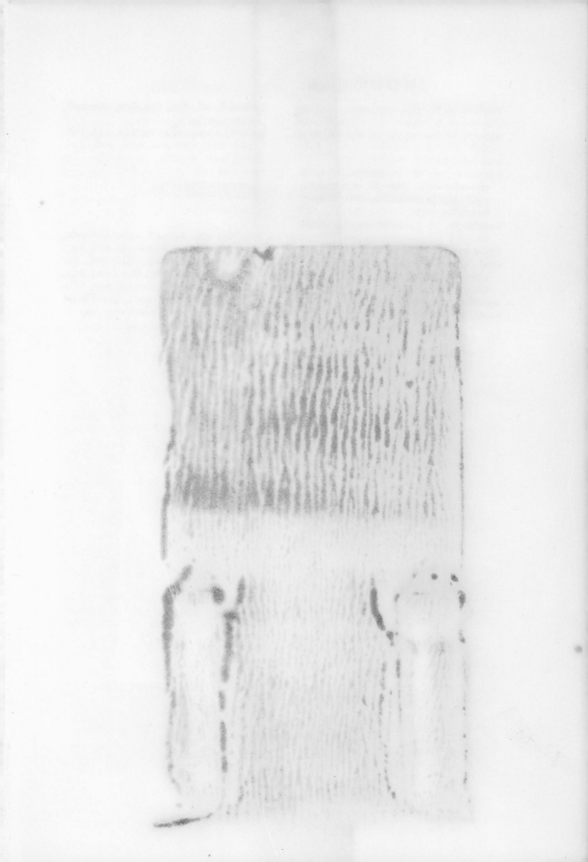

This book may be kept

FOURTEEN DAYS

A fine will be charged for each day the book is kept overtime.
